PURSUING PERFECTION

PURSUING PERFECTION

People, Groups, and Society

Leonard W. Doob

Westport, Connecticut
London

Library of Congress Cataloging-in-Publication Data

Doob, Leonard William, 1909–
     Pursuing perfection : people, groups, and society / Leonard W.
Doob.
        p.   cm.
     Includes bibliographical references and index.
     ISBN 0–275–96448–5 (alk. paper)
     1. Perfection—Moral and ethical aspects.   I. Title.
     BJ1533.P36D66   1999
     170'.44—dc21   98–33610

British Library Cataloguing in Publication Data is available.

Library of Congress Catalog Card Number: 98–33610
ISBN: 0–275–96448–5

First published in 1999

Praeger Publishers, 88 Post Road West, Westport, CT 06881
An imprint of Greenwood Publishing Group, Inc.

Printed in the United States of America

⊗™

The paper used in this book complies with the
Permanent Paper Standard issued by the National
Information Standards Organization (Z39.48–1984).

10 9 8 7 6 5 4 3 2 1

Copyright Acknowledgments

The author and publisher gratefully acknowledge permission for use of the following material:

Excerpts from A. C. Jordan, *Towards an African Literature*. Copyright © 1973 by The Regents of the
University of California. Reprinted by permission of the University of California Press, Berkeley.

Excerpts from W. Evans-Wentz, *Tibetan Yoga and Secret Doctrines*, pp. 67–79. London: Oxford University Press, 1935. Reprinted by permission of Oxford University Press.

Contents

Preface

Perforce at my age I tend to think privately about a prolonged past more than I do about a shorter future. In such reverie I am usually overwhelmed by feelings about various persons and by some of the experiences I have had. There have been my sufficiently patient parents; my ever devoted wife Eveline and a few friends throughout many decades; my three sons and their wives and children, all loving and distinctively capable; professional educators during student years at Dartmouth College, Duke University, the Johann Wolfgang Goethe University in Germany, and finally Harvard University, particularly with inspiration from Professor Gordon W. Allport, James MacKaye, William McDougall, Karl Mannheim, and Max Wertheimer; and interdisciplinary colleagues at Yale University for more than sixty years. Then I remember vividly, if not always accurately, many experiences: as a graduate student attending a few of Hitler's meetings during his political campaign to attain power; while a government "servant" successively in three federal agencies during World War II, with admiration for Nelson Rockefeller, Elmer Davis, and Edward Barrett; amid friends, students, and research participants in Uganda, Tanzania, South Africa, and Ghana; and among those who helped colleagues and me seek, not very successfully, greater mutual understanding for peoples in the Horn of Africa, Northern Ireland, and Cyprus. Wisdom has come from the truly great, especially from the New Testament, Karl Marx, Mohandas Gandhi, Robert Browning (yes, really), John Dewey, and books and articles by or related to them.

With whatever perspective and confidence I have achieved from these activities and sources, I would emphasize now that I seek not blindly but deliberately ways to diminish the imperfections in which all of us are engulfed. With difficulty and with vigor, therefore, this book has emerged. I am saying to myself and I hope to you in the following pages: let us ask ourselves, all those "experts," and others who struggle, at a minimum let us ask what everyone must know and do to achieve what we seek. None of us, none of them, can have an eternally valid panacea for people, groups, and society. We and they can only edge slowly, tentatively, and imperfectly toward an elusive perfection.

This book indicates and summarizes the viewpoints as well as data from some of the promising sources within social science very broadly defined and from the glimpses of philosophers and others pertaining to many of the problems that forever plague and goad us, deliberately or not. The assemblage may be consulted if one desires either to become acquainted with relevant phases of past research or to push forward and try to improve what we know or think we know. Guidelines, not pat or easy solutions, are proposed.

Readers may pursue this pursuit of perfection in various ways. No one approach is prescribed because that would violate the spirit of the book. One may choose to grasp the overall challenges and browse through the text without consulting the evidence or its sources that are discreetly segregated in notes at the end of the book. One may concentrate on beliefs rather than actions, or the reverse and postpone half of the exposition to some later moment or mood. One may examine the pursuit by finite individuals such as oneself and leave the bigger challenges for groups and the enormous, insoluble reformation of society (defined in so many different ways) to others who courageously and foolishly believe they know what is wrong or what is right. Or else each of the two chapters here devoted to groups or the remaining two to society can be the principal focus. Either way, the trio of people, groups, and society eventually must be knit together, otherwise the pursuit is too imperfect.

Less imperfect, not plain perfect, is then the goal of the book. Dogmatic views and prescriptions may seem inviting, but no one, least of all this writer and the sources he has consulted, can guarantee eternal success. Our modesty, therefore, would be realistic but, in both the long and short run, more achievable and satisfying. Do you agree? Read on, please, before you decide, before you go outside and bicycle toward whatever it is you guess you should pursue.

CHAPTER 1

The Pursuit

Another book; why? The title reveals its perennial goal: to secure better, freer, happier, and hence more perfect people, whether they be the self, others, or members of some society. But the pursuer will not achieve perfection; persons may become less imperfect without attaining complete or everlasting perfection. The goal, therefore, is elusive, as are the means to be employed. The pursuit, nevertheless, must continue, as dissatisfaction with any aspect of living quickly suggests and demands. Knowledge is gathered and probes are offered.

In English, with an almost exact or equivalent expression in other languages, there is one word, *meliorate*, that reflects and expresses this pursuit. That word and its variants—meliorate, melioration, ameliorate—can be traced to the Latin word for "better." As a doctrine so named, meliorism was proposed by George Eliot more than a century ago. Its dictionary definition is clearly related to its root: "The doctrine, indeterminate between optimism and pessimism, which affirms that the world may be made much better by human effort."[1] Note "indeterminate" and "may." The doctrine as such has inspired very few writers or activists; it is generally ignored in philosophical treatises. For William James in an influential discussion of pragmatism, meliorism is "less" a doctrine than "an attitude in human affairs" that is "midway" between the optimistic view that considers "the world's salvation inevitable" and a pessimistic view that human goals are not likely to be attained; likewise it reflects and advocates a position between free will and determinism.[2] Consistently meliorism contains the same central thought—hope—but with uncertainty expressed in various ways: "the world is neither good nor evil, but can be improved on the condition that its parts do their best to improve it"[3]; "the faith which affirms not merely our power of lessening evil—this nobody questions—but also our ability to increase the amount of positive good."[4]

Whoever subscribes to the optimistic-pessimistic viewpoint of meliorism is challenged to discover ways to advance the doctrine's goal. What must one know, what must one value, what must one do? Utopian, maybe, but how else can we improve our existence? In this book the indicative mode of its verbs suggests a constituent aspect of meliorism; the imperative mode recommends changes or actions. This is what we know, value, or do; this is what we must, should, or ought to do. Reality quickly intrudes: who are or should be the meliorists, the individuals who subscribe to meliorism and act upon its edicts? They are fallible persons who squeeze out of their limited knowledge and experience at least glimpses of utopian meliorism. It is not necessary to believe that one is superior to Aristotle or Mohammed, Newton or Einstein, Marx or a conservative neighbor to engage in the pursuit; rather we utilize their and our own insights, wisdom, challenges, and experience in pursuing more perfect people now and in the near and far future.

Nobody, especially this writer, knows or can be expected to know all there is to know about the past and the present, about the facts and theories from the disciplines of history and the natural or social sciences, and about the relevant practical and impractical actions. One is not infallible; one cannot and will not digest all that is to be found in encyclopedias or libraries and on the Internet.

In view of these limitations, three precautionary devices are employed in this book to serve as warnings to ourselves and meliorists concerning many statements being offered. First, the adverb *once* is often inserted into sentences to suggest the possibility of the temporal uniqueness or non-generalizability of a viewpoint or study. What was once true may not be true again. Second, the abbreviation "cf." is used in the notes—all at the end of this book—when the cited author or authors inspired the idea or contention at least partially: the actual, fallible responsibility is the present writer's. The same designation, however, at least suggests where documentation can be found. In deference to the original sources and also to convey their style and flavor, whether qualified or dogmatic, direct quotations from them are frequently given. Suddenly and quite frequently other single words or phrases are enclosed in quotation marks when no source is cited: this primitive contrivance suggests that the writer is challenging himself, common jargon, the author being mentioned, or the reader concerning the probably slippery meaning of a trite word or phrase.

Third, and strangely, often sources do not appear to be available or else they have not been discovered or digested by this particular writer. In such a desperate situation, the reader is given the name of "you" and is called upon for assistance to add wisdom and experience to the thought at hand: rhetorical questions are raised and then deliberately no answers are or can be supplied. This last device is supposed to be challenging: look, it says in effect, we do not know, we are uncertain, more evidence is desirable or required; the problem involves you, who likewise may or may not have information or a viewpoint worth noting; what do you as another human being think? Rhetorical questions thus allow this writer to express his own uncertainty and to pass the responsibility of replying or improving the ideas to others and to you, the devoted reader, whoever you happen to be.

UNCERTAINTY

By definition meliorism portrays uncertainty in a pursuit that is both realizable and unrealizable. Again and again it is acknowledged that truths are elusive, dogmatism must always or almost always be avoided, uncertainty is inevitable. An erudite British sociologist who has sought and has not found "the basic units of thought" concludes his analysis with the reminder that "the attitudes and characters of all people are incomplete": they continually use rhetoric and they themselves are "objects of rhetorical argument"; therefore, as we search for certainty, we are reminded that "so long as human thought continues, the last word should be unattainable, for there is always more than that can be said." Believing otherwise is to succumb to "vanity."[5] It is frustrating at the moment to withhold judgment and to promise ourselves and others that in the future the "real" solution will eventually arrive and it will then be possible to uncover previous mistakes. Accepting a subsequent statement or generalization may also be hazardous. One psychologist, after making notable contributions to experimental psychology in which variables were carefully controlled and conclusions were generally confined to the problem being investigated, retired from this scholarly approach and wrote a stimulating book describing the evolution of human beings and their achievements after they emerged into "full bipedalism" (a fancy word for walking on two feet rather than crawling on all fours). One of the difficulties preventing additional change or progress, he claimed, is that "we, as a species, have an easy time convincing ourselves and each other that our current ethic, morality, and way of living is not just good or better but comes close to being Truth."[6] We think and proclaim just that; really?

The realistic pessimism of uncertainty raises compelling challenges for meliorists. On the one hand, the "perils" associated with principles and generalizations are disturbing: meliorists, being human, crave "truth"; they wish to be certain that an endeavor will succeed in spite of attending difficulties and frustrations. Another psychologist remembers that "information is obtained by a reduction of uncertainty": you reach your destination on the route you finally select, you find the medicine or the procedure that relieves your pain after you have wondered whether you really have the remedy. On the other hand, uncertainty may be exciting or gratifying: you overcome odds; "meaning in music" may be identified "with uncertainty of melodic pattern," whereas in simple melodies we know what is coming and then experience no or fewer intriguing surprises.[7]

Meliorists cannot depend completely or forever upon principles that keep changing: exceptions are noted and new discoveries emerge. In charting human affairs, as an astute and deservedly respected political scientist has suggested, "mechanical precision" may not be attainable, instead "pure luck" may play a role which persons "of good judgments seem to enjoy."[8] After reviewing various scientific experiments, such as those testing theories of relativity and gravitational rotation, and after alluding to serious accidents such as the nuclear disaster at Chernobyl in 1986 and the explosion of the American space shuttle the same year, two social scientists conclude that "when things go wrong, it is not because human error could have been avoided but because things will always go wrong in any human activity."[9] Will they; and always? That statement, however, makes a valid suggestion to meliorists: errors can and must be anticipated, yet they are not completely inevitable or final and often may not occur. Indeed there are "advances" in science and technology: errors, yes, also greater precision and increasing accuracy.

There is likely then to be no simple, ever effective solution to human problems. Even on the level of troubled individuals, available therapies usually are not standardized. Yes, if a person is drowning, we know that he or she must be saved. But what should or must be done about a high fever? Lower it, yes, but how? The answer depends upon discovering the nature of the condition or illness for which the fever is a symptom. Challenging likewise are psychiatric difficulties varying from petty anxieties to suicidal impulses. In many instances a pure or modified psychoanalytic approach may be useful: slowly, patiently, painfully help the client or patient to become aware of the nature and origin of his or her difficulties as Freud clearly advocated and practiced. But often this "basic" approach is neither necessary nor effective, instead attention is concentrated only upon symptoms, an approach called behavior or multimodal therapy.[10] Who decides, how does one decide?

GUIDES

In spite or because of uncertainty, decisions concerning the validity of knowledge, the importance to be attached to values, and the selection of actions to pursue or reject are continually and inevitably made by all human beings. In the absence of imperfect principles, meliorists do not abandon the good fight or resign themselves to hopelessness or suicide. What they can do, in the absence of everlastingly valid principles, is to search for useful if imperfect guides. More than a verbal change is accomplished when open-ended guides are substituted for principles: they preclude uncertainty; they cannot, may not, must not, should not always be followed without anticipating exceptions. With somewhat confident hesitancy, then, the following guides are not decreed but only proposed, however patent their imperfections.

Guide 1: Determinism

A deterministic guide, which for many moments rejects or skeptically views "freedom," is a first step toward acquiring knowledge and planning action. Unavoidably people blink when a bright light suddenly strikes their retinas; another explanation must account for their prior presence at the spot where the light suddenly appears or for a possible subsequent judgment or action that may or may not include a value judgment suggesting that the light is harmless or dangerous. Although the sequence of first-cause and then-effect is the essence of determinism, cautiously avoided may be the fallacy that carries Latin "post hoc, ergo propter hoc" (after this, therefore, because of this).[11] That man, it is said, is healthy because he exercises so regularly. Less than a moment's thought suggests that his health cannot be attributed to exercise or exclusively so: his diet, philosophy, and way of life may have contributed to his health, which may be a cause and not the effect of the exercise; also many persons who exercise are not healthy. The cause-and-effect sequence, therefore, must be specified or limited. Another more common Latin phrase suggests a different explanatory route: "ex post facto" (from what is done afterward). Surely we know, but only after the fact, that whoever or whatever flashed that bright light is a cause of the eye-blinking event mentioned a few sentences ago, but we have that knowledge only retrospectively or after the occurrence of the blinking. And individuals, while subscribing to determinism, and ex post facto explanations in many situations, nevertheless share a conviction with many philosophers, theologians, and common sense that often—not always—they themselves "cause" the events.

Guide 2: Imperfection

Immediately or ultimately (however defined) every person, object, and "thing" (again, however defined) is imperfect (and defined?). Many reasons have been offered in the natural, social, and psychological sciences for the imperfections of people and hence for their inability either to understand themselves, and the "real" world, or to anticipate generally and accurately actions and interactions: the complexity of the problems being raised, variations in the technical jargon employed to describe other persons and events, and the compartmentalization of knowledge in different scholarly and technical disciplines. Not unexpectedly, a philosopher also once argued that scientists, scholars, and all of us have varying conceptions of morality that affect—or should affect?—what transpires when different theoretical and practical problems emerge.[12] In addition, within one's own group, including often among those pursuing or advancing knowledge, there may be a tendency to conform to its prevailing norms. After combining two common words, a psychologist once semi-dramatically emerged with the concept of what he appropriately called "groupthink" to refer to the tendency of persons in a group to strive for unanimity regarding a decision by "overriding" realistic alternatives offered by some of its members. Thus John F. Kennedy and his associates more or less agreed with one another when they decided to invade Cuba (the sad, unsuccessful "Bay of Pigs" in the spring of 1961): they did not consult qualified associates, they adopted the "preferred solution" of their president.[13] The self-esteem of a group's members thus may override "critical thinking." Occasionally, but increasingly frequently, social scientists admit their own imperfections and hence their uncertainty about the progression of events. An astute French writer once confessed:

> While the student of Nature can rejoice in the fundamental harmony he discovers beneath disorderly appearances, such aesthetic enjoyment is denied to the student of Politics. . . . It is impossible to foretell that a given investigation will be efficient whoever the subject may be.[14]

Even the not unopinionated H. G. Wells, in the final paragraph of his two huge volumes on *The Work, Wealth, and Happiness of Mankind* moaned that "our most fundamental ideas are provisional ideas, no doubt, but as yet there is nothing to replace them."[15]

Guide 3: Singularity

Generalizations based on the description and investigation of any phenomenon, however valid and reliable, are very likely to be incomplete or imperfect because the statements perforce may neglect particular or singular instances or exceptions, while those focusing upon singularity cannot include all other relevant instances. On the level of generalization it is probably true that all "normal" adult Americans of American parents who have been born and educated in the United States speak English, but the somewhat distinctive way in which any one of them uses and abuses that language—pronunciation, vocabulary, fluency, and so on—is part of his or her individuality. This guide does not deny the value of generalization but cautions against a common and tempting error of jumping from a limited number of individual instances to a general statement that also includes instances that have not been similarly appraised in their own right. A study of one, three, or a dozen wars in great detail permits a general statement about those particular wars but not about all wars ever fought. Whoever is concerned with a particular person—whether as a psychiatrist, psychologist, or friend—is confronted with the problem of individual differences. For many purposes, any person is unique; from another standpoint or for some other purpose, that uniqueness can be challenged and is part of some generality.

Guide 4: Perspective

Always, often, or whenever possible an effort is made to comprehend the relation of knowledge and action to whatever has been, is, will or could or must be relevant. This guide is both sweeping and vague, and deliberately so: perspective is required to anticipate the possible imperfections of generalizations since they may be imperfect or will be altered in the future and since they perforce are likely to neglect exceptions. Concretely perennial problems are related to personality and environment in different ways. A challenge of special interest to psychiatrists and anthropologists is whether "the high prevalence of psychiatric disorder is associated to a marked degree with sociocultural disintegration."[16] That association is postulated again and again and includes "the apparent effect of low socio-

economic status on mental health which many investigators have observed." The cause-and-effect sequence, however, can go either way:
depressed social conditions may facilitate personal disorders, and those
with such disorders may choose or be compelled to live under such social
conditions. Meliorists recognize the actual or potential importance of both
factors, appreciate that they interact, anticipate that in various situations
they have different weights, and do not ignore the possibility of genetic
(hereditary) determinants. What is essential is perspective defined as "the
range of content alternatives an individual takes into account when rating
his own attitude"[17] as well as the underlying knowledge, value, and action:
do persons decide to approve or disapprove of what they think or do by considering a few or many reasons associated therewith?

Guide 5: Evaluation

Every person, group, society, and object when perceived is, can, or
should then be evaluated; nothing is neutral. The guide does not decree the
value or values to be utilized, but indicates only the presence or potentiality
of some value as well as a responsibility for its recognition. No evaluation is
also a value, that of worthlessness, carelessness, inexperience, or indeci-
sion. Call it whatever one will, individuals are confronted with metaphysical or moral challenges, whether or not they or others believe and suggest
that there are no complete, satisfactory, or eternal values. Both the found-
ers and followers of religions everywhere, in Western as well as non-
Western societies, and philosophers in ancient and classic times or at this
very moment raise evaluative challenges. From their own standpoints they
try again and again to resolve similar resolvable or unresolvable challenges.
In the present era one philosopher has sought to stir interest by employing
the neologism of "Metamind" as the basis for evaluations. He points to "a
thought about a thought, about a feeling, or about an emotion" as a human
attribute, and he firmly believes that with such a frame of reference individuals confront and resolve challenges to themselves.[18] They normally
may not raise significant questions, yet at some point in their existence
they do and must wonder about the values guiding them. Relevant and important for this guide is also the distinction between explanations and justifications.[19] Explanations seek to be dispassionate by involving some
"objective" principle: one tries to discover why she was sleepy, why he had
too much beer to drink, why they are always listless, why the weather is un-
seasonable. They likewise pose an empirical challenge concerning their
validity or completeness: correct or not, have all factors been taken into ac-

count? Justification, on the other hand, requires an accompanying value, expressed or unexpressed, deliberate or not. He maintains that he was following a dictum of his religion when he helped that older person. Explanations and justifications frequently overlap. An explanation serves as a justification: she had to do that, her set of beliefs prevented her from doing otherwise, hence in one observer's view she was justified. Or she made the decision and later found reasons to explain that she believed she had no alternative.

Guide 6: Searching

Both despite and because of uncertainty it is necessary to search continuously for old, revised, and new knowledge, values, and actions. According to one of America's most distinguished and influential philosophers, the "ambition of moralists" is to have "ready-made rules available at a moment's notice for settling any kind of moral difficulty and reducing every species of moral doubt."[20] Immediately it is evident that most persons only glance at the overwhelming number of attempts to discover and adhere to general or particular principles and values. Consider the schools of philosophy and religions that have arisen. Certainly at a moment's notice or over time individuals cannot be expected to survey such a mélange and to uncover the best or exclusive guides for themselves. What meliorists do is either remain skeptical concerning the possibility of an ultimate, enduring decision in any given instance; or, for stated or unstated reasons best known to themselves, they select guides and cling to them on the basis of their own or others' experience or their private conceptions of validity. Unsettled ever is the aforementioned issue of certainty and uncertainty. With certainty individuals feel confident and perhaps secure, yet events may prove them wrong. With uncertainty they are insecure at the moment, yet perhaps less likely to be unpleasantly surprised by future events. Again in the words of the same philosopher, "principles" exist "as hypotheses with which to experiment"[21]—at least when the future seems unknowable. The melioristic search continues, even though meliorists know that they themselves and all others suffer from limitations imposed by their bodies, inheritance, society, opportunities, life span—on and on. Meliorists assume they share these limitations, while knowing and doing what their position in society permits, fosters, and requires. They exercise self-control when they believe they have the opportunity to do so; likewise they assume responsibility for their own actions when a choice appears available.

Guide 7: Surprise

Some aspect of every event—retrospectively, prospectively, or both—has not been, could not, or will not be anticipated. The guide may not be useful or helpful unless knowledge is imperfect, perspective is limited, responsibility is avoided, or the relevant value is muddled. A simple example: you throw an object into the air some distance from where you are standing; it falls to the ground. Surely you knew beforehand that it would fall; if its fall is your only concern and if the object is not a balloon filled with hydrogen or helium, then there is no surprise and the guide is useless or, unless qualified, the anticipation is incorrect. Still, if you reconsider or if someone else views the event, an unexpected surprise could have been anticipated: the effect of the descent on the falling object or on its landing place; the reason the object has been dropped; the reaction of a bystander (human or animal) to the event at some point in time. Forget the dropped object and turn to Marx and Engels, who forecast the coming of communism in the future and thus did not anticipate events similar and dissimilar to those they were not describing. In one of their best-known and frequently cited scholarly treatises, they suggested, after a "distribution of labour in capitalist societies," that human "activity is not voluntarily but naturally divided," with the result that "each man has a particular, exclusive sphere of activity which is forced upon him and from which he cannot escape"; thus he is "a hunter, a fisherman, a shepherd, or a critical critic, and must remain so if he does not want to lose his means of livelihood." Under communism, however, "where nobody has one exclusive sphere of activity but each can become accomplished in any branch he wishes, society regulates the general production and thus makes it possible for me to do one thing today and another tomorrow, to hunt in the morning, fish in the afternoon, rear cattle in the evening, criticize after dinner, just as I have a mind, without becoming hunter, fisherman, shepherd or critic."[22] Is that what once happened in Soviet and other modern communist societies? Is the description applicable to the People's Republic of China? Would Engels or even Marx have not been surprised?

Seven guides have now been unveiled. They are mentioned explicitly or coyly in every chapter throughout this book. Sometimes references to them are made unobtrusively by placing in parentheses the letter G followed by the number of the guide.

The guides purport to be promising bases for meliorism, melioristic knowledge, and melioristic actions. Evidence varying from the historical and religious to the empirical and experimental is supplied in each chapter.

Often that evidence is not new but trite, for which no apology is offered. Triteness is not always false; rather it may often reflect a hard-won truism that permeates peoples' beliefs and values and hence cannot be instantly or poetically outlawed. We have here an effort to synthesize unoriginal and possible original thoughts, elementary and not so elementary findings, and personal opinions that may achieve—possibly, hopefully, if improbably—a wisp of new insight at least temporarily. One never knows; carry on. Again, however, meliorism must be a joint enterprise between designated or self-appointed spokesmen or spokeswomen and an audience. You, the reader, you are the audience; you are thus challenged to improve every thought, proposal, or contention that follows.

But how can anyone, including the present writer, be sufficiently audacious or foolhardy to provide guides to meliorism in view of well-respected efforts throughout the centuries to achieve the same or a similar objective? In this lonely, unconventional paragraph, let private misgivings be expressed and confessed; thus at least the writer seeks to be melioristically forthright. Yes, critics will find deep holes to poke in the presentation. Yes, being an American with English as his mother tongue, he has tended to concentrate on English-language sources, and only occasionally on those in the two other languages he adequately understands, German and French. Yes, being a social psychologist and social scientist, he is largely wedded to those disciplines which are not infallible, although at least they deal directly with people who are a chief concern of meliorism. Yes, he has somewhat arbitrarily selected sources that have come his way or that he has located throughout many years in libraries and in conversations with colleagues and other sensible or not so sensible persons. Most paragraphs should be labeled "cf.": they are perhaps really only tentative, explorative, or illustrative. Yes, there are too many references to Hitler and his Nazis; why? The writer has had extensive experience with Germany; as an American graduate student he lived there for two years in 1930–32 as that man and his party struggled to attain power; and during and immediately after World War II he assisted the efforts of the United States and its allies to engage in "psychological warfare" against their enemies and to help evaluate those efforts. Amen.

After appraising these guides, let us relax—certainly a value—and observe quickly how other guides can be variously located. A South African scholar once cited Maxim Gorky: "The writer is like the eyes and ears of his epoch." He then suggested that one of his own countrymen had pointed to a similar guiding value at the beginning of a poem:

I aim not to quench any gleaming light
In this land of shadow and darkness;
I deride not the light of a flickering star
When the sun and the moon are no more.
There being no light from the sun and the moon,
I will hail the lone star of evening,
And the flash of the floating fire-fly
Little bird that glows in the night.[23]

A tablet concerning Gilgamesh, the Sumerian ruler thirty centuries ago, conveyed a feeling that mortal human beings, unlike the sun, are unable ever to travel across mountains in the dark and at night.[24]

Open, wide open, must be the query whether poetic guides of this sort emerging from the deeply felt observations and intuitions of conscientious nonscholars and nonscientists are more or less valuable than those from scientific laboratories or from research based on scholarly findings from small samples of human beings that are statistically significant at some conventional level. Was Shakespeare only a poet—should we listen to his beliefs or act as he implies?

CHALLENGES

Whether meliorists pursue past, present, or future problems and whether they are postulating egocentric or utopian solutions, they are confronted and confront themselves with three—yes, another three—challenges: elusive solutions, inadequate knowledge, and their own existence. A discouraging bell strikes truthfully those times, is illustrated here, and tolls longer and more loudly in subsequent chapters. Do stop and listen.

First, meliorists seek the utopian goal of peace on earth, yet the great intellects are unable to decide exactly why wars continue and foster horrors and death:

The number and variety of schemes for classifying and sorting out possible causes of war is quite large, and the typology selected depends not only on a range of scientific considerations but upon many extra-scientific ones: nationality, age, sex, basic personality, education, prior research experiences, and not surprisingly the fads and fashions of the moment as exemplified by those who employ us to teach, who finance our research, and who otherwise are in a position to pass judgment on our plans and our performance.[25]

And the remedy? Think for a moment of attempts to curb wars by individuals, organizations, and governments; then decide whether "progress" has been made. Since 1945 atomic weapons have not—or not yet—been dropped on enemies, but . . .

Another closely related, unresolved challenge is crime, in some ways more despicable than war. Criminals of any kind are disliked and feared or, if not by their victims, pitied. Medical and other therapies may be directed toward specific persons considered to be risks. The formal means adopted to curb crimes and criminals range from warnings concerning and actual punishments for criminal actions to educational and psychiatric treatment of the criminals and those allegedly so inclined. Involved are moral and social implications for the type, severity, and "justice" of the punishment and the reforms as well as their cost and ultimate effect on those convicted.[26] Thus the outpourings on that supreme punishment of capital punishment wander from deterrence to moral indignation. Corporal punishment of children who misbehave? A survey once revealed 16 percent of a sample of Germans completely opposed this method, 36 percent considered the punishment a part of training, 46 percent called such punishment a last resort, and a mere 2 percent claimed they were undecided. All the beliefs varied slightly with gender and a bit more so with age.[27] Stop crime, lower the crime rate; how?

A second frustration, inadequate knowledge, is epitomized by ignorance or uncertainty concerning persons who have played important roles in their own or other societies. The motive is not to satisfy curiosity, but to discover when, where, and in what circumstances such persons function so that in the present and future others like them can be either cultivated or curbed. Let Hitler serve as an illustration. Perhaps one knows how and why he was able to attract millions of Germans to support his Nazis, then with his Party to function as a dictator during a war foisted on Europeans and most of the rest of the world, and to encourage his followers to commit such atrocities as concentration camps, murders, the Holocaust, and other deliberate deeds of hatred. "The Search for Hitler" is the title of a preface to a scholarly book that once utilized, more than two decades ago, available archival materials. Its first sentence states: "It seems likely that more will be written about Adolf Hitler than about anyone else in history with the exception of Jesus Christ." Even on issues that may partially "explain" Hitler psychiatrically, there is "insufficient evidence to warrant the conclusion that Hitler was an overt homosexual," although "it seems clear that he had latent homosexual tendencies, and it is certain that he worried a great deal about them."[28] Conclusions about other details to "explain" Hitler likewise remain tentative and inconclusive. Suppose he had been psychoanalyzed!

The third peal of the challenging bell requires only a sentence because eventually it is so final for all of us: death, the ultimate consequence of age, disease, disappointment, deprivation, accidents.

In summary: this book is a strenuous, imperfect, too personal attempt to cull from a large, if necessarily incomplete, collection of sources the "best" wisdom and advice concerning what we know or must know if only fleetingly in order to lead a more satisfactory, happier existence and to achieve more utopian objectives. The arbitrary nature of the selection is again freely admitted. There is no alternative: almost anyone who has ever thought or written about human beings directly or indirectly has provided information that is or can be made to seem relevant. Here is one view, one attempt to glance at what has been, is, perhaps should be known concerning meliorism. Let us try, and try to do better, in Part I, "Tools" (Chapters 2, 3, 4); Part II, "People" (Chapters 5, 6, 7); and Part III, "Actions" (Chapters 8, 9). The title of the Epilogue (Chapter 10) is, appropriately, "Nevertheless."

PART I

TOOLS

CHAPTER 2

Nature of Knowledge

Knowledge is a key factor in meliorism: it concerns ourselves, others, the environment, and society; it is associated with joys and sorrows; and often, but not always, it leads to appropriate or inappropriate action. Knowledge engulfs us. We are satisfied and dissatisfied with our accomplishments. Persons we love or hate impart their "wisdom" to us. We catch glimpses of philosophical, religious, and scientific beliefs formulated centuries ago or recently and transmitted in ways we may never discover. Through our own language and translations of varying precision, knowledge reaches us.

The sun rises and sets every day. We believe the statement to be true. But of course infants do not possess that belief. From a scientific viewpoint the statement is also incomplete: the sun rises and sets at different times throughout the year. The rising and setting are a subjective, inaccurate way to refer to the position of the earth with relation to the sun. For meliorism is it always essential to "explain" or modify the first statement above about the rising and setting of the sun? In this chapter and the next, knowledge in general is appraised by considering its nature and functions; and its metaphysical aspects dare not be overlooked. Whatever its content or objective, knowledge is usually or can be expressed in everyday, technical, or symbolic language. A discussion of the perilous challenges of language is impatiently delayed until Chapter 4.

Initially knowledge is explored to "explain" events that have occurred or to anticipate their recurrence later. Confusion and uncertainty may thus be avoided. We know that Mexican workers have migrated to the United States since World War II in increasing numbers, whether legally or illegally. Why? One conscientious analysis reveals that at home in Mexico the migrants have been suffering from "the lack of cultivatable land, the increasing financial cost of farming, low income levels, lack of credit, the absence of price guarantees, and a low productivity of land caused by poor soil or poor cultural practices." With that knowledge meliorists also discover that such conditions in Mexico persist; hence leaders of the two countries seek, realistically or halfheartedly, to curb or regulate the migration by agreements and laws that have been only partially enforced. A quick statement by one Mexican provides memorable knowledge to explain his behavior at least to nonexperts: "Our necessity knows no law."[1]

Knowledge originates from external sources and personal experience. Externally you note that the wind blows off your hat; a friend praises you; the price of eggs or gasoline rises. Personally you know your throat aches; that a dream of yours haunts you the next day; that a flower or a friend is attractive. The sources may be combined. The wind blows off your hat, yes, but why were you wearing a hat, why were you wearing a hat that did not fit securely on your head, why were you then outdoors and not indoors? Your throat aches, poor you; have you been given the wrong advice or medicine to avoid or soothe that aching? At a given moment the impetus for acquiring knowledge may be personal, although originally the external source may have included the environment as previously affected or arranged not only by other human beings but also contemporarily by family members, peers, the powerful, and the mass media. Knowledge in an individual's group or society may be acquired without deliberate effort or almost effortlessly. In the West and elsewhere one probably knows that the concept of "gravity" or a similar term can be invoked when explaining why objects thrown in the air, unless somehow suspended aloft, drop to the ground. Likewise embedded in common knowledge are relatively new theories in the history of human thought that may or may not be considered completely valid right now or in the future. Conspicuous in the West and elsewhere is Darwin's approach to evolution, especially his emphasis upon "the survival of the fittest" (the pungent phrase of Herbert Spencer he cited approvingly): accurately or not, this explanation of change by living organisms has diffused in some form to most "educated" persons when they refer to the survival or the loss of species, groups, and even ideas.

VALIDITY

The chief melioristic challenge is to determine whether knowledge at hand is valid. But what is meant by validity? Valid knowledge is true;

invalid knowledge is false. But what is meant by truth or falsity? Truly we have bumped into an ancient problem to which there has always been some kind of solution, however pragmatic. Knowledge is true when it is claimed by competent persons on the basis of evidence. But when are claimers competent, and what evidence do they employ? We experience yet another bump or two. Halt: claimers are persons whose competence is judged by someone to be adequate in a given situation or generation; variability is thus acknowledged, and we can go no further. Also evidence varies but always—yes, always—stems from observable facts, however ascertained or collected.

After such twistings meliorists force themselves to contemplate various forms of validity, such as the following offered only for illustrative purposes:

Title	Claimer	Referent	Verifier
Objective	competent	anything	competent
Subjective	self	self	self
Projective	self	anything	not self
Unknowable	anybody	anything	nobody

Herewith quick examples: "people eat cheese" (objective); "I like cheese" (subjective); "I think they prefer Cheddar cheese" (projective); "donkeys don't like cheese" (unknowable).

Obviously each of the above or any form of validity requires careful elaboration. If you say projectively that they like Cheddar cheese, you may or may not be making a valid statement: you may be biased or be making only a careless observation of their cheese-eating, hence now or eventually somebody else, a competent observer, must verify your statement before the knowledge embedded in it may be considered valid. A report by you concerning a personal experience is subjectively valid only when you maintain you have had the experience and no one can or will deny that fact; but asserting that others or human beings generally also have a similar experience under allegedly similar conditions may or may not be objectively valid.

Unknowable validity is especially puzzling and may also be applicable to other forms of verification. The precise, private, internal reactions of any other human being besides yourself or of any living animal or plant will never be known to someone else. What are the reactions of that person, whether they be those of your mate or a stranger, to any situation including a printed communication or the sounds of a sonata? When you pet your dog or when you chase a bug that has invaded your private sanctum, what does the animal's behavior suggest concerning how it feels subjectively as you pet or persecute? You pull out a "weed" from your carefully cultivated garden: does that plant experience pain in its own terms? Some of such information may be known, but all of it is unknowable, and instead only wise or foolish guessing serves as the substitute. I can examine specific reactions or properties here or there, yet I can never get inside you, a pet, a bug, or a plant; and they cannot get inside of me. Even when you and scores of other geniuses observe that hundreds of donkeys shy away from cheese, you and they may only infer on the basis of their behavior that they dislike that food, but 'tis only an inference and you don't know their feelings. Similarly if I say I like cheese and you then believe that I do, only a portion of your knowledge is objectively valid: you competently understand me, you assume that I am telling the truth, and you believe there is a relation between what I say and what I feel. There is, however, an unknowable aspect of such validity: you will never know precisely how I feel when I claim I like cheese or anything else; you may believe my feeling about cheese is like yours, yet that is a guess and its validity is unknowable (G4).

Another precaution concerning validity stems from the false conviction that whatever we truly believe with emotional intensity must have resulted from our own experience and thought, hence it must be valid. Nonsense. It may not be valid in the view of someone else; it may be gainsaid by those who have not had similar experiences and who do or do not know whether that knowledge has been systematically obtained and tested. Such validity, consequently, is only subjective: I believe it; it must be so. The people you have met from the XYZ country have seemed jolly; there have been no exceptions, they all have been jolly; you believe, consequently and strongly, that XYZ produces only jolly persons; yet the belief based on your subjective experience may be wrong, you may project your own joviality upon them, you have met only unrepresentative samples of XYZs.

Common sense, intuition (both masculine and feminine), or straight guessing is often employed as a way to validate knowledge about human beings and their actions. The moment a specific study is examined, such as one from experimental psychologists or sociologists, surprises are likely to occur; and almost certainly no sweeping generalization without exceptions emerges. What happens when one wins a substantial sum of money in a lottery? One's lifestyle may certainly change, yes, but only about two-thirds of substantial winners in an American lottery once reported that they actually had made changes; less than a quarter believed they really had not changed at all. Some winners stated they did not feel happier after the financial windfall, and most of them then claimed they derived less pleasure from present or past satisfactions. The same investigator interviewed paraplegic and quadriplegic Americans who had suffered serious accidents; not unexpectedly these individuals tended not to anticipate great joys in their future, and they believed they were magnifying those joys they had experienced before being incapacitated.[2] Thus good old common sense conceivably might have been a guide for the sufferers but not for lottery winners.

SOURCES

"Probably since the dawn of human reflection people have been searching for the ultimate causes of events, the driving motors of phenomena and processes, the forces responsible for their fate," according to a modern Polish sociologist (G1). At first, he suggests, they pursued information to explain supernatural or animistic forces. Then they turned to natural forces now called "physical, chemical, biological, climatic, geographic, even astronomical." Eventually responsibility and hence causality have been attributed to Great Men, other leaders, scholars, scientists, and "geniuses." The final agent has been "society itself" and hence the growth of sociology and other social sciences.[3]

Knowledge from any source may or may not be deliberately acquired by its possessors. Young children slowly, gradually, unwittingly eventually learn that their welfare depends upon their parents and guardians. You discover that you do not reach a destination; you have followed the wrong route, which you try to avoid in the future. Most of what must be known to function effectively in an occupation usually must be consciously learned; but the information required to repair shoes or cars differs from what kindergarten teachers and politicians learn from experience. Physicians master knowledge that has little in common with what attorneys must know, although occasionally the interests of the two professions coincide and then each discovers or seeks knowledge about the other's way of functioning.

There follows a brief and not always fascinating description of the sources of knowledge together with suggestions regarding reasons for their possible validity or invalidity in one or more of its meanings. Individuals do not necessarily categorize the sources of their knowledge, but when they do, the evaluation thus obtained may itself be positive or negative. The dicta of parents may be more highly valued than those from strangers; yet the judgment also depends on the attitude toward parents and the others, doesn't it? In the West the highly educated are tempted to bow more respectfully to scientific knowledge than to traditional folklore; yet the wisdom of the ages sometimes commands more subjective respect than the whimsy of alleged upstarts in science.

1. Casual Knowledge

Knowledge not only from the self, relatives, and peers but also from views prevailing within a society is casual knowledge. Such knowledge, whether subjectively or objectively valid, can come in a flash, whether or not its communicator intends the learning to be effortless. "The devil can quote scripture," and his utterance may or may not be convincing. Seemingly profound knowledge, such as beliefs related to patriotism (is our country making "progress"?) or metaphysics (is there a god or gods, who or what created this universe or other universes?), may originate externally within the family or society but then may be modified, amended, or lightly or markedly changed by the learners themselves. In the United States and often in other countries, the chief culprits for communicating superficial, inaccurate, or misleading knowledge are some public commentators and advertisers, especially those associated with mass audiences on television and radio. A "popular" writer once contrasted the "more than a thousand hours" of TV he recorded on a single day in 1990 with information coming to him on another occasion when he was atop a mountain and he could allegedly perceive only the countryside all about him. Most, not quite all, the TV communications were superficial and incomplete, offered as entertainment or commercial inducements; alone on the mountain, he asserts, he was in a mood to experience his surroundings and to obtain new insights into himself. He also noted other obvious ways of obtaining less superficial or fleeting information leading to more complete and hence valid impressions, such as by reading rather than by quickly riding by a billboard in a car or even on a bicycle.[4]

Knowledge of the self by the self, regardless of its own or socially objective validity, affects that self's behavior. Presume that an aging person believes that absentmindedness increases with age and that strangers, when they perceive others' advancing age, are more friendly or polite than they are toward younger people. This person then notes instances of being absentminded which previously might have been ignored or may be generally less attentive to details because he or she believes that such behavior is as inevitable as gray hair or wrinkles. And the friendliness and politeness of strangers, whether or not it be objectively valid, is likely to be appreciated or to suggest another reason to be ashamed of advancing age. This phenomenon has been aptly named "self-fulfilling prophecy" and has given rise to considerable research especially with American college students.

What one perceives, hears, or reads informally, especially out of context, requires careful evaluation. Glance quickly at two examples. The first: "Since the days of Hobbes, man's view of the world has changed and man's concept of the forces of history has changed accordingly," so that "history may prove which side is right and which wrong in the struggle against communism."[5] The second: "It is one of the great paradoxes of our time that man, who began the period we call 'modernity' with a self-confident assertion of his 'coming of age' and 'autonomy,' approaches the end of the 20th century fearful of himself, fearful of what he might be capable of, fearful of the future."[6] The first comes from a deputy prime minister of Greece in an introduction to a book reporting papers from a conference on international relations of Asian and African countries in the early 1960s; the second from Pope John Paul II toward the end of his address to the United Nations in October 1995. Which statement do you believe or do you believe both; was your judgment affected when you were given the sources of the statements and their publication dates?

Obtaining informal knowledge about other persons, especially strangers, is especially perilous: they may be questioned or observed in situations that for them are "atypical"; they may deliberately respond in a manner that conceals what they think or feel or in their opinion creates a favorable if misleading impression of themselves. So-called "unobtrusive measures," therefore, have been devised by scholars, social scientists, and psychiatrists to try to obtain seemingly valid information without advising informants concerning its purposes[7]; later they may be informed concerning the deception when investigators believe it is "unethical" not to do so. Also filed reports can be used to learn about persons on the basis of their recorded past behavior: the popularity of books on particular subjects as determined from sales or library records; the directories of clubs and organizations; voting outcomes; spontaneous responses to the mass media. In each instance the validity of the inferences is unknowable if reasonable. "Simple" observation of individuals as they pass by or as they attend or participate in games and public gatherings may be interpreted by observers, whose assessment may or may not be completely or sufficiently valid.

New or slightly new knowledge may be acquired by reasoning from experience or other previous knowledge. At first an individual appears shy, and his shyness is attributed to the situation in which he is being observed; but later, if he appears shy in many different situations, the observer may conclude that shyness is one of his traits. Generally syllogistic reasoning may be employed, without recognizing the syllogism as a paradigm, in order to conclude that Aristotle is mortal after hearing the premises that "All men are mortal" and that indeed "Aristotle is a man." After "residents of isolated villages in Central Asia" during the 1930s were told that "in the north where there is snow all year, the bears are white" and that "Town X is there in the north," they were then asked, "Are the bears white in that town or not?" Their typical reply was reported to be: "No, I don't know what kind of bears are there; I have not been there and I don't want to lie."[8]

2. Arts

The arts provide deliberate or nondeliberate knowledge from fiction, poetry, and other art forms. Suddenly one learns: "But so it is, and nature has contrived / To struggle on without a break thus far, / Whether or not we find what we are seeking / Is idle, biologically speaking."[9] That wisdom thus conveyed is expressed in a form likely to be remembered; does it possess objective or only subjective validity?

A competent historian reminds her scholarly colleagues and the rest of us that "Shakespeare's Macbeth is not an exact portrait of a certain eleventh-century King of Scotland but is a profound and illuminating study of a living and comprehensible man, weak, not without nobility, gradually corrupted by ambition."[10] A quick glance at or pensive contemplation of a painting or sculpture, whether it be realistic, impressionistic, or expressionistic, can provide intuitive knowledge about a human being or human problems perhaps less likely to be obtained in formal communications. And music? Other flagging questions protrude from the arts. How "typical" is that character in a novel or portrait; can its creator be trusted as an informant? And memorability does not always contribute to wisdom and mental health; we remember easily and unwittingly the contrived "artistic" content of commercially motivated advertisements.

3. Philosophy

This source of knowledge is seldom communicated liltingly but is usually packed with references to predecessors and speculations about the present and future from undocumented, undocumentable, and documented observations of the universe, society, human beings, and other philosophers. The progress achieved by this source of knowledge depends on the use of precise concepts and illuminating illustrations. Even the wildest and oldest of philosophical ideas, however, whatever their validity, may be inspiring. Meliorists may often turn to the ancients and to respectable writers and thinkers venerated by their ancestors, as they find or seek to find suitable and cogently formulated guides to their own era and the future (G6).

4. History

This source of knowledge recounts, with scholarly or other formal or informal standards or explanations, past events of all kinds. Such information may be useful to know. The present stems from the past and cannot be fully grasped or appreciated unless at least some of its origins are known. Knowledge of past actions that have succeeded or failed to achieve their objectives may provide guides to the selection of similar or dissimilar actions at the moment. It may thus be useful to review the ancient and perpetual problems and solutions already discussed in the past, such as those in both testaments of the Bible or the Koran and in the writings of such persons as Plato, Rousseau, Thoreau, and Einstein. Any list of the magnificents, however, is arbitrary; why not include Shakespeare, Goethe, Dante, or a playwright whose drama or comedy opened on or off Broadway the day before yesterday? There is no good reason to exclude any source, when the author offers reasons or evidence for the observation or viewpoint. Insights from old sources can be accepted or rejected without affecting their utility at a later date.

Almost always, then, history is a slippery guide. So many "facts" from the past are known or may become available so that nobody, including even professional historians, can be expected to be acquainted with all of them. Considerable historical knowledge is not easily or glibly acquired: a quick glance at the various theories of history espoused by historians and others indicates that the life work of a scholar may sometimes be required to try to unravel all available information on a single topic. Historians may not agree with one another concerning what past knowledge must be salvaged to understand the present. Which sources should be consulted? Then new historical knowledge may become available that requires the past to be interpreted differently. Thus as the Japanese surrendered in 1945, it seemed clear in the West that they were responding, at least in part, to the destruction of two of their major cities by the atomic bombs dropped by the Americans. That popular belief now contains more than a trace of projective validity as revealed subsequently. American physicists and others in the 1940s worked feverishly to develop that lethal weapon before the Germans could do so; and American authorities knew "the Nazis would not be able to build more than a research reactor." It was clear, according to secret sources, that "Japan would have surrendered if atomic bombs had not been dropped" because the "Japanese were already defeated and ready to surrender." Surrender may have been hastened; but, as indicated by classified information, that deadly weapon both then and in the postwar period served as "a trump card against the Soviet Union."[11] More generally, some origins and events may never be known. Napoleon's inner thoughts when he was banished finally to the island of St. Helena can be resurrected only in fiction.

The existence of a persistent religious or social belief or practice for centuries in a society does not mean that all persons now believe or behave accordingly: some do, some do not; and both the belief and practice may be weaker or stronger than it formerly was. A historian once concluded an analysis of history with a devastating challenge: "If one thing is certain, it is that history's forces have reached a power utterly unlike that of our sheltered past, and that the changes those forces portend are very different from the propitious historic transformations they brought about in our past."[12] And he was writing in the early 1960s, not during the even more chaotic times toward the end of our century. And now a simple, personal question: have you ever noticed differences between your memory of an event and the way it has been reported by your best friend, by journalists, and by historians?

5. Polls and Surveys

That source of knowledge is from "instruments" employed by social science, governments, research organizations, and industry; it is usually concerned with actions of human beings, the prime targets of meliorism. In this research it is frequently essential to know and appraise the sample of persons from and for whom the data have been obtained. To achieve a generalization that has objective or even subjective validity, the sample must be representative of the group that has been selected or designated people generally. Some, not all, published social science studies involving the opinions, attitudes, and actions of Americans are based on samples of American students in American universities who are easily available, with or without their prior consent, in classes being taught by the investigators. The latter assemble the data and usually eventually write articles which, when published in a scholarly journal, add to their professional standing or income. These samples may not be representative even of American students, of Americans generally, or, more probably, of persons in other societies on earth; nevertheless, their collectors may be tempted to believe otherwise and give the misleading impression of a more extensive implication of the findings by couching them in the present tense that sounds universal, rather than in the past tense which indicates that these participants were investigated only once and that the findings may or may not be obtainable a second time. One precautionary device to avoid such misleading errors has previously been suggested in this book: the use of "once" at least to place a finding in its temporal and research period. Another reminder hereafter will be to call investigation of American students on one occasion *dingdong samples*: the usually helpless students may be reflecting only their culture, status, and era. Dingdong does not ring senselessly: the appellation would politely warn that other human beings, methods, and time periods are not considered. Imperfect as it may be, dingdong research at least provides preliminary knowledge that may be valid more widely. The same label is usually, maybe always, applicable with modification to research in other countries conducted by governments.

The phrasing of questions in such surveys and in similar research affects informants' replies. Do you believe in such-and-such? The investigator's wording of the question may or may not evoke the informants' own way of viewing the phenomena being investigated. To try to prevent misunderstanding, such-and-such may be spelled out in detail, so that at least it is known that the responses come from the particular collection of verbal vibrations but not from subtler or cruder expressions. Also participants' interpretation of a complete sentence may differ from that of the investigator. Even more perplexing, some or many of the informants may not have had a previous opinion, so that raising the question produces a reaction to which a considered or spontaneous opinion is given. The reply can be "don't know," or some persons feel embarrassed not to express an opinion in front of a stranger so that what they say comes quickly, may be unreliable, or different on another occasion. The real purpose of polls and surveys, either determined in advance or after the data become available and computerized, is not communicated to those in the sample when it is unnecessary or impossible to do so. Like researchers employing unobtrusive methods, however, pollsters and experimenters may feel ethically obligated to reveal the rationale of their study after collecting the data. Concealed recording on tape does not disturb the "natural" nature of an investigation, and then later the same ethical challenge may appear: must we tell them what we were really doing?

An apparent or alleged advantage of polling is that outcomes are expressed in quantitative terms, so that one knows or believes what the majority of the sample think or claim they think. Numbers suggest precision and are part of experience whenever reference is made to the passing of time during a specified period that varies from a brief interval to the spread of history.[13] Quantification, however, describes only the outcome of the gathering of data, and meliorists must search for possible errors and shortcomings involved in the gathering.

Differences between individuals in a group or society can be ascertained cautiously from surveys and replace reckless generalizations. Yes, "Americans" were horrified when President John F. Kennedy was assassinated in 1963, but careful surveying revealed "differences between children and adults, between younger and older children, boys and girls, normal and disturbed, upper and lower class, science students and liberal arts students, as well as a great variety of individual differences."[14] Deviations of some kind from central tendencies usually exist likewise and may be important to report and to know.

When surveys or any measures or observations reveal differences between two groups or between samples from two areas or countries, the obtained differences must then be "explained." They can be attributed to membership in the two groups or samples only when other differences are irrelevant and when they alone are related to that membership. Thus a survey revealing that Group A is more "religious" than Group B establishes that difference, but the difference may be due not to group membership but to the fact that a powerful preacher has been active in A and not in B; or religiosity of the two groups may have been "measured" at different times of the year with A having been closer to a religious festival and B during another month. In addition, whenever the findings of two samples—whether ascertained in survey or through a rigorous scientific method—differ, the question arises whether an obtained difference between them could have arisen by chance resulting from the sampling method or some other irrelevant cause. The investigator determines whether differences are "statistically significant" by means of standard mathematical formulas. By sensible convention the greatest confidence is expressed when it can thus be ascertained that the obtained differences could have arisen "by chance" only once in 100 times. Some investigators, nevertheless, may attach significance to differences that could have arisen by chance 5 times in 100: but, it has been vigorously argued, such differences are marginal and should inspire little or no confidence that other than chance could have been the explanation to account for the obtained differences.[15]

6. Experimentation

This source of knowledge is based on investigations in which the variable of interest is measured or observed under different conditions so that its effectiveness or importance can be ascertained. Ideally there are two groups: the experimental group in which the variable is or is thought to be operating and a control group in which that variable is not operating or operating differently. In the natural sciences the investigator deliberately manipulates the conditions so that the variable functions in the experimental group but not in the control group. What happens to a compound when a specified chemical is present or absent? For the social and psychological sciences, human beings may be randomly assigned to one of two groups; thereafter the experimental group receives some treatment (a communication) and the control group is ignored; or past events have been different for two groups (an educational method favored by officials has been followed in one group but not in the other). In any case, whether the investigator or some other source has employed whatever the variable suggests, the basic assumption must be that the two groups have been equivalent before the experimental group has been treated or affected differently.

The value of knowledge obtained from experimentation, like other methods, must be carefully and critically examined. Originally were the experimental and control groups or conditions really equivalent? Is any obtained difference between the groups statistically significant in the sense described above in connection with surveys? What is the relation between the manipulated or observed variable in the experiment and in "real life"? Since real wars thankfully are not engineered for the sake of research, what does one learn generally about wars from a "simulated war" staged for an experimental and control group of American high school students or ding-dong samples in comfortable laboratory settings?[16] In addition, meliorists do not forget that experimentation in the strict sense enables investigators to control the sequence of events and to establish causal sequences, but that many significant events cannot be controlled and hence their causes and effects remain elusive. One way to achieve objective or greater objective validity is to repeat an experiment to determine whether similar or dissimilar findings emerge. With chemicals, usually with animals, and sometimes with people such replication is possible and feasible, but often on a human level the replication cannot be exact: in the meantime the individuals are different, or historical changes or the costs of the research prevent the past from being repeated.

Indeed a control group to compare with an experimental group may not be available in many circumstances. What kind of person would you now be if you had been one of seven siblings in your family? What would have happened in the United States and elsewhere if Presidents Lincoln or Kennedy had not been assassinated? Would there have been World War II if the

British and French had not accepted the Munich Pact with Hitler in September 1938? Such counterfactual thinking can be employed to stimulate the imagination and also, of greater importance, to sharpen perception of events that in fact have occurred. Guiding principles have been suggested that can render the approach more valid and useful, such as: "Sound counterfactuals require sound theories that provide the lawlike generalizations that fill in the missing data points in our thought experiments." The imaginary thinking may also have an effect upon personal values: "Things may not be great, but think how bad things could have been if x or y had occurred."[17]

Science based on experiments produces theories that cannot be uncritically acclaimed and usually require additional experimentation or research. In a book with the melioristically inviting subtitle of *What Everyone Should Know about Science* and claiming to be written "for the general reader who wants to know about how science really works and to know how much authority to grant to experts," two sociologists examine such topics as relativity, cold fusion, gravitational radiation, and the origin of life. They indicate dramatically not only the complications involved in those studies but also the rivalries and claims of different theorists working in the same area and seeking in small or large part to bolster their own credibility as they pursue "truth." In the critics' own words: "Reporting an experimental result is itself not enough to give credibility to an unusual claim"; "It is said that scientists claimed too much, based on too little, and in front of too many people"; "When things go wrong, it is not because human error could have been avoided but because things will always go wrong in any human enterprise." In short: "scientists are neither Gods nor charlatans; they are merely experts, like every other expert on the political stage."[18] Meliorists review such travails even in science and thus retain and strengthen their own convictions concerning uncertainty.

Experiments in the abstract and concrete continue to increase as the environment in every sense and its inhabitants are probed and reveal or are induced to reveal new knowledge. Perhaps it is tempting to think that "the sciences are by their nature subject to eventual decay" as they "come up against unbreakable barriers of understanding, beyond which we shall always remain ignorant." Einstein, according to one historian of science, however, possessed what must be considered here to be the melioristic view that science is "a program with an aim toward which one can advance but it has no ending in the foreseeable future"; it can function "only with one's subjective capacities and with essentially arbitrary concepts."[19] Hail to this modest but determined approach.

Einstein's view is likewise suggested by the observation that "all events are unique" or at least seem to be unique at first or second glance, but this observation or interpretation "does not imply that their explanation cannot be based on general theories."[20] Meliorists are able to acknowledge uniqueness, therefore, yet in almost every unique event they can find some components similar or related to other events (G3). Uniqueness involves all the components of the event and particularly their combination; from the combination some, but not all, components can be extracted that resemble other events.

Scientists who have recognized limitations within their disciplines have sought various remedies. One is to combine two disciplines, as in the case of biochemistry or sociohistory, so that new kinds of syntheses can be achieved and different kinds of data gathered. A relatively recent methodological technique, "meta-analysis," has been proposed and extensively utilized, not only to avoid generalizing from a single or small number of studies or observations but also to deal with the challenge arising when many relevant studies are available.[21] All studies are collected on a given topic or problem, and then are carefully coded to determine whether they meet acceptable standard criteria such as number of informants, type of measuring instrument, and statistical technique. Those not meeting the standards are discarded; those then remaining are weighted and combined so that eventually generalizations emerge that are based on the selected studies. The generalization, therefore, represents the findings of those studies and hence is a way of integrating empirical knowledge.[22] Although such meta-analytical generalizations are of great value in understanding groups or particular phenomena, sometimes meliorists and others must concentrate on specific persons and glimpse their individuality.

This chapter's skirmish with knowledge ends challengingly with a reference to a conscientious, well-accredited astronomer who once addressed the topic of communication among animals such as dolphins and whales and the possibility that they also may deliberately communicate to human beings: he speculated too about the possibility of "extraterrestrial life" and of visits to the earth by organisms from other planets.[23] He arrived at no firm conclusions about the communication of animals or such visits; instead he offered supporting and contrary evidence. A serpent tempted Eve to eat from the tree of knowledge, she tempted Adam, and after succumbing they both were banished from Eden; and a thousand years earlier another serpent stole a plant from Gilgamesh that would have given him eternal life.

CHAPTER 3

Functions of Knowledge

Before and after the functions of knowledge are known and appreciated, two relevant challenges appear: is knowledge in fact available and, if so, is or is it not utilized or utilizable by the self, others, and society? Again there are no definitive replies to these questions, and the pursuit can be viewed optimistically or pessimistically. Meliorism always intrudes.

AVAILABILITY

Quite obviously, as a problem arises, the relevant knowledge must be available to the person or persons for whom it is a guide; its validity must be appraised. Sources of statements, especially when provided as footnotes or their equivalent, may be placed along a continuum of trustworthiness and objective validity, with casual knowledge or philosophy at one end and experimentation in the natural sciences at the other. You and your neighbor disagree whether your guide to action should come from Aristotle or a Nobel Prize–winning chemist, and the two of you differ concerning the accomplishments of any two persons. Can one trust a well-written, serious "travel book" by an apparently conscientious journalist who recounts his "personal experience" in various African and Asian countries after "a brief romp through a swatch of the globe"?[1] Personal knowledge of that sort is easily and frequently available, yet may or may not be trustworthy. You tell a joke and people laugh; thereafter you may be subjectively correct or incorrect if you believe that the same joke, when repeated with a different audience, will also seem funny.

Before accepting or utilizing available knowledge, meliorists seek to de-termine its validity. Skepticism is essential especially concerning a pro-posed explanation of events and the sequence of causes and effects. "No one disputes that the welfare state is here to stay," a confident sociologist once explained during a scattered, compelling discussion of how modern states had been attempting to cope with the unfortunate or misguided per-sons requiring assistance from governing authorities.[2] Meliorists must im-mediately wonder whether the statement itself is correct: "no one," but surely we can discover somebody who rejects the statement, even as in the intervening years some persons in former Soviet states indicated their dis-agreement with its flat claim. Perhaps, as has been suggested, political and social movements like communism, "classless society," and democracy have attracted large numbers of people because their promises and the con-notations of their concepts have been sufficiently vague to enable followers to exercise imagination and fantasy concerning what they believe would soon or eventually be thereby accomplished.[3] Certainty derived from ob-jectively valid knowledge is generally desirable; yet, as previously sug-gested, the surprise or excitement after or during periods of uncertainty can be pleasantly gratifying. Even pure scientists make mistakes, and some are prone to commit what has been called "irrational belief persistence" or "the tendency to search for evidence, and to use evidence, in a way that supports beliefs that are already strong for us (prior beliefs) or beliefs that we want to be true."[4] Replicating an investigation of any kind, as previously men-tioned, is clearly one way to test hypotheses or assess generalizations when and if replication is manageable.

Often, perhaps too often, objectively valid knowledge is not available even to experts anywhere (G2). Does life in any form exist elsewhere in the universe and, if so, where and in what form? Cures for some diseases remain elusive in spite of extensive investigations by medical and health profes-sionals. The outcome of some events may be impossible to anticipate: what are the effects of early childhood experiences on adult behavior? A psycho-analyst has examined the diaries of Heinrich Himmler, the Nazi leader of the SS troops who was responsible for carrying out Hitler's command to murder Jews and real and alleged opponents of the regime. In his early years and then later, Himmler "could be as loving or as aggressive as the person with whom he was identifying." That description and analysis of him was written years after he had been arrested by British troops and committed suicide. "Could one have predicted from his adolescence that this youth would grow up to be the greatest mass murderer of all time?" The proposed answer: "Clearly such prediction is beyond the scope of either history or psychoanalysis." Why? "The variables are too numerous."[5] Likewise, more generally, it would be similarly useful to know the conditions that produce depressions in individuals and societies as well as possible cures. Any one treatise cannot provide the details concerning their genesis and possible therapies or socialization practices. Volumes for each topic are at hand, but no agreement concerning origins or treatment may be found. Frustration, disappointments, the "essential aloneness" of all persons, and "the decline in vital energies" with increasing age are inevitable. An American psychiatrist once admitted that no single therapy could be recommended to alleviate any one or all of those four dismal conditions; and so he emphasized the downs and ups of conventional psychiatry, psychoanalysis, antidepressant drugs, and electric shock therapy as possible methods to restore a satisfactory existence or at least to diminish, maybe even eliminate, some of the distressing symptoms.[6]

Some knowledge may be available but incomplete. Individuals travel for the fun of it, don't they? Perhaps thereby they learn and retain additional knowledge concerning the peoples and countries they visit. More than the travelers themselves obviously are involved in their adventures. Tourism is a large industry for companies and travel agencies that help to arrange trips as well as for hotels, restaurant owners, and souvenir hawkers in the places being visited. Its analysis has become another minor scholarly pursuit with commendable studies emerging especially in anthropology.[7] The benefits and injuries accruing to the hosts and their governments can also be cautiously assessed. Non-Western countries gain money and may learn seemingly therapeutic techniques from their visitors, while being to some degree Westernized; is support thus being given to the value of "one world" that becomes more homogeneous so that cultural and other nuances gradually or abruptly disappear?

Generally knowledge of a problem may stem from what is known concerning its components, but their interrelationship transcends them and demands comprehension of the total configuration. Thus knowledge about the physical environment or about the zoning regulations of communities requires that attention be paid to many factors, tempting as it may be to mention, respectively, only the composition of the soil or the status of people living or excluded from a particular locality. It may be very well to believe or to know that "everything is connected to everything else," but objectively valid knowledge also determines "which connections are stronger and more significant than others."[8]

Conceivably, one must immediately if tentatively add, some knowledge may never become available. A founder of American sociology once claimed at the beginning of the twentieth century that "all origins are lost in mystery, and it seems vain to hope that from any origin the veil of mystery will ever be raised."[9] Such a view may be generally objectively valid for most social and other topics and can serve as a general precautionary warning concerning most other knowledge. At a given point in time, however, some hypotheses appear probable, tempting, and hence perhaps convincing; efforts do and must continue to probe apparent mysteries. Meliorists ever remind themselves, in the challenging words of a historian, that there are "limitations of human knowledge"; if there are "immutable laws of nature," they are "not always knowable to us, and most certainly not knowable—or rarely knowable—at the time frames necessary to right the wrong of the past and prevent future harm."[10]

Knowledge may be provocative without providing the complete coverage required by objective validity. Correlations indicating the probability of a relation between two phenomena are useful but require critical examination. Height is correlated with weight; taller persons tend to be heavier than shorter persons. The degree of the relation between two variables can be expressed by a statistical correlation that ranges from zero to 100 and that may be positive or negative. The degree of the association established between the two phenomena depends upon the size of the correlation itself as well as the number of cases on which it is based. But knowing the correlation is only a first step in determining the utility of the information thus obtained. Then one must ask: why is the correlation positive or negative? Why are heavier individuals taller; why does smoking "cause" lung cancer, that is, why is cancer associated with smoking; why does the crime rate go down, if it does, as countries "prosper"?[11] In any case, further investigation and additional knowledge are essential. Essential to whom? Essential to the experts and meliorists and also to those who would improve or disprove the correlation. For the nonexperts unable to seek explanations for correlations, knowledge of some association between events may suffice, provided they can or will appreciate that they thus are only acquainted with a statement of a problem. A key word (or its equivalent) that is employed by scholars and meliorists and that must likewise be grasped and appreciated is that of *tend*: a relationship moves or appears to be in the specified direction but only imperfectly so; a central tendency is noted, yet there are also large or small deviations.

Correlations, consequently, provide tentative knowledge without indicating the causal sequence of events. In Western countries poverty and many ills ranging from poor health and stunted growth to criminality and drug addiction exist side by side; but which is cause and which is effect? Do meliorists subscribe to a modern standpoint that for most persons, by and large, poverty must be the cause and that the ills are the consequence? A careful analysis of Britain in the nineteenth century indicates that infant mortality, the health of children in poor families (including a general decrease of height among boys), as well as "immorality and disorganization" worsened as poverty increased during that century, especially among urban dwellers.[12] The statistical finding calls attention to "the quality of life" offered the lower strata in society and may suggest only that over time both poverty and the attributes of impoverishment may have fluctuated.

Some, perhaps even all, knowledge must remain inexact for a variety of reasons. Replication, however desirable, may not be possible, and counterfactual reasoning is not a completely satisfactory substitute for a control group. The beginning of the earth or of the universe cannot be duplicated; instead inferences must be made from efforts to simulate what, it is thought, may have occurred billions of years ago. The scientists may provide a different version of events that may be variously interpreted as a "glimpse of divinity," their "purpose" may be a source of wonderment,[13] but the interpretation may actually come from unprovable wishful, subjective thinking. Except under experimental conditions designed by natural scientists, two events involving human beings can never be "exactly" identical: even when surrounding conditions appear or are made to appear the same, the later event occurs after the first one and hence may have been affected by the passing of time or interim events. You continue to like a particular person a day or week later, yet you are now older and may have had pertinent experiences between the two occasions that have made you wiser or more foolish. In short, quickly but memorably, Heraclitus told us centuries ago: "You cannot step into the same river twice." And a modern scientist shouts in a heading within a penetrating book: "The future is unlike the past because it has not happened yet"; in addition, "any prediction about human affairs necessarily rests on a very large number of assumptions" and "populations, the environment, economics, and culture all interact jointly."[14] Tritely, however, we try to do the best we can, yet perfection never ceases to be elusive.

Available knowledge may become less inexact and more objectively valid, nevertheless, when new data are gathered by investigators or when improved techniques are devised. Biology and other sciences and disciplines have been able to advance on the basis of observation and measurements rendered feasible by microscopes. New theories can be similarly productive. Thus Chaos theory—with a capital C—emphasizes "the importance of interdependence in shaping the world at all levels from the molecular to the societal," so that "science, pragmatism, and spirituality are in fact becoming intertwined."[15] One adherent of the theory argues that what appears random may not be stochastic, but can be systematically formulated; yet increased information may produce not less but "greater" uncertainty.[16] For many scientists in governmental organizations, universities, and industries engaging in research, additional knowledge may require minor or drastic revision in general and specific theories. Toward the end of this century new words such as pollution, biosphere, desertification, ecosystem, endangered species, herbicides, and radon call attention to important discoveries requiring the revision of knowledge, principles, and innovative actions.

Facts or data may remain unchanged, but the knowledge they make available may be interpreted or conceptualized differently as new modes of thinking or designation arise. Even simple storytelling "consists in going back to some selected beginning and carrying forward a narrative of happenings from that point to the situation which the narrator has undertaken to make clear,"[17] and the same is true of the stories that constitute formal history as well as any discipline that moves from the past to the present when a sequence of cause-and-effect is postulated. As time passes, different events or values that may have been previously available are selected to be included in the story or the theory. The stories and the data behind the principles have not been experienced by every individual who relates or subscribes to them. The details come from the past, represent the interactions of known and unknown persons, and hence are subject to change. "It is self-evident that people share memories of events and objects that are social in origin."[18] The metaphor of what has been called "Collective Remembering," consequently, is subject to revision, illustrated dramatically and perhaps convincingly in the United States by "the ebb and flow of Lincoln's reputation . . . from his death in 1865 to the present": as president not "overwhelmingly popular"; then "grief and condolence" after the assassination but "an imperfect martyr," so that the nation did not suffer "an irreparable loss"; thereafter characterized only as mediocre (especially in comparison with George Washington) until the beginning of the present century, when he has generally emerged as a "national idol" and among "the most cherished of national possessions."[19]

Whatever the reason for their significance, topics and problems may inspire investigations and thus alter the relevant knowledge or its interpretations. Frequently mentioned are gender differences that are forever apparent and are explained or conceptualized differently in every society and over time. In a current view, behavioral differences between the sexes must first be appraised cross-culturally. In Europe and most Western countries, women and men perform distinctive roles; often from the Western standpoint the gap between the privileges and responsibilities assigned them is considerable. Gender equality even in the West is certainly not achievable overnight; the inequalities and differences must first be acknowledged before they can be diminished or eliminated. On the basis of American hospital corpsmen and corpswomen who once responded to standardized questionnaires and to experimental situations involving the environment, a social scientist reported: "Given the similarity of the age and social background of our respondents, the sex differences in time perception suggest that women may be more sensitive than men to the temporal features of their environment." The same investigator also reports other gender differences, based exclusively upon dingdong samples except for one study in Austria and another based on "Indian students."[20] Many of these differences barely reach or do not reach the conventional level of statistical significance; and studies elsewhere can be found that do or do not suggest gender differences with respect to temporal judgments.[21] Usually gender differences are explained in terms of different responsibilities assumed by men and women with a resulting difference in concern for the present or future. Recently, however, preliminary evidence for differences in the brain activity of the two sexes while performing verbal tasks has been carefully noted,[22] so that some skepticism concerning environmental or cultural differences as the complete, final explanation is essential. Generally men are taller and stronger than women, and of course only women give birth to children; these are physiological differences that perhaps, yes perhaps, have implications for the possibility of subtler sexual differences in beliefs and actions.

People's knowledge usually changes as they experience new events. No illustration of this banal platitude is truly necessary because any adult, for melioristic or other reasons, must agree that "reality" as so defined may be compelling. Nevertheless, let it be quickly mentioned that in the early months of 1945 few Germans, even patriotic ones, could not imagine that defeat was avoidable: their armies had been driven back from Stalingrad and Tunisia; the strong Allied forces were steadily advancing in Europe; their ally Mussolini had been deposed and killed; numerous German and German-occupied cities were being heavily and frequently bombed. An official report at the time noted that "nobody believes anymore that we will win" and even Hitler "is included more and more every day in the question of confidence and in criticism." Hope that secret weapons could change the situation had faded. Instead, in Germany, "utter despair could be seen

in day-to-day existence, in wild carousing or thoughts of suicide." Even
anti-Nazi jokes were repeated; more Germans listened to foreign radio
broadcasts.[23] Events made it clear that Germany was losing the war; for an
unknown number of Germans, "reality" prevailed.

Knowledge may also change when attention is called to available and
hitherto neglected sources (G7). In the West, educated adults may later
read again or for the first time classics, especially those created by notable
persons such as Homer and Shakespeare. The splendid epics and plays were
available to their contemporaries, as we know from surviving tales and
other evidence, but do we have the right to assume that the moral values
they reflected and described were understood in a manner resembling your
present interpretation or mine? Projecting later reactions upon the original
and later audiences is precarious, perhaps incorrect, or clearly without convincing evidence. Our strong convictions are ours, not necessarily theirs.

UTILIZATION

At first glance it might appear that a single guide or principle is all meliorists must possess regarding the topic of this section: knowledge, whether
the best available or not, is utilized and acquired in order to pass judgment
or engage in action to achieve an appropriate goal. Usually when you are
hungry or thirsty you know what to do to satisfy those basic needs. If an adolescent is to drive a car, clearly he or she must first acquire verbal knowledge
about driving and practice driving under supervision. If you are to travel
abroad, you must know whether you need a passport and visas, what the
costs will be, and too many other boring details. The statement at the outset of this paragraph, however, is useful if much too simple: utilizability may
be complicated by factors as numerous as those involved in all human behavior.

Individuals may be inclined to use knowledge in the present that has
proven to be useful or valid in the past, but they may be wrong (G6). You
feel comfortable in doing what you have always done; when you then fail to
reach an objective or are otherwise frustrated, your previous knowledge
may need to be changed. Knowledge obtained from others or from the self
must be evaluated now. Even objectively valid knowledge from the past
may not be likewise valid in the present: we are no longer a prosperous
country; others are more efficient and surpass us. Times change and so does
venerated knowledge. Individuals, being human, may simply forget what
they have previously learned either because they are unable to recall what

they once knew or because previously they have been inadequately taught or indoctrinated.

Meliorists and the rest of us find ourselves on a slippery and perilous slope as we contemplate utilizing knowledge to determine action because the very utilization may become the factor affecting its validation. If economists have a theory concerning depressions and if their current knowledge suggests that a depression is soon to occur, they may induce their government to adopt measures that prevent or at least mitigate the predicted depression. After adopting the measures, the depression does not occur. Was the theory then valid because the depression was avoided; or would there have been the predicted depression if the measures had not been taken? More simply: an individual expects to succeed or fail to achieve a goal and therefore exerts, respectively, more or less energy while performing the relevant action. Or a theory about oneself is "proven" by acting according to its prescriptions and becomes self-fulfilling: I knew I would be afraid if such-and-such occurred and, lo and behold, I was indeed afraid when that happened. In these instances human expectations from a principle interfere with the validation process, unlike the theories being tested in chemistry or even in most research with animals where the investigator's bias affects the modes of investigation but not the reactions of the objects or the subjects of the investigation.

In any society, many different sources are usually available for consultation, so that one or some may be selected and the others ignored. Too much knowledge may be available, in the West especially in libraries, in the mass media, and from the formal and informal communications from friends and foes. In recent decades, Internets in various forms provide glib or detailed knowledge to millions of people on the planet from almost all imaginable sources, and thus they supplement or replace other mass media, scholarly and popular journals, and books. In the typically enthusiastic words of one unblushing expert, "the Internet gives you access to more people and more information faster than you can imagine, including online catalogs from most major U.S. academic and research libraries and from more and more foreign libraries."[24] Similarly uninhibited observations once appeared in a four hundred-page book offered by an American sociologist: "By merging communities of discourse, television has made every topic and issue a valid subject of interest and concern for virtually every member of the public."[25] The Internet can transcend conventional schools so that entire courses of instruction are communicated; students and adults in distant places or countries can communicate with one another as if they were in the same room together, provided of course they or their organization possess or have access to the necessary equipment. An obvious caution: as mentioned previously, some or many items on the Internet and in the mass media, particularly advertisements, come from self-serving persons and have not been evaluated by another more or less independent source. In more restricted media such as books or journals, the contents are previously appraised either by competent or incompetent peers but at least by editors, publishers, and proofreaders. Again: the source of knowledge is relevant and is to be ascertained.

A relaxed cynic must wonder whether available knowledge easily located and almost effortlessly obtained may be valued less and forgotten more readily than information arduously procured. In olden times, define them as you wish, there may have been less to learn and to remember; what was obtained may have seemed precious because of the effort required to make it available by reading books and journals in a comfortable chair and after going to a shop or library to procure them. Before the advent of printing presses and duplicating machines, preliminary labor and prior arrangements were necessary to reach people at a distance. Perhaps one is less "profound" and less inclined to admit one's doubts and feelings in an e-mail message dashed off rather than in a letter that often must be carefully handwritten, typed, or dictated. Internet and similar information, being efficient and often seemingly or actually more objective, necessarily omits the social contacts among persons required by the older media: you do not see friends or acquaintances before sealing an envelope and you do not meet someone when mailing your gems.

Nonsense, another relaxed or tense noncynic or cynic must immediately add, masses of prejudices and trivia were available in those old days, whereas now—now what? Furthermore, those who dislike innovations and Internets are on shaky ground as they laud the contributions of other persons and themselves to more conventional media. Ages back, even written communications as they evolved may have been likewise rejected by traditionalists who preferred the traditional economy and coziness of squeals and grunts rather than articulated speech for purposes of expression and communication.

The challenge, especially in modern times, is dramatized by a quick or steady glance at the fifty or more odd and non-odd books, written or edited by one not very timid scholar, often together with colleagues and assistants. The experience is sufficient to indicate that, at least in the West, many or most "Great Ideas" (the title of one of those volumes) can be utilized to supply knowledge that may justify many actions, provided that somehow a choice can be made. The ideas—he lists 102, no more, no less—in alphabetical order range from Angel, Animal, and Aristocracy to Will, Wisdom, and World. The problem for meliorists is to locate and select particular subjects that are, must be, should be relevant. How does one do that with any degree of confidence?

The same scholar has made an equally staggering "close analysis of 434 works by 73 authors" that have appeared during the last twenty-five centuries in "the Western World." He supervised "a staff of specialized indexers," and he himself wrote the 102 accompanying essays. The present writer would try to indicate here the broad scope of the "thoughts" therein by arbitrarily dividing them into five topics, each of which—also arbitrarily—is illustrated here thrice: human attributes (courage, emotion, love); human activities (art, poetry, revolution); politics (constitutions, democracy, law); knowledge (history, language, science); values (good and evil, justice, truth). Admittedly all the topics are "Western," and hence insights from elsewhere have been slighted or excluded. A casual or serious reading of any one of the concepts, however, leaves the respectful impression of controversy and marked disagreement among the persons being cited. Uncertain meliorists may patiently search through the particular sections of interest in the 958 pages in an effort to find utopian means to utopian goals. Agreed with a salute and applause: this tremendously diligent author has raised but never intended to resolve important issues.[26]

The existence of a scholarly approach with 102 ideas induces a shudder as any single abstract is carefully appraised. We are or should feel challenged to provide a historical analysis of the idea and to indicate concretely how and why it is being invoked in a particular context. In some instances generally, and even also here in this book, thoughts are employed without being explored for two principal reasons. Each of the "Great Thoughts" and ones not so great require part of a volume in its own right, its usage without explication challenges both the communicator and the audience to supply the significant details. The concept of the West (or Western) may appear to focus on countries and customs that have developed in such a way that they differ from "traditional" areas and cultures elsewhere, especially—at least often until recently—in Asia and Africa. It is sufficient to assume that West may mean Canada or Germany and not Sri Lanka or Gabon. Other concepts in some context may be challenging and demand only a pause for detailed explication. Thus Christianity may often be quickly mentioned without distinguishing between Catholicism and Protestantism or the numerous and vital divisions and sects therein. Likewise it is possible and useful to refer to animals and human beings without digressions concerning their evolutionary developments or their similarities and differences.

Within each conventionally defined scholarly discipline, the same surplus of valid and invalid knowledge exists (G4). A typical example perhaps: in 1992 two American psychologists stated: "Over 520 experimental and 100 correlational studies on social interdependence have been conducted over the past nine decades" and "generally, the results suggested that . . ."[27] Both this first sentence and only that fraction of the second raise tantalizing and perplexing problems for meliorists. First, "over" 600 studies is a challenging number; how can any summary be adequate; how does the summary differentiate between studies that range from the excellent to the probably invalid? Why not provide a meta-analysis? Should studies conducted ten or more decades ago be consulted? Especially challenging is the authors' word "generally," suggesting some disagreement among the collectors of data. Two other psychologists believe that well-controlled and managed experiments may be difficult or almost impossible to replicate since replications are affected not only when but also by whom and how they are conducted. This "when" they confine to the historical development of a particular research problem, but from a broader perspective "when" includes the developmental state in the society as well as its prevailing standards.[28] If all replications, therefore, as they and some psychologists also argue, are only "relatively exact," knowledge generally, and certainly including the research cited in the present volume, serve in a humbling way to call attention to the nature of the problem at hand; meliorists appreciate the futility of seeking eternal exactitude, although that goal is desirable and often partially or completely attained.

Locating the best available information is thus seldom easy. Relatively well or quite well educated persons in the West and occasionally elsewhere have access to libraries and networks requiring choices to be made. The advances of most scientific and some scholarly knowledge are usually reported initially in technical journals before the books, if there are books, are published. Likewise government reports, whether objective, seemingly objective, or biased, may be aired informally before being finally approved or published. Books and journal articles obviously communicate knowledge more completely and, if designed for a general "public," more intelligibly for nonspecialists. In Western societies and elsewhere, an article, book, or some evidence can usually be located somewhere to justify what one wishes to believe or communicate. Scientists and all of us must cautiously appraise the publication being consulted. In the last decade of the present century, a distinguished biologist, a member of the National Academy of Science in the United States, argued in print, to the dismay of his qualified colleagues, that AIDS does not result from HIV infection.[29] Only specialists could then refute his claim, but what would nonspecialists do if that claim were the only one brought to their attention?

Individuals may be unable to utilize knowledge they cannot comprehend when they lack the competence to evaluate or grasp its technical or methodological contents. Or the information may appear in a language they cannot comprehend. There is also the possibility that they cling to beliefs even when they realize adequate evidence is lacking or other evidence has shown them to be false: they favor what has been communicated to them by approved sources, they believe there is no alternative, or they simply prefer not to change. Is there life after death?

The manner in which adequate or inadequate knowledge is available may affect its acceptability as well as its utilization. Statements may be communicated without evidence or, for subjective validity, with a qualification such as "I think," "it seems," or "probably." The evidence or qualification must then be appraised. The mode of expression may suggest its validity or determine its intelligibility. Chemical or mathematical terms can be appreciated only by those trained in those disciplines; to the untrained the expressions may be puzzling or misleadingly impressive. When one's own language is English, the language to which many persons almost anywhere now have access and which in recent years has replaced French informally as the international language, it is tempting, perhaps necessary but shortsighted, to overlook the information appearing in other languages. Indeed "not all significance can be evoked by inspection nor is all significance accessible to casual observation." That quotation comes from the preface to a scholarly book in which authors once explained in precise detail how to analyze the content of various communications in order systematically to determine their content and the trends within. Ordinarily most mortals cannot employ the accompanying elaborate, careful, statistical techniques because they lack the background or the time to do so; and they may shy away from employing less formal methodologies or drawing inferences from "unconventional" sources like popular love songs.[30]

For all the reasons now mentioned, available knowledge may be ignored and not utilized by and large because it does not appear useful or because new or other knowledge seems more promising. A traffic light turns red as a motorist approaches: he knows he is supposed to stop to avoid an accident or a penalty if observed by the police, but he quickly decides to run a minor risk and drives straight on. To be able to write and read English or any of the Romance or Germanic languages, surely you do not need to know why their script differs from scripts in Asian and other languages or why the sound evoked by the letter "t" is designated by that letter and not by some other letter such as "b" or "w." The straightforward question arises as phrased by a historian: "What do we need to know?"[31] And the reply must include much of human existence extending from precious values to be achieved and requirements of one's occupation to ways of dealing with one's family and routes to follow to reach shops that sell food. How do you decide which of two competing, available products to purchase; whose advice do you follow when you feel ill and you do not consult a physician or when one is not available? To these and many other questions that have now been raised, let the final challenging word be given to an American novelist who wrote in his private journal less than three months before he died, "Me, I only want to know what I need to know to do what I need to do."[32]

CHAPTER 4

Language and Values

The principal functions of language are to designate and store in accessible form people's knowledge not only about themselves, other persons, and society very broadly defined but also about the values they and others would achieve or avoid. An earthquake erupts and initiates a series of human responses. Its occurrence is reported in the mass media; it is an event to be remembered, especially by those in the area or in similarly vulnerable locations. Relevant scientists may wonder whether their discipline merits praise for having predicted the possibility or probability of that event or merit criticism for not having done so. Expressive language occurs when persons "involuntarily" communicate or designate a value and give vent to their horror or dismay.

Language and values are almost always so interlocked that herein they are considered in the same chapter. "He is a good person": the sentence conveys or implies knowledge about him, and obviously the much-used and abused adjective "good" indicates an approving value. That earthquake may be viewed by its victims fatalistically as evidence of bad luck or of a god's retribution for evils previously committed, and it may be designated by scientists as evidence for their geological theory or for their own astuteness. Merely "making" any statement is likely to involve a value or to facilitate a desirable or undesirable action: "if you know that Anne Frank is hiding in the attic" and you say in the presence of a Nazi search party that, "if you look in the attic you'll find Anne Frank," the anonymous you is advocating, though not directly, the action to which the not "value-neutral statement" inevitably leads.[1] Value-laden phrases such as "human dignity," "the rights of minorities," and "freedom and justice" slip forth easily, often too easily.

Statements may express values only implicitly and yet suggest the need for both additional knowledge and relevant action. The preface to a book once claimed to examine "the prospect for all species on earth, 5–10 million of them" and immediately suggested that "we stand to lose at least one million by the end of the century," perhaps at the rate of "one species per day."[2] The author of course deplored this trend (his value), provided compelling evidence for the loss (knowledge), and suggested ways to counter the trend (action) in the chapters that followed (language).

On a simple but impressive level the relation of value and language can be noted by observing the ways in which children learn to communicate in their own manner without being misunderstood. They may know the correct meaning of a word, phrase, or sentence before mastering its standardized, polished expression in the language of their parents and the society. At an early age they sometimes employ their modes of expression to indicate what adults call the tenses of verbs. In a social context a child can say "milk allgone" or "more milk" to indicate, respectively, the past and the present or future tense in the absence of complete or conventional grammatical sentences.[3] A child of three and one almost six were once asked to repeat grammatical sentences, two of which were: "Are you nice?" and "I'll give it to you if you want it." The three-year-old said "Nice?" for the first sentence and "Want it" for the second; the older child's versions were "You nice?" and "You want it."[4] In each instance the child cooperated with the adult by using fewer but expressive words accompanied by an appropriate intonation.

As efforts are made to comprehend human values, it is useful to observe their prototypes among animals. Altruism, it has been argued, is "not limited to our species," and other human values—alliance formation, aspects of morality, nurturance for others, imitation, sympathy, hierarchical ties, sharing, reconciliation, teasing, recognizing the self in a mirror—may be ascribed to animals, especially to the "higher" ones (chimpanzees, gorillas, orangutans, baboons, monkeys). The ascription is based upon the animal's observable behavior: body positions and movements, facial expressions, and sounds uttered to which other animals as well as human beings may react. Whether animals consciously organize or integrate past experiences as values for similar situations in the future remains unknowable; it is sufficient to note objectively and socially that all living creatures possess a biological basis for what may be designated as their values.[5]

VERBAL QUESTS

"At the bottom of all human activities are 'values,' the conviction that some things 'ought to be' and others not." This assertion is from an influential German psychologist who emphasizes again that nothing happens to people "indifferently," even though "from person to person, from tribe to tribe, and from historical period to historical period, accepted values seem to vary enormously."[6] Ordinary, everyday language, therefore, has a staggeringly vast vocabulary that reveals and functions as a guide to values. The designation of "evil" or its equivalent is applied to disease, death, crime, war, and "anything that we all dread" in contrast with such a value as the "dignity and worth of the human person."[7] Negative verbal concepts must be utilized cautiously, meliorists know, lest they be "mere" expressions of prejudice: the criteria for the "wrong choices" can be expressed and then in turn evaluated.

In their communications and especially in publications, individuals suggest values leading to actions that are sought or avoided. A deservedly conspicuous illustration comes from Sir Thomas More, who was not only a theologian but also a diplomat, poet, and lawyer. He first criticized trends in his own sixteenth century, then, perhaps seriously and always pleasantly, he suggested universal ideals for human beings in "Utopia," the word that he coined for "No Place" and that is being brought up to date in the present book by being called meliorism. These arbitrarily selected examples appear chronologically in More's Book II[8]:

> The Utopians marvel that any mortal can take pleasure in the weak sparkle of a little gem or bright pebble when he has a star, or the sun itself, to look at.
>
> By pleasure they understand every state or movement of body or mind in which man finds delight according to nature . . . it is a delight that does not injure others, does not preclude a greater pleasure, and is not followed by pain.
>
> But if the disease is not only incurable, but excruciatingly and unremittingly painful, then the priests and public officials come and urge the invalid not to endure further agony . . . he should not hesitate to free himself, or let others free him, from the rack of living.
>
> They despise war as an activity fit only for beasts, yet practised more by man than by any other animal.
>
> Pride is too deeply fixed in human nature to be plucked out.

The last prescription of Sir Thomas concerning pride stems from his conception of a biological or genetic component of human beings. More important is his and often our tendency to point toward a future with values realized more completely or at least differently from those in the present, whether the hope or the striving refers to the Judeo-Christian conception of Heaven or the Buddhist view of Nirvana. But utopia may be pushed into the past, so that Eden or "the good old days" are associated with greater contentment or more positive values.

As noted in the previous chapter, philosophers can be a source of knowledge which, though undocumented and undocumentable, provides stimulating wisdom. A quick reference to Socrates, Plato, and Aristotle is sufficient to evoke values in the judgment, if not in the actions, of persons centuries later (G4). Often in the declaration of philosophers linguistic challenges are found that forever plague other philosophers, individuals, and especially meliorists. One of them suggests that we can "try to remove the vagueness of the everyday word 'city' by stipulating that a community is a city if and only if it has at least 50,000 inhabitants." Fine, but then we are faced with another question: under what conditions is a person to be counted as an inhabitant of a community and hence assumed to have urban values? Yes, if he or she resides and works there; and those who live there temporarily as summer residents, students, and long-term visitors?[9] This straining illustration raises problems that can be settled, yet may be ignored when the word "city" appears in casual, somewhat slovenly sentences.

Probably the source of values frequently consulted by persons in any society is that of "religion."[10] Consider the number of religions on the planet as well as local sects and other organizations. Most religionists sincerely believe they possess "the" most valid knowledge and best value: and there are also theists and atheists with stronger beliefs. Here are illustrations of the suggested actions and stern values in the translated language of the New Testament:

And now abide faith, hope, love, these three; but the greatest of these is love.

Be kindly affectionate to one another with brotherly love.

Blessed *are* the meek, for they shall inherit the earth.

And this I pray. . . . That you may approve the things that are excellent, that you may be sincere and without offense till the day of Christ.

Honor all people. Love the brotherhood. Fear God. Honor the King.

Greater love has no one than this, than to lay down one's life for his friends.

And there are suggestions for the self to apply to the self, such as the following which, not incidentally, the present writer communicates to himself endlessly:

> Lord, my heart is not haughty, nor my eyes lofty. Neither do I concern myself with great matters, nor with things too profound for me. / Surely I have calmed and quieted my soul, like a weaned child with his mother, like a weaned child is my soul within me.[11]

The prophets and others who advocated these actions and fostered the values communicated by Christianity were expressing not only their own views but also, more important, those of their mentors and followers.

Embedded in the structure of language are syntactic modes that explicitly or implicitly advocate values and that are served by the auxiliaries attached to verbs. For illustrative purposes, let the verb be the simple "do," the referent the universal "I," and the language perforce English:

A. *Judgment*
    1. present: what *do* I do?
    2. past: what *did* I do?
    3. future: what *shall* I do?
B. *Evaluation*
    4. alternative: what *may* I do?
    5. requirement: what *must* I do?
    6. value: what *should* (ought) I do?
C. *Action*
    7. anticipation: what *would* be the consequences of doing X?
    8. probability: what *might* be the consequences of doing X?
    9. intention: what *will* I do?

The auxiliaries are similarly employed to apply to others (what do they do, what did they do, etc.?) and to society (what do people in that country do, what did they do, etc.?). They are, however, carelessly and ambiguously and not always strictly used as suggested above and hence provide another example of how language and values are enmeshed. Even with the first three regarding verbal tenses ambiguity lurks. "He is honest," yes, but surely his honesty springs out of the past and may be evident in the future: his actions also are being evaluated positively. The most used and abused auxiliary is "should" and its equivalent "ought," two words likely to suggest positively valued action. "Must" and "should" are often employed as synonyms and thus create either confusion or additional, if ambiguous, emphasis. A parent tells his or her child, "You must always tell the truth." Why tell the truth? If the child does not tell the truth, he or she will be punished, will be disliked for being a liar, will be departing from what people anticipate or require, or is violating a code of behavior considered desirable for religious or philosophical reasons. Perhaps "should" and "ought" can be confined to moral values and "must" to present but effective rationales; but only mild convention, not laws, would impose such a linguistic distinction.

Once a psychologist asked a sample of Americans to examine various statements containing the auxiliary "ought" and to place them into piles "according to the nature of the oughts" they expressed. On the basis of the opinions of his "most sophisticated judges," he emerged with ten different and more or less self-explanatory categories of "ought" to which he gave appropriate names; each category is followed here by an arbitrarily selected illustrative statement from that investigator's own list:

1. Inference: This ought to be about where I lost it.
2. Completeness: We won the game and we ought to celebrate.
3. Beauty: You ought to have your hair cut.
4. Social welfare: Every man ought to have a chance to work.
5. Utility: Garden peas ought to be soaked before planting.
6. Duty: Every man ought to keep his promise.
7. Safety: One ought to be careful in the choice of friends.
8. Custom: In America a driver ought to keep to the right side of the road.
9. Justice: Women and men ought to receive the same pay.
10. Legislation: To vote in November you ought to be twenty-one years of age.

The meaning of the ten sentences may be clear, but the various oughts suggest quite different actions or desirable values. In a study called "Measurement of Ethical Insight," the same psychologist asked respondents, again only Americans, to classify fifty statements according "to which variety or category of OUGHT that proposition belongs"; the reference was to the same ten oughts. Each ought categorization of the statements by the respondents was then called correct or incorrect as previously characterized by the sophisticated judges who had originally classified them. On one of the two forms in which there was supposed to be a single "correct" reply for forty-nine of the fifty statements, the correct answer to "Everyone ought to keep his promises" was said to be "duty." Why not "custom" or even "welfare"? The number of correct responses increased as the educational level rose.[12] Once more: language and values are intertwined.

With or without auxiliaries, language communicates information that may be ambiguous and convey varying values (G6). "He is honest": not tense but the meaning of "honest" must (or should or will) be questioned and evaluated in comparison with other values like truth or accomplishment. Too easily other important, value-saturated concepts slip forth and vary from beautiful to ugly, from democracy to fascism, and from "good" to "bad."

In the verbal quest for values it is useful, as one of the initial steps to evaluate values, to indicate their possible or probable referents that may be categorized, in the following ways:

1. *natural:* values referring to the assumed biological, physiological, or presumably innate nature of human beings
2. *endemic:* values referring to a historical, sociopolitical, or cultural context
3. *personal:* values referring to preferences by one or more specified persons

Usually it is difficult to locate a value's referent because it may be unmentioned, categorized as a dogmatism or common sense, or ascribed to intuition, as when Plutarch and some Platonists are said to have stated that "to be like God" is the aim of "every successful life."[13] Herewith are hypothetical illustrations of the three referents above: food of some kind, beer, and coffee are endemic values in many Western societies; marked preference by specific persons and not by other persons, such as vegetarianism in a particular group, has personal value that is also partially natural (people must eat and drink) and also endemic (vegetarians have their own clubs and organizations).

COMMUNICATION

New or unusual words communicate knowledge and values to the self and others that might otherwise be slighted, overlooked, or ignored. "Souperism" is unlikely to appear in many English-speaking persons' vocabularies; it is included in only a few dictionaries. It refers to the belief or charge that clergy, especially Protestants, promised food—the *soup* in the word—to starving people in Ireland during the 1840s and at other times in order not primarily to keep them alive but to convert them and have them join the established church (established by and for England) and to oppose

Catholicism. A passionate historical account of existing evidence from that period indicates that souperism was not a motivating value of most clergy of either denomination, although it does forcefully describe a few.[14] The concept, therefore, can easily be defined but requires a wealth of information before being applied to a particular pastor or clergy of that or any other period; yet, when understood, it may induce some persons at least to challenge the "real," primary or secondary, value of good deeds by the clergy or persons in any profession.

Somewhat similarly the concept of "sexism" performs an enlightening function today in the West. When it is clear that the neologism refers to endemic biases favoring males over females, examples thereof may then be observed and appropriate measures advocated or taken. Earlier in American society the same bias of sexism was "always expressible by syntactic constructs" that were less concise. "Sexism" itself was coined as "the contemporary women's movement" grew more prominent. "Meanings," therefore, "become lexicalized as a result of social change" and then their "lexicalization can accelerate the rate of change and perhaps produce changes which otherwise might not happen, or would happen with greater difficulty."[15]

The recognition of sexism or other linguistic usages, however, does not guarantee appropriate action. In English it has been recently complained that too many persons have failed to adopt an antisexist change: "The use of *man* to include both women and men may be grammatically 'correct,' but it is constantly in conflict with the more common use of *man* as distinguished from *woman*."[16] No one, certainly not a male, in this age can deny the accuracy of that observation. The remedy is close at hand: when both genders are the referents, use "they" or its equivalent (yet what about the last three letters of "human"?), "he and she" (or "she and he"), or—if aesthetically insensitive—"s/he." One wonders about those speakers of German who would avoid sexism: in their language "man" and "Mann" are nouns in the third person singular, and have identical pronunciations, but the first word without an article is the equivalent of the nonsexist "one" in English and the second refers to a specific male. What must or can nonsexist Germans do?

Even though they involve "the pretense that something is the case when it is not," metaphors usefully call attention to phenomena that otherwise might not be perceived. Both their users and recipients may not be aware of their own linguistic assumptions (G7). The expression "metal fatigue" is or is not immediately recognized as a metaphor derived from "muscle fatigue"; the metaphor becomes clearer when both designations are combined, "metal and muscle fatigue."[17] Obviously there are abstract similarities but also marked concrete differences between the two referents.

Speakers of the same language use more or less the same grammar for elementary objectives, such as verbal tenses or changing nouns from the singular to the plural, yet ordinary speech requires interpretation and value judgments that vary from person to person. A psychiatrist in the psychoanalytic tradition once employed simple expressions to dramatize the point:

> All communications have, as one of their characteristics, the capacity to invite greater intimacy or to function as distancing devices. The casual communication, such as "Good morning" or "How are you?" or the responsive, "I'm feeling fine," are approaches to another person of a rather casual and peripheral nature but, viewed in another context, they are intended to be non-communicative and distancing devices. They even suggest, in some contexts, that further inquiry would be intrusive and that the level of intimacy must be maintained at a very superficial level.[18]

Similarly the words and sentence structure of the priest who asks the prisoner why he has robbed banks are thoroughly and accurately understood, but the latter's reply of "Well, that's where the money is" indicates that exactly the same question has evoked both similar and different referents: obviously the priest seeks an explanation of why the man robs, the prisoner gives a sensible reason for selecting a bank and not some other building.[19] Two sociologists once felt compelled to devote part of a book to suggest how scientists in one specialized field of biochemistry, that of bioenergetics, must carefully "use distinctive interpretative forms as they construe their actions and beliefs in different social contexts" usually to their colleagues in English and sometimes assisted by diagrams and photographs.[20]

Communication in language by one or more persons can induce changes in the beliefs and values of other persons and affect their actions. Some but not all persons respond to the advertisement of a bargain by buying the article or patronizing the service being publicized. Devices galore are at hand to promote an intended response. One approach to understanding suggests that the "framing" of the communication affects an audience's response,[21] as the following non-rhetorical questions would suggest. In fostering health, is it efficacious to specify what is or will be gained by cooperating with dietary recommendations, what will be lost from not doing so? Is it better to emphasize actions to be taken to prevent or to cure illnesses? Can members of potential audiences be alerted to conditions resulting from non-cooperation so that the dangers to health can be detected? May the benefits to be derived from any action (whether learned in advance or detected later) be trumpeted with or without mentioning the risks, expenses, or other costs?

Knowledge concerning effective communication through language, therefore, is elusive. Will a communication be effective when it does or does not conform to an audience's expectation? The answer may fall either way, as it perhaps indeed should. Thus empirical data from Americans once suggested that in varying circumstances the repetition of communications in accord or not with what has been expected from communicators may or may not elicit agreement with what is communicated.[22] Do note the qualification or "varying circumstances": one may admire communicators because they are consistent or because they change with changing circumstances. Also there may be no "best" way to communicate with or without language, yet such uncertainty does not mean that the effort to improve communication for a melioristic or any other end is or should be abandoned.

An unhappy conclusion is inevitable: it is usually or at least often either perilous or impossible to decide whether a communication has succeeded or failed or what its effect will be. From whose viewpoint is the success or failure judged—that of the communicator or of other persons? Criteria differ and are numerous: the nature and content of the communication and the medium through which it is communicated; its perception or nonperception; acceptance or rejection by the audience which changes or does not change over time; its relation, if any, to some value or action. And repetition: communicators have the resources to repeat their communication; are they permitted to do so; and if they do repeat, do they introduce variations of content and value and, if so, why and on what basis? Do repetitions bore audiences? Why have or have not previously advocated changes been induced?

Communicating by translating from one language to another has its special challenges. According to one of his devoted disciples, there have been mistranslations of Freud from his original German to English. The title of one of his books in English, *The Psychopathology of Everyday Life*, omits his first qualifying German word, "Zur," which literally means "on the" and which suggests Freud's own modest evaluation that he was providing only "A contribution to the . . ." or "Reflections on the . . ." Also the translation of "Seele" as "mind" and not "soul" alters the metaphysical value of Freud's thinking.[23]

The struggle to translate, however, may communicate new knowledge about another society as well as reflections concerning one's own. The German words "Erfahrung" and "Erlebnis" can both be translated as "experience." According to one most meticulous translator,[24] however, the former refers to "past experience" and the latter to "current happening," so that a distinction can be made by means of another English word such as "occurrence" or "event," which then adds other noteworthy and challenging complications. Perhaps a bit more is learned about British imperialism in Africa by discovering that the name of one of its former colonies there, Uganda, has been carelessly adapted from the language of a prominent ethnic group there when in fact *ganda* as a suffix is used with different prefixes (Muganda for one person, Baganda for persons, Luganda for the language, Kiganda for objects and things, Buganda for the country) but never beginning with a "U."

Translations from very dissimilar languages may be challenging and lead to new judgments and experiences. The Ewe in West Africa use the same word to refer to what are called black and blue in Western languages or their equivalent. The Zulu, also in Africa, have a single word that in English refers to red and some shades of yellow. Speakers of both languages, however, can perceive the differences in color but communicate them with difficulty. An Ewe woman, asked to report the difference between a blue and black cardboard square, struggled to reply to the investigator: "I see the difference, this is dark, that too is dark, but is like this; it puzzles me; I have lost the names of them." And traditionally Zulu can call a yellow object "*bomvu* like corn" and a red one "*bomvu* like blood."[25] The more or less distinctive vocabulary and structure of a language, therefore, may not prevent individuals from perceiving differences that their own language then enables them to express and communicate. Neutral appraisers, if they exist, may not easily decide which cultural mode is to be melioristically preferred. Thus among the Wolof in Africa it was once reported that in contrived situations traditional adults and children without formal schooling tended to observe differences in color more frequently than other Wolof children in Western schools or than Westerners who reported perceiving not color but shape and function more frequently.[26] Which is more desirable for these people, sensitivity to colors or Western-style education?

In addition, the ease and frequency with which a word or phrase is employed may affect its usage and the meaning or value thereby attached. Again, please refer to German, which has the word "Zeitgeist" that requires more than a single word—such as "spirit of the time"—to be translated; are Germans, therefore, more likely to characterize a total era more glibly or profoundly than English speakers who do not possess the convenient if trite term?

Not metaphorically but realistically similar problems of communication arise among persons who have the same so-called mother tongue. Like knowledge, meanings of words and phrases change over time, and one participant in a conversation may not be up to date, so that another person misses the meaning or nuance being communicated. An educator has written an entire book about four words and "their associated words": self, growth, relative, relationship. Those words have been used differently by writers in various areas as well as in popular and scholarly systems with resulting confusion or ambiguity. "Einstein not only gave *relativity* the title in both of his theories . . . but he also made it play a big part in his explanations of what the theories are about."[27] Are the words for foods, customs, values always relative? You favor democracy, do you not? Were the American colonies a democracy before rebelling from England; is Sweden a democracy; is the People's Republic of China a democracy; what do you "mean" by democracy?

"Educated" persons and others appreciate the existence of dictionaries as guides to meanings, but one-volume and convenient pocket dictionaries function only in a preliminary way: what is listed therein depends on an editor's decision at the time of publication, and later the volume may not be up to date. More extensive information can be found in larger dictionaries, books, and encyclopedias, where accounts are given concerning the derivation of words with examples by different writers and sources. But brand-new usages may not be thus reported by publications that lag behind the language of the moment; the not necessarily reliable Internet can then be consulted. Also readers and speakers themselves select the connotation or denotation to be remembered and utilized. The wealth of possible meanings can be confusing, as previously suggested concerning all knowledge. Above all, most persons do not have the incentive, patience, or time to refer to authoritative sources. Talking, thinking, and even writing may or can be spontaneous; and audience reactions usually are or must be likewise. Historical slogans, detached from their original sources even if known, may be remembered and cited carelessly and may affect values and actions: *veni, vidi, vici*; Give Me Liberty or Give Me Death; Life, Liberty, and the Pursuit of Happiness.

While it may be true, according to a distinguished linguist, that "extralinguistic beliefs concerning the speaker and the situation play a fundamental role in determining how speech is produced,"[28] simple, straightforward literacy can be of paramount importance in communication and hence for achieving melioristic goals. Probably nowhere, or almost nowhere, are most individuals in any society only somewhat literate;

they have no choice if they seek some of the benefits of their society or if they or their children attend schools at least partially leaning in the Western tradition.[29] Meliorists do more than pay lip service to literacy. An experienced educational psychologist once proclaimed at the outset of a book titled *Endangered Minds*: "The state of literacy in the United States today is declining so precipitously, while video and computer technologies are becoming so powerful that the act of reading itself may well be on the way to obsolescence." After filling three hundred pages with illustrations of the decline in specific instances of literacy regarding specialized knowledge and of efforts to improve educational systems, the author concluded that "new developments are both needed and inevitable," and hence "parents and teachers will need to broaden, perhaps even redefine traditional parameters of intelligence and learning."[30] The search for realizing values, especially verbally, goes on and on and on.

Each society, moreover, has its own standards concerning literacy which, according to the author of a book with a flaming title (*What Every American Needs to Know*), "lies *above* the everyday levels of knowledge that everyone possesses and *below* the expert level known only to specialists." Possibly, as anecdotal evidence indicates, such literacy is declining in the United States: schoolchildren could not supply dates for World War I or II; while they probably recognized the name of Martin Luther King and his "I have a dream" speech, they probably did not grasp his references to American "documents" in that oration. This author and two of his colleagues have provided, as of the late 1980s, almost five thousand words and phrases that had been appearing "in newspapers, magazines, and books without explanation." The list begins with six dates (1066, 1492, 1776, and those of the Civil War and the two world wars). Samples of the terms selected by the present writer for each letter of the alphabet included Abraham and Isaac, bail, cabinet (government), Dachau, e = mc^2, Fahrenheit, galaxy, habeas corpus, iambic pentameter, Jack Frost, kamikaze, Labor Day, Douglas MacArthur, NAACP, Occam's razor, pacifism, Quaker, rabbi, Sacco-Vanzetti case, tabula rasa, U-boat, vaccine, wage scale, xenophobia, Yankee, and Zeitgeist.[31] May one ask, as of today are you familiar with those words, what does "kamikaze" mean, what was the "Sacco-Vanzetti case"?

PURSUED VALUES

"Why are you doing this?" The immediate reply to the question or one emerging after probing indicates the ostensible values being pursued. The same question can be posed by the self about the self or by the self and others about other persons or societies. The schemas of values being natural, endemic, and personal referents obtained through inquiries are as numerous as the languages in which they are expressed, so that meliorists must be content with an overview that indicates arbitrarily selected examples of what has been, is being, or must be pursued. The pursuit here first examines relevant methods to catch a glimpse of values, searches for a supreme value, and returns to methods in behalf of such a value. Evidence may indicate that a species of fish or plant is in danger of being extinguished as a result of specified actions (overfishing or the use of a particular fertilizer) by certain human individuals; the fact and value of biodiversity is thus being threatened. But why is the value of biodiversity desirable or necessary? That question must be referred to other values, the specification of which leads to political, economic, religious, and generally endemic referents. Similarly it is melioristically insufficient merely to assert that ozone depletion or overpopulation should be deplored or regulated without delving into their rationale. Ask again: why are you doing that? That is my custom, that is the way I always do it. A reason has been offered which assumes as personal referent the value of habit or experience; but why?

For meliorism values require empirical, perhaps verifiable, evidence (G5). Three approaches are herewith noted. First, common sense and experience assume that every individual at some point evaluates what the self pursues whether in the past, now, or ultimately. Or a value is postulated for everyone including the self. All of us, it is assumed and documented, pursue one or more values that vary from the highest spiritual value in an established or personal religion to a subtle or crude form of materialism alluding to market or Marxist objectives. A second approach is to infer value from objective or behavioral actions. Most of us would remain healthy and retain whatever personal possessions bring satisfaction, so that we occasionally or conscientiously eat "sensible" food and exercise, and also take measures to prevent accidents or the losses for which insurance policies are supposed to compensate. Values may be similarly ascribed even to the actions of animals by observing the actions of their bodies or hearing the sounds they emit, although they cannot verbally explain to human beings the rationale behind what they do:

> Aiding others at a cost or risk to oneself is widespread in the animal world. The warning calls of birds allow other birds to escape a predator's talons, but attract attention to the caller. . . . When chasing arboreal monkeys, chimpanzees often work in pairs, trios, or larger teams.[32]

A third approach is favored by scholars and by those having a personal interest in values for political or personal reasons. The plunge into the rough sea of measured values may arbitrarily begin with a German philosopher who early in this century proposed six "attitudes" toward values as "the ideally basic types of individuality" here listed together with scattered, descriptive words and phrases selected by the present writer:

1. Theoretic: objectivity; complete individualist; empiricism, rationalism, criticism

2. Economic: preservation of biological life; as producer or as consumer; utility

3. Aesthetic: the expression of an impression; color, mood, rhythm; a life related to nature

4. Social: interest in another being and the taking-the-place-of-another; limiting of individuation; use of power only for love

5. Political: imprinting of one's own will; power of knowledge; avoidance of being exposed

6. Religious: the highest possible value to be experienced; a wholly subjective product of soul; searching for the supreme value of mental life

The above typology is claimed to be based on "a psychological investigation," although almost no sources then available are given. Presumably the author was claiming a natural and endemic basis for the schema, yet some of the categories—especially the last two—seem to have been "personal" as defined here a few pages ago. He sensibly warns that the six attitudes do not describe human beings generally but are "mere constructions" characterizing each person at different times or in different situations: "Man is not one of those creatures who live only in one class of values." He also tries mightily to relate his sixfold division to ethics, but forces himself to admit "the actual psychic structure of man can never be the standard of the rank order of values." Ethics concerns not the individual but society: "Only the man who acknowledges society and its estate can recognize socio-ethical demands." Nevertheless, he argues, "the pronounced religious set is the highest among the formation of the ideal mind," and "no great religion" can be "without myths which combine all three aspects, religious, theoretic, and aesthetic."[33]

This six-shooter has become popular among academic psychologists, especially Americans, after being embodied in a questionnaire that can be conveniently administered to cooperating dingdong samples. That "instrument," therefore, according to one of its co-authors, simply "invites you to indicate the relative strength of these six values in your own personality," but the emerging score "cannot be compared with anyone else's because the test reflects relative strengths of those values only within your own personality"—only? A person with a low score on a value, he suggested, may more energetically pursue or express that value than someone with a high score who does so less energetically.[34] According to another psychologist, as a measuring device this questionnaire does "not permit a clear distinction between value standards and preferences that lack the force of 'ought,' "[35] another way of indicating that values can be portrayed and classified without being advocated.

Yet a third psychologist, seemingly interested in values with a heavily endemic component and probably prevalent only in Western societies, provides a mode of categorizing values on a verbal level. A distinction is made between terminal values ("end-states of existence") and instrumental values ("desirable modes of conduct"). Over the years he has emerged with eighteen terminal and, miraculously, also with exactly eighteen instrumental values. Terminal values include, in his language, a comfortable life, an exciting life, a sense of accomplishment, social recognition, true friendship, and wisdom. And instrumental values are designated as ambitious, broadminded, capable, polite, responsible, and self-controlled. The two sets of eighteen values have been ranked by American respondents when applied to themselves ("arrange them in order of their importance to YOU") and to fellow students and to "nonscientists." Of course, such rankings have been shown to vary with gender, income, education, ethnicity, religion, political ideology, and almost any other breakdown conceived by the author and other researchers. Two tables of data even indicate the "frequency of mention and rank order" of both the terminal and instrumental values "found in writings by socialists, Hitler, Goldwater, and Lenin." Among Americans the same so-called instrument has been employed to indicate changes in the values with the passing of time and among empirically induced experimental but not control samples.[36] More than four hundred of the 630 members of the British House of Commons once ranked the thirty-six values arranged, in order to simplify the task, in four groups of nine values each.[37] Another careful survey of large samples of Americans was introduced as follows: "In this study we are interested in measuring the quality of life of people in this country—that is, the things people like and dislike about their homes, cities, neighborhoods, jobs, and so on."[38]

SUPREME VALUES

It is almost impossible to avoid postulating ultimate values whenever a writer considers the "serious" problem of human existence. A humanistic physician believes the goal of the self is to achieve a "quality of life" that consists of a fluctuating "balance between privacy and a sense of community."[39] A Catholic priest subscribes professionally to the personal view of Descartes that "cogito, ergo sum" and then provides "a set of directives that serve to guide a process towards a result."[40] A supreme value also appears in ostensibly empirical research. Thus a dingdong study once revealed that "desensitization" tended to be more effective than "insight": those in the sample were helped more when they both learned about the history and status of their problem in the past and were specifically taught to relax than were others who were merely given "help" to discover ways in which they were functioning. As ever, exceptions were noted: some departed from the reported trend but improved more after achieving insight.[41]

Empirical investigations such as the ones mentioned and many others indicate only the endemic values that actually or allegedly guide individuals; they avoid, often deliberately in order to appear objective or scientific, the normative challenge of what should be sought for a rationale related to some other or "higher" value. One tries to discern the value behind the violence or destruction of "terrorists" and then condemns their value. Is there a supreme value, are there supreme values that transcend immediate values? That question, however phrased, obliges meliorists and others at least to conduct a search.

Even before the search begins, however, meliorists confront themselves with what philosophers and others have called the "naturalistic fallacy," which occurs, according to one view, when the designated value has been located empirically and then claimed to "justify" the actions to which it conceivably gives rise. The "ought" or the "should" in that sense (but not in the other diverse meanings attached to the auxiliary as outlined earlier in this chapter) is thus derived from the "is." You crave caviar, is it "fallacious" to maintain that you should have caviar only because you crave it? But—permit a farfetched suggestion—suppose you would really perish without caviar because your digestive system at the moment can tolerate only caviar, so that without this delicacy you will indeed starve, grow even more ill, perhaps even perish. Mentioning your survival is necessary to justify the "ought" for you; even so, however, your survival must be placed in perspective; it could be that caviar-producing sturgeons are an endangered species that somehow must be preserved for the benefit of the entire planet and hence should not be caught and perish in order to obtain their roe. The naturalistic fallacy is to be avoided when it justifies a particular need or practice, yet it is not completely avoidable when attention is concentrated on the overall nature of a natural (not an endemic or personal) value and not on its present means of attainment. Endemic or personal values may be called fallacious by persons in the past, present, or future who have a different value when it is postulated to be essential for others besides themselves or for all people. The followers of absolute monarchy in England and the United States centuries ago would have called or did call values favoring democratic institutions fallacious.

If meliorists would avoid that form of the naturalistic fallacy, they must reach out to locate supreme values that are not confined to the specific beliefs or actions being justified. The search for supreme values leads them to diverse sources that include religion, poetry, literature, philosophy, and the systematic disciplines of social and natural science. According to one Christian publisher, here are the supreme values to be attached to a "glorious tomorrow":

Absolute End of War

Freedom from Death

Freedom from Want

Freedom from Sickness

Freedom from Fear[42]

The endemic referent for those values is said to be the Christian Bible that outlines the nature of "God's World." Other supreme values can be snatched, of course, from the truly great such as Omar Khayyam and Virgil, but instead the procedure here is about to focus upon particular values that seem to transcend particular sources and to possess data more convincing, perhaps, to the present or any generation.

One prominent supreme natural value is that of survival. Every person usually wishes to continue living and not perish. Those racked in pain who would die or commit suicide presumably would prefer survival if their pain could be reduced or removed. Survival is a natural value, to be sure, but only in part because it also must—or should?—have endemic or personal bases. When survival includes the subsidiary or contributing value of one's present income that is dependent on a particular occupation, the supreme value becomes that occupation but only for those so employed. Lumbering companies and their employees may thus value more highly their income than species of animals like a bug or a bird threatened by the destruction of forests; those favoring biodiversity at the expense of lumbering possess a different value that they believe has a higher priority in the short or long run and hence is supreme.

Survival, however, presupposes yet an even more supreme value, perhaps a rational one, related to individuals' feelings. One values survival highly, but when . . . when what? The meaningful reply is communicated in language. One values many values highly only under conditions of "well-being," especially "subjective well-being"; only when one is happy. And so happiness is introduced as the paramount supreme value to unravel. Consider the following beryl ascribed to a French oceanographer by his son: "The happiness of the bee and the dolphin is to exist. For man it is to know that and to wonder at it."[43] Happiness, then, can be employed tentatively by meliorists as the concept, more promising perhaps than any other, to function as a guide to action. This writer, like many thinkers and nonthinkers, agrees with a modern philosopher who has footnoted the view that "the notion of happiness as a satisfactory and well-lived life, an objective well worked out in ancient ethics, has more footing in our ethical thinking than most ethical discussion allows."[44]

Any hymn to happiness as the supreme value is immediately confronted with at least four challenges. The first is metaphysical: the relation between happiness here and now and happiness in a possible (probable, certain—as you will) afterlife. One can only nod or bow respectfully and leave to the reader or someone else the view or faith to follow. Any other supreme value, including survival and well-being, faces the same perplexity: survival, well-being, happiness during one's lifetime or forever after?

Then, second, it may be useful to exclude from the referent of happiness or any supreme value the connotations of another concept that may appear in the same context, namely, that of hedonism. That word comes originally from Greek and is usually translated as the pursuit of pleasure. "Pleasure" suggests only momentary satisfaction and hence a selfish or self-centered feeling unrelated to more enduring moments as well as to other values in the individual's immediate or far-flung society. Can one be truly non-hedonistically happy when it is known that others suffer?

Third, words from a modest, brilliant, philosophical engineer ring out:

Happiness or pleasure may be said to be the common quality of experiences which are per se to be preferred to oblivion or no experience at all, and unhappiness or pain to be the common quality of experiences to which oblivion or no experiences at all is per se to be preferred.[45]

And again from the same author in a different book:

Happiness is the one thing that people never get tired of; but they confound it with its causes—eating or drinking, or kissing or playing a harp—and so

they mistake the thing they are tired of. They are tired of the cause for the
very reason that it has ceased to be a cause of happiness. Hence they are saying exactly the opposite of what they mean. They say they don't like happiness when they mean they don't like unhappiness.[46]

The solution to that provocative challenge must be a more careful assessment of happiness, especially its attributes and duration over time. According to one investigator, during "the flow experience" accompanying
periods of human creativity, individuals do not feel happy but are immersed
in the activity itself; yet the attributes of that "flow" (such as having a goal,
receiving feedback from the action, absence of distractions and of self-
consciousness,[47] and other mental states), it is suggested here, can be
viewed as happiness-producing.

Another interruption at this point is necessary. It is irrational to think
for a moment that any individual can postulate supreme values eternally
for all human beings. An effort like the present in the last few pages must be
qualified, as all similar have been, are, and will be qualified. Here the
qualms of conscience are softened by outlining in a brief appendix to this
chapter other "Credos" as enunciated, or considered to be so enunciated,
by the following giants: Plato, Aristotle, Yoga, and Albert Schweitzer. We
would thus experience a sample of how the truly great strive to comprehend and guide human existence.

The fourth and last challenge calls attention to the ways in which happiness is ascertained. Like other values considered in this section, the same
methodological opportunities are available and must be assessed. Happiness
may be assumed when the natural or endemic basis for human beings is suggested. A humane, brilliant psychologist once departed from his usual factual
reports on surveys in various countries and titled a book The "Why" of Man's
Existence; in his words from that book and other books as well as essays by him:

1. [After relating a youthful experience of an American jurist] Here we have an
    example of the quality of being human—the ceaseless striving for a more com-
    plete, a richer satisfaction in experience, the desire to experience new conse-
    quences of action we initiate,

2. Human beings continuously seek to enlarge the range and to enrich the quality
    of their satisfactions,

3. Man more than any other animal is faced with the problem of choice,

4. All observations of man indicate that most people who are attuned to anything
    approximating normal life will not be satisfied with their role unless it offers
    some potentiality for one experience to lead to another, for change to occur in
    some apparent direction,

5. . . . we find people everywhere reaching for certain universals, certain ultimates which seem operationally so similar when their function is understood.[48]

Politely and respectfully one must wonder. Statement 4 above refers to "all observations": by whom, when, where? Statement 2 generalizes about "human beings" who "continuously seek": every person, all of the time? What we have here, then, is one man's sincere, unsubstantiated views but based upon personal, sensitive observations and the numerous authors (especially those from literature and philosophy) he cites. Presumably the above five prerequisites for happiness reflect human strivings.

Similarly it is possible to salvage by implication many declarations pointing to values and assume they are justified when they have only a latent foundation in happiness. Thus the first sentence in *An Introduction to Social Ethics* once stated the following most bluntly: "The fundamental problem of human life is the social problem or the problem of living together in a social order with the least friction and the richest possible conservation and development of human powers."[49] The self, too, is presumably happy under the conditions specified for others and within society.

After postulating happiness as the supreme value, it is necessary to indicate or discover the methods adopted to achieve that value. Both the drug addict and a cloistered nun are pursuing happiness, if by different means. The addict's pursuit may be momentarily or ultimately unsuccessful when he cannot procure the drug or when the addiction prevents him from achieving other happy states such as those associated with his career or relations with other persons; then he is unhappy. Likewise a nun does not experience certain joys like those associated with a hearty meal, a delectable wine, or marriage; yet such deprivations, it may be assumed, do not make her unhappy because her faith and way of life remain satisfactory and undisturbed. For neither individual is it misleading, profane, or sacrilegious to employ the value of happiness to describe their goals, ways of living, or hedonic states: the nun presumably is happier or more successful than the addict, although neither of them describes his or her existence precisely in terms of happiness or success.

Numerous direct, empirical approaches to the critical concept of happiness and concepts closely related thereto have been offered by scholars and others, a sample of which is reviewed here to demonstrate how that worthy, slippery value has been pursued. The review is somewhat long and repetitious in order to emphasize the varieties of the struggle. If the recital becomes too long or boring, do skip happily to the end of the present section.

One investigator and his collaborators in the Netherlands, having proclaimed at the outset that "most people agree that it is better to enjoy life than to suffer" and that "modest investigators" define happiness as "subjective appreciation of life-as-a-whole," has called attention to no less than "7,838 findings from 603 studies in 69 nations 1911–1994"; these "correlates of happiness" are summarized schematically and adequately in 2,028 pages in one relatively thick and two very thick volumes.[50] Generally the self is confronted directly with the spoken or written word "happiness" and then with probing questions. "How elated or depressed, happy or unhappy, did you feel today?" was followed by ten alternatives ranging from "rapturous joy and soaring ecstasy" to "utter depression and gloom."[51]

It was once reported that "well over" 100,000 Americans replied to questions in two popular magazines and to those posed by a polling agency and by academic investigators. Twenty topics were included, beginning with "In general how happy have you been" ("Over the past few months?" "Over the past five years?" "During your life up to now?"); moving eventually to specific items such as "What effect do you think making more money would have on your happiness?" and ending with "Is there anything I haven't asked you that you think is important to happiness?" The overall conclusions: "There is no simple recipe for producing happiness, but all the research indicated that for almost everyone a necessary ingredient is some kind of satisfying, intimate relationship." Also: "Many people have personal visions of the happy life."[52] A summary of empirical data once had the smart title "Happiness is Everything; Or Is It?"[53]

The direct approach to happiness has been varied for other informants, usually dingdong samples, but some have come from other countries besides the United States.[54] In a book with the unflinching title *The Pursuit of Happiness* and the subtitle *Who is Happy—and Why*, samples of Americans were asked whether they believed they were "satisfied" with various aspects of their lives such as their friendships and marriages. In an "epilogue" the author generously provides ten "things that *do* enable happiness" to occur. Some of those ten are definitely beliefs referring to diverse actions ("positive self-esteem," "feelings of control"); others suggest beliefs about more specific actions ("supportive friendships," "a socially intimate, sexually warm, equitable marriage").[55] In an older and more extensive study, Americans and samples in other countries (including Japan and Norway) rated and then ranked thirteen different kinds of life "you personally would like to live." On the questionnaire, each of the ways was described in about

150 words. In the investigator's very own phrasing, Way 1 has been summarized as "preserve the best that man has attained"; Way 7, "integrate action, enjoyment, and contemplation"; and Way 13, "obey the cosmic purposes." A factor analysis of data from the American students revealed that the thirteen kinds could be reduced to five factors arbitrarily labeled Social Restraint and Self-Control, Enjoyment and Progress in Action, Withdrawal and Self-Sufficiency, Receptivity and Sympathetic Concern, and Self-Indulgence or Sensuous Enjoyment. Similar factors emerged from Indian and Chinese data.[56]

Using an even simpler approach toward the same end, another investigator once included among numerous verbal scales administered to Americans seven drawings introduced with this statement: "Here are some faces expressing various feelings." The informants were then asked six questions: "Which face comes closest to expressing how you feel about your life as a whole?", followed by the same query "about your house or apartment," "about what our national government is doing," "about your spare time activities," about your independence or freedom," and "about your standard of living." All seven sketches consisted of a circle with two dots representing eyes and a line the mouth. The dots were all the same, but the lines of the mouth varied from one curved upward (presumably the happiest) to one facing downward (the unhappiest).[57]

In the 1930s almost 2,500 Americans, married or divorced, and more than one-third of them men with a "professional" occupation, submitted themselves to 71 questions concerning their behavior and their feelings and attitudes; 128 items sought to determine their "general likes and preferences," and 34 concentrated on their "views about the ideal marriage." An example of the last scale: "If you had your life to live over, do you think you would marry the same person; marry a different person; not marry at all." Herewith a summary of some of the principal findings:

> . . . it is especially characteristic of unhappy subjects to be touchy or grouchy; to lose their tempers easily; to fight to get their own way; to be critical of others; to be careless of others' feelings; to chafe under discipline or to rebel against orders; to show any dislike that they may happen to feel; to be easily affected by praise or blame; to lack self-confidence; to be dominating in their relations with the opposite sex; to be little interested in old people, children, teaching, charity, or uplift activities; to be unconventional in their attitudes toward religion, drinking, and sexual ethics; to be bothered by useless thoughts; to be often in a state of excitement; and to alternate between happiness and sadness without apparent cause.[58]

A slightly different approach concentrates on the relation between scores on a supreme-value schedule and demographic factors. Again the meliorist drowns in the studies being offered; in this paragraph the reader is spared that experience by reporting only the studies by one American sociologist which are of special interest because they come from careful analyses not of dingdong samples but of populations throughout the United States. Relations of varying significance were found between "well-being" as measured by seven questions regarding how "happy" individuals felt in general and specifically with reference to place of residence, non-working conditions, family, friends, health, and financial status as well as marital status, education, "race" (black vs. white), religion and membership in religious organizations, age, etc.[59]—and the "etc." must be added since additional factors have been and will be discovered in other studies. The "etc." also inspires the final word coming from a social scientist who once made the world-shaking announcement that "physical necessities are not the only basic human needs." After that bit of originality he attempted to list in a single paragraph the additional needs (and hence values) to be satisfied if happiness is to be attained in American society and "sometimes" in "other large-scale systems":

> . . . we need to love and be loved. We need sharing, tenderness, and to be needed by others. As a species, we need to reproduce and to rear our children. We need to learn the ways of our society, and hopefully others, and to learn and share the heritages of our past. We need to learn who we are, to develop self-respect and appreciation of our capacities and worth. We need joys, relaxation, creativity, opportunities to grow and change, and to satisfy our curiosities as we seek new knowledge, insights, and truths. We need to develop our minds, our intellectual capacities, our ability to think and reason. Our capacities to relate to each other, to other forms of life, and to the world and universe of which we are a part, all need developing. We need to identify with others, to belong to groups, and to have group pride. We need protection from dangers and attacks and from threats to our lives. Our groups need to survive against both cultural and physical threats.[60]

Into this gulp are jammed pleas on behalf of individuals and their groups as well as the interrelation between them. Noticeable, too, is the verifiable assumption that all these needs at the moment are not satisfied and hence that the desirable urge to strive to do so should continue. Packed into the few words are contentions concerning needs that are being, are not being, and should be satisfied, certainly a legitimate and understandable instance of the naturalistic fallacy. And yet it is easy, too easy, to wonder why other satisfying activities are not included, such as the satisfaction derived from completing a task, whether or not praise comes from others for doing so, or anticipating a gratifying experience in the near or far future, particularly when that experience seems probable.

Stop, enough, enough. Available to the skeptical are competent summaries of studies on human happiness in the past and in the recent present, usually based—as ever—on American and sometimes British samples.[61] Can such studies and those mentioned here be succinctly summarized? Compulsively here is one effort:

1. Happiness can be tentatively assessed by means that vary from a simple, direct question to a series of probes and that employ the concept itself or an equivalent such as "well-being."
2. So measured, the feeling of being happy or unhappy fluctuates over time, even though people report their "normal" or modal state rather than fluctuations therefrom and even though they are more likely to recall positive rather than negative events, to underestimate satisfying events and to overestimate depressing events, and to emphasize frequent rather than infrequent experiences associated with their own actions and feelings of joy or gloom.[62]
3. Certain conditions and events are or are not associated frequently or infrequently with happiness in people's lives or everyday existence: ethnicity; family background; health; experiences; leisure, boredom, loneliness; and social relations in a general or specific sense.[63] Translation: it all depends!

And once more in another gulp:

According to my personal priorities and to the best of my ability, my judgments and their appropriate, anticipated actions bring me deep satisfactions while remaining in harmony in varying ways with a complete set of values that include responsibility to other persons and the groups of immediate and far-reaching significance to me.[64]

UNCERTAINTIES

After pursuing values generally and happiness in particular, the unhappy conclusion must be that uncertainties appear and characterize values as well as the language being used and abused. Utopia is not at hand or imminent. Many of the difficulties arise in the interaction between communicators and their audiences.

For communicators the challenges begin during infancy and during the socialization of youth: the learning process is gradual and fraught with errors from an adult standpoint. An analysis following one writer's essay

called "How Shall a Thing Be Called?" once suggested the ways in which
human beings must and do learn to use language in order to abstract from
an environment teeming with objects and events the particular referents of
interest and value to them at the moment. With humorous and serious exceptions, it is suggested that short rather than long and concrete rather
than abstract words tend to be used more readily in English and hence are
taught to and learned by children as they are socialized.[65] Such words thus
offer a preliminary clue to perceptions, values, and actions in a society.
"That tall person is drinking milk." You and I are confident that the sentence is "understood" without revealing whether the person, besides being
"tall," is young or old, bright or stupid, lavishly or simply clothed (if only
the extremes are considered); and whether the milk is cold or hot, pasteur-
ized or homogenized, fresh or curdled; and why the person is drinking that
innocent beverage and not a whiskey-and-soda. Somewhat arbitrarily,
though with some research backing, it has been suggested that the values
behind actions change through "stages" as children develop. The stages are
listed here in some of one author's words: (1) obedience and punishment;
(2) naively egoist; (3) pleasing and helping others; (4) authority and social
order maintaining; (5) contractual legalistic; (6) conscience or principle.[66]
All individuals do not reach the final stage and throughout their existence
employ idiosyncratically a smattering of the values inherent in each stage.

Communicators may justify their own actions to themselves and to others by falsely citing a value they claim to be implementing. They really
could not afford to contribute money to his cause, but they told the solici-
tor that they disagreed with the objective being sought. Verbal labels are
convenient and useful, but in non-trivial contexts can be misleading and
hazardous. She may be called a reactionary or a radical, but—even when
the label is accurate from someone's viewpoint—she has many other attributes in addition to those being conveyed by the political sentence; isn't she
also charming and beautiful? Verbal labels may be deliberately employed to
discredit opponents when in the West they are called communists or fas-
cists; or, in reverse, to bolster or conceal one's own view. The "National
Wilderness Institute," which opposes restrictions on exploiting forests, has
used a name close to that of "The Wilderness Society," which has the opposite objective.[67] Dare one be certain that any verbal message has been "correctly" understood?

Value-laden stereotypes or prejudices are likely to be employed especially in describing groups. Anthropological textbooks rightly suggest[68]
that much more is needed than its name to identify another society: the
origin of that name, the methods used in determining descent (matrilineal

or patrilineal?); the extent to which traditional practices are retained and "modern" or "Western" ones have been adopted; the modal ways in which children are socialized—any identifying list is both arbitrary and endless. Single words alone may be ethnocentric. According to one standard dictionary, a shaman is "a priest-doctor who uses magic to cure the sick, to divine the hidden, and to control events that affect the welfare of the people." The words in the formal definition, "magic" and "divine," may immediately discredit shamans from a Western viewpoint and thus preclude the possibility of discovering among them new and useful drugs for Western medical practice and for exploring the unexplorable in human consciousness.[69]

Similarly, verbal characterizations may omit important concomitants that may be of interest or value. When someone is called "religious," what do we then know about him or her? A scholarly African theologian examined many traditional religions in sub-Saharan Africa and found that "religion, more than anything else . . . colours their understanding of the universe and their empirical participation in that universe, making life a profoundly religious phenomenon." But those religions for centuries have been competing with Christianity, Islam, and other religions originating elsewhere, and they have tended to "yield more and more their hold in shaping people's values, identities and meaning in life." Together with changes from elsewhere, consequently, "Africa must now search for new values, new identities, and a new self-consciousness."[70] Is any such anthropological information conveyed when the term "religious" is attached to a person or society? Certainly not, but what then is conveyed?

Uncertainty about past events is pushed aside when people would cling to their version of events, when in fact they lack the time, patience, knowledge, or desire to catch more than a glimpse of what has transpired. According to a political scientist and his collaborator who have produced a massive tome on the history of anti-Semitism, most recently "there is a tendency to assume that the problem of Jewish security and the attitudes of Jews toward their survival grows from the Holocaust alone." This sweeping misconception results from the fact that the "actions of the Nazis and their collaborators are of such a scale and horror as to obscure the long history of anti-Semitism." These writers' own careful historical account and analysis indicate that for a multitude of reasons "anti-Semitism has been a continuous and pervasive element of Western history and culture" long before the Nazis.[71] Writing at the outset of World War II and in this instance without quotations or documentation, another American psychologist suggested that "each major piece of Nazi propaganda undertook to drive into the consciousness of the man in the street an irresistibly alluring image, assaulting his senses from all sides day and night and getting him dizzy with the lure of easy winnings."[72] This and similar statements cannot be ignored not because they illustrate the author's unrestrained style of writing but perhaps because they reflect the reactions of many Germans at that time to attacks on Jews and others and to Hitler's promises.

Knowledge and value judgments concerning every mass phenomenon involving many persons require hesitation before their validity can be asserted with certainty. Yes, wars have negative consequences: death, destruction, waste, injustice—on and on. But the devil's or the angel's advocate in some instances can note other associations: heroism, independence, punishment of evil—likewise on and on, including even justice. There is always more to perceive and to communicate after the generalization or exhortation ends.

APPENDIX: CREDOS

I. Plato: *Republic*

I think a city comes to be because none of us is self-sufficient, but we all need many things. . . . Surely our first and greatest need is to provide food to sustain life. . . . Our second is for shelter, and our third for clothes and such . . . we aren't all born alike, but each of us differs somewhat in nature from the others, one being suited to one task, another to another.

First, then, let's see what sort of life our citizens will lead when they've been provided for in the way we have been describing. They'll produce bread, wine, clothes, and shoes, won't they? . . . They'll put their honest cakes and loaves on reeds or clean leaves, and, reclining on beds strewn with yew and myrtle, they'll feast with their children, drink their wine, and, crowned with wreaths, hymn the gods. They'll enjoy sex with one another but bear no more children than their resources allow, lest they fall either into poverty or war.

Do you think that a potter who has become wealthy will still be willing to pay attention to his craft? . . . And surely if poverty prevents him from having tools or any of the other things he needs for his craft, he'll produce poorer work and will teach his sons or anyone else he teaches, to be worse craftsmen. . . . So poverty and wealth make a craftsman and his products worse.[73]

Noteworthy is the way in which Plato interweaves his statements: in effect he discusses the nature of the self and many of the observable attributes of others before, during, and after he specifies the attributes of that self, others, and their values.

II. Aristotle: *Politics*

Before we can undertake properly the investigation of . . . the nature of an ideal constitution, it is necessary for us first to determine the nature of the most desirable way of life. . . . We must . . . first of all find some agreed conception of the way of life which is most desirable for all men and in all cases; and we must then discover whether or not the same way of life is desirable in the cast of the community as in that of the individual. . . .

(1) The constituent elements of the best life which it is certain that no one would challenge . . . is the classification . . . into external goods; goods of the body; and goods of the soul.

(2) No one would call a man happy who had no particle of fortitude, temperance, justice, or wisdom . . . who would ruin his dearest friends for the sake of a farthing.

(3) . . . we ask, "How much of each good should men have?" . . . Any modicum of goodness is regarded as adequate; but wealth and property, power, reputation, and all such things are coveted to an excess which knows no bounds or limits.

(4) You can see for yourselves that the goods of soul are not gained or maintained by external goods. It is the other way round.

(5) We may therefore join in agreeing that the amount of felicity which falls to the lot of each individual man is equal to the amount of his goodness and his wisdom, and of the good and wise acts that he does.

(6) The fortitude of a state, and the justice and wisdom of a state, have the same energy, and the same character, as the qualities which cause individuals who possess them to be brave, just, and wise.[74]

Aristotle, Plato's most distinguished student, likewise and somewhat similarly considered the relation between the self and the attributes of others and of the ideal society at the outset of a discussion of political ideals and educational principles in Book VII of his treatise on politics.

III. Tibetan Yoga: Elegant Sayings

Men of little ability, too,
By depending upon the great, may prosper;
A drop of water is a little thing,
But when will it dry away if united to a lake?

1. Causes of Regret: Having obtained the difficult-to-obtain, free, and endowed human body, it would be a cause of regret to fritter life away.

2. Requirements: Having estimated one's own capabilities, one requireth a sure line of action.

3. Things to be Done: Seek friends who have beliefs and habits like thine own, and in whom thou canst place thy trust.

4. Things to be Avoided: Avoid gaining thy livelihood by means of deceit and theft.

5. Things not to be Avoided: Ideas, being radiance of the mind, are not to be avoided.

6. Things One Must Know: One must know that the effects of past actions, whence cometh all sorrow, are inevitable.

7. Things to be Practised: Once having experienced spiritual illumination, commune with it in solitude, relinquishing the worldly activities of the multitude.

8. Things to be Persevered in: Should various misfortunes assail thee, persevere in patience of body, speech, and mind.

9. Incentives: By reflecting upon death and the impermanence of life, mayest thou be incited to live piously.

10. Errors: Strength of faith combined with weakness of intellect are apt to lead to the error of narrow-minded dogmatism.

11. Resemblances Wherein One May Err: Desire may be mistaken for faith.

12. Things Wherein One Erreth Not: In having greatness of intellect and smallness of pride one does not err.

13. Grievous Failures: To preach religion and not practise it is to be like a parrot saying a prayer.

14. Weaknesses: A religious devotee showeth weakness if he barter sacred truths for food and money.[75]

Yoga doctrines have been traditionally collected in seven "books," only from the first of which the citations above have been obtained. The first four lines of poetry have been lifted from more than two hundred stanzas. The fourteen "categories of Yogic precepts" are the first half of the twenty-eight that are available. Each precept is labeled as indicated here and contains at least ten specific elaborations, only one of which in each instance has been cited.

IV. Albert Schweitzer: *Reverence for Life*

Don't vex your minds by trying to explain the suffering you have to endure in this life.

In action lies wisdom and confidence.

The older we grow, the more we realize that true power and happiness come to us only from those who spiritually mean something to us.

It appears that men have always instinctively known that God needed their thanks.

To hope, to keep quiet, and to work alone—that is what we must learn to do if we really want to labor in the true spirit.

We must make atonement for all the terrible crimes we read of in the newspapers.

Only familiarity with the thought of death creates true, inward freedom from material things.

The interior joy we feel when we have done a good deed . . . is the nourishment the soul requires.

"Be true to men as they are true to you."

The primary insight is man's awareness that his destiny is not synonymous with his daily experiences.

Reverence for the infinity of life means removal of the alienation, restoration of empathy, compassion, sympathy.

Never put off gratitude.[76]

Seventeen of the numerous sermons by this extraordinary philosopher, theologian, musician, organist, biographer, accredited physician, and humanitarian who functioned in Europe and Gabon in the first part of the present century have been collected in a book with the English title as translated from German. That title comes from one of his sermons, was bracketed with "sympathy with other lives," and considered by him to be "of supreme importance for this world of ours." Above are some of the actions and values extolled therein.

PART II

PEOPLE

CHAPTER 5

Self

In a quest for perfect people meliorists begin by targeting themselves. Without some self-knowledge, individuals under- or overestimate their own capabilities, causing them to misjudge others and society as well as the actions they would undertake. An American theologian who actively pursued desirable values opens an analysis of the self by observing that "the human animal is the only creature that talks to itself" so that a conscience develops in which the self judges its own "actions and attitudes" and expresses "a sense of obligation in contrast to inclination." Then that "self is in constant dialogue with various neighbors," including communities that are "beyond" direct observation. Ultimately the self has or should have a "dialogue with God" in order to "overcome the threat to the meaning of its life by finding that the one mystery, the ultimate or divine mystery," is "a key to the understanding of the mystery of the self's transcendent freedom."[1]

For whatever reason, the word "I" (or ego) is used to call attention to or summarize the self by the self. The almost metaphysical question is posed, "Who am I?",[2] the referent to which may be experiencing stress, contemplation, or merriment. I know I am hungry or thirsty, and I know what I do or believe I should do in some but not all circumstances as I cope with a need or desire. A problem arises when a judgment is faulty, inaccurate, or uncertain: I was not really aware that I disturbed you by talking too loud. But who is passing judgment on my action, who decides I have created a disturbance or that I am less than perfect? Another person observes or judges my action, and I myself may do so without a contribution or intervention by others. Self-awareness may not be accurate as judged by those others or even on a later occasion by the self.

Some concepts referring to the self that are employed in ordinary communication, and also in the natural and especially the social sciences, must be called fashionable without detracting from their importance at the moment or later. Psychologists and those they influenced, including persons associated with the mass media and market surveys, have been inspired by expressions such as instinct, conditioning, aggression, habit, wishful thinking, locus of control, repression—well, the list is long. Meliorists appreciate the beliefs, research, and attitudes to which the concepts give rise but try to recognize their possibly fleeting significance. Would that there were terms for human beings to which we could usefully cling as we do over generations to words like weight, color, and gravity.

SELF-APPRAISAL

The self is always one center of attention by the self and frequently by other persons. Meliorists must begin an analysis somewhere; here let us begin with that self. A modern, somewhat fancy concept that includes nontheological values as well as aspects of self-appraisal is that of metacognition, a reference to "a person's cognition about cognition, that is, the person's knowledge of cognitive processes and states such as memory, attention, knowledge, conjecture, illusion."[3] Meliorists recognize that human beings, including mature adults, are encased in private cocoons from which there is no everlasting escape and into which other persons are unable to penetrate most of the time. "Self-reports of such common sensations as shortness of breath, racing heart, and tense muscles have different meanings to different people" and hence are experienced and interpreted differently. Such appraisals vary with age, gender, marital and occupational status, residence, socioeconomic status, ethnicity, and culture.[4] Because of its variability, the discrete processes are organized more or less uniquely so that, as Gestalt psychologists have been intoning for decades,[5] their characteristic properties cannot always be determined from the individual components.

Who or what is the self who communicates information about that self to the self and to others? The perplexing, involuted question raises so many philosophical questions that a relatively new discipline called "narratology" ("narrative discourse") has been evolved to deal with communications about the self in literature; unsurprisingly studies on "self-monitoring" are now available.[6] Here attention is called to three ways to describe the appraisal of and by the self and hence may be useful to meliorists: self-efficacy, self-esteem, and identification with one or more groups.

The first appraisal, that of self-efficacy, refers to an individual's belief in his or her own power or ability to achieve desirable goals. A "theoretical analysis" of largely experimental studies employing that concept concludes that "people who think they can perform well on a task do better than those who think they will fail."[7] Thus the initial actions and motivation of a dingdong sample in a bowling game were once affected by their own ratings of their self-efficacy in that experimental situation.[8]

Self-esteem, a second mode of appraisal, has an obvious and close connection with the goal of meliorism. Some psychologists and others agree that "human beings have a pervading need to maintain an adequate level" of such esteem which is affected by events and hence is maintained when and if experiences therefrom generally are satisfactory and when societal conditions lead to satisfaction. Esteem can be applied generally to the self or, perhaps especially among adolescents, to the self in comparison with others in the family, school, or different social groups. Jealousy may occur when self-esteem is threatened: she is more successful than I ever can be; he loves another person more than he does me. Studies in Britain and elsewhere have indicated a significant if not overpoweringly close relation between low self-esteem and prejudice toward other persons and groups. Some individuals, including schoolchildren, may "enhance" their self-esteem by reevaluating themselves and their own actions[9]; self-esteem may be damaged by one or more failures resulting from one's own actions or from unavoidable conditions in society.

Self-esteem, as one knows from introspection, varies from very high to very low. It can be tapped—"measured"—by replies to self-imposed questions such as "On the whole, I am satisfied with myself," "I wish I could have more respect for myself," "I am able to do things as well as most other people." An extensive study of this variable, based on questionnaires containing such items, was distributed to more than five hundred high school students in New York state during the 1960s. Not unanticipated among the findings were differences based on gender (more girls than boys believing it important to be "sympathetic and understanding") and on religious affiliation (more Catholic and Jewish than Protestant boys giving a high value to being "efficient, practical"). The participants with high rather than low self-esteem tended to be more interested in national or international affairs and to follow events in the mass media. Meliorists thus disappointedly learn again that a desirable trait is likely either to be or not to be associated with other general or desirable beliefs and attitudes.[10]

A straightforward, subtle technique has also been employed to estimate self-esteem among American children. "Tell us about yourself," a child is told, and then the individual either replies freely while his or her words are recorded or writes, also freely, in a booklet provided in the classroom. The personal responses are later content-analyzed and reveal references to physical characteristics (height, weight, hair and eye color, handedness, wearing of eyeglasses), ethnicity, and demographic attributes (age, gender). One boy in grade 7 provided a "particularly evocative and provocative" account:

> I am a kid that has nothing and gets nothing. When I was born, I born trouble. My mother said to me that I was born just for trouble. I was born in New York. I used to think to myself that I should be dead. I never had a good time for long. When I come home I just get fust at. I was born just to be born. I am a kid that is hardly known to the world. I am a human just like everybody you know and I should be treated like one. Please be my friend.

For this boy a follow-up request, "Tell me about your family," elicited the following:

> My family is the nicest parents in the world. Sometimes they can be mean and I think they no good. My mother said she hated me so I thought I shouldn't like her but I do. I love her very much and she loves me but doesn't know it.[11]

Empirical research of this sort indicates the importance of extensive probing to elicit more of the context in which sentiments are embedded.

A third appraisal, that of group identification, has a cause-and-effect relation to self-esteem. Each individual plasters upon him- or herself—or is so plastered by others—a designation indicating membership in a specified group that is formally or informally recognized by that self or most persons somewhere in the society. The person is smart or stupid, young or old, liberal or conservative, white or dark, well or poorly educated, successful or unsuccessful—and the list of designations is long, with each designation ranging between the indicated extremes. Also additional challenges arise when an individual's group identification is to be comprehended:

a. source: has the self or another person made the identification?
b. attitude: does the self consider the identification favorable or unfavorable from his or her own standpoint?
c. usage: does the self make the identification only occasionally as the situation demands or frequently or continually in many situations?

You or someone else may consider you to be X, you may or may not like to be called an X, you may think of yourself frequently as an X or only briefly as a particular situation demands.

SUBJECTIVE VALIDITY

The self and others who appraise the self's self-appraisal are or must be concerned with the validity of the appraisal and other attributes of that self. Like the self, let us first immediately consider self-judgments. Very probably the self is likely to be biased in favor of judgments by the self rather than by others: they have subjective validity. This is what I am; this is what I have done; this is the kind of person I am; no one knows me as well as I know myself; others cannot judge me because their knowledge of me, compared with my own, is superficial. Impressive research in different countries suggests how a society's emphasis on collectivism, the distribution of power therein, and general expectations related to gender have repercussions on individuals' personalities and how they view themselves as they develop.[12] Especially crucial is a society's system of education regarding the self. It has been suggested, also on the basis of extensive research, though almost completely in the United States, that there may be six stages in the development of moral judgment ranging from the "preconventional" and the "conventional" and ending with the "postconventional or principled." The "reasons for doing right" change from stage to stage. Stage 1 involves the "avoidance of punishment, and the superior power of authorities." Stage 3, the first of the conventional reasons, ranges from the "need to be a good person in your eyes and those of others" to the "desire to maintain rules and authority which support stereotypically good behavior." Stage 6 is characterized by "the belief as a rational person in the validity of universal moral principles, and a sense of personal commitment to them." Experience with this framework suggests that children can be encouraged to move from one to a "higher" stage not only by what they have been formally taught but also by participating, together with their parents and especially with their teachers, in the educational process.[13] Are earlier stages less objectively valid than later stages?

For reasons piled high throughout the centuries and advocated or provided by theologians and philosophers, strangers and friends, parents and individuals themselves, self-judgments may not be objectively valid. Sometimes, but not always, there is a tendency to remember successes more readily than failures. All memories of the past may possess only projective validity in part or in whole. The entire experience and the details connected thereto may be forgotten with the passing of time, or they are not likely to be recalled or function as guides to goals being sought or avoided. What is remembered may emerge in a form different from the original experience, but may be in accord with whatever is of concern at the moment of recall.

Memories of events, therefore, often differ from the original perception concerning vividness or details. The changes resulting from interim experiences and present interests may magnify or reduce the significance of the past. Later on you suddenly realize subjectively that a trivial event in your childhood really has played a critical role in determining some of your present interests; and with effort you remember or think you remember what you have forgotten. These differences between experience and memory are especially crucial when individuals themselves have not experienced the events of which they have become aware through formal and informal histories or through less detailed accounts accompanying the traditions of a society. You will never really know how it felt to be present ages ago during that war or revolution in your society which is now praised or condemned, no matter how strong or weak your present feelings are; you are dependent upon second hand accounts that cannot communicate all the details and feelings you might have experienced or perceived if you had been present. In spite of their pitfalls, however, memories must frequently be trusted, perhaps at least skeptically, because there may be no alternative.

Not surprisingly, evidence from persons in the West and dingdong samples indicate that self-appraisals may be self-serving and self-flattering, and they often are designated ambiguously or idiosyncratically.[14] "Everyone," it has been asserted, "can cite instances of wishful thinking, of overconfidence, of people who refuse to recognize their own faults, often despite a penetrating awareness of the same faults in anyone else."[15] Objectivity may be ignored or trumpeted as an ideal.

The conflict between wishful and realistic self-appraisal leads to a challenge to the self: "Can we trust ourselves to be honest with ourselves, especially if we understand that self-deceivers do think themselves honest with themselves?" But the author just quoted gropes toward salvation and notes that "we are endowed with a capacity to reflect on our action, and this permits us to act morally and to correct ourselves"; "a sign of moral health as well as psychological health" is the ability "to confront oneself with the truth about oneself." The "*possibility* [the italics are his] of eliminating self-deception is realized through the "self-transcendence of faith . . . grounded in God." With such faith one acquires "certain attitudes" such as irony that become "a stance against pretense and self-approval." Humor is a "marker of the religious person" who overcomes self-deception; one can laugh at one's own efforts and realize that "without God one can do nothing."[16] Amen, but also changes induced by events and aging may be recognized during sudden or prolonged, actual or reported interactions with strangers or while in groups or societies differing profoundly or superficially from one's own. Young children can engage in "pretend play" for the fun of it or, from an adult's standpoint, for therapeutic purposes.[17]

In addition, individuals may lie to themselves, deliberately or not. Strongly held beliefs, though impressive to passersby, are not necessarily even subjectively valid: psychoanalysis seeks to probe such beliefs to determine their rationale and the function they perform for the self, which may be different from what the self claims. A commendably rigorous psychologist has criticized therapists and clinicians who accept too readily and uncritically what they learn from their patients or research participants, so that their theories are based on invalid data. He himself has effectively used case histories and his own experiments to suggest that theories validated backwards are much less promising than those that look forward; utilize, if possible, not what these persons have done but forecast what they will do and see whether in fact they do so.[18]

For the same or very similar reasons, the judgments of others concerning the self may not be objectively valid (G2). They too may be biased in favor of their own judgments about the self: they believe they know better than he or she does. They may have their own conscious or unconscious wishes that induce them to render favorable or unfavorable judgments. They may recall false judgments they have made about that person on other occasions because they also are affected by their own present needs and goals. They may acknowledge that they are strangers in some or many senses to the self and lack the experience to render more competent judgments.

Usually but not always, though almost always, invalid judgments of various kinds occur when most human phenomena are attributed to a single variable and thus additional, relevant, and available knowledge may be overlooked. Regardless of your own conviction, do glance quickly at the policy of affirmative action now generally if sporadically popular in many Western countries. Surely the policy is desirable because it is "just": more individuals who have been suffering from discrimination, such as blacks and minority groups in the United States and women everywhere, are able to achieve positions or goals from which they have previously been barred or which few of them have been permitted or been able to achieve; discrimination thereby at least can be reduced, and minorities or the "victims" may well be happier. The theory equating discrimination with some form of misery, however, is too simple. Those thought by an observer to be suffering discrimination may not be suffering; they may not be blaming their oppressors, they may hold themselves responsible; and the others enjoying affirmative action may not feel elated unless they believe that the advantage thus gained has also resulted from their own merit and not alone from a government's policy.[19] Similarly many challenges, such as prejudice, depression, political partisanship, may be associated with a single factor for a particular person, but generally more than one factor may be required to provide an adequate general explanation.

EXPLICATION

Not only to comprehend but also to explore judgments concerning the self by the self and by others it is necessary to select the self's attributes to be designated. Herewith for illustrative purposes a brief list indicating the possible nature and scope of such attributes:

1. *content*: beliefs, ideas, ideologies, principles, explanations
2. *subjectivity*: feelings, emotions, desires, attitudes, values
3. *action*: behavior, conduct, demeanor, movement

All three variables may be delineated with respect to

a. *importance*: from high to low
b. *salience*: from total to negligible
c. *organization*: relation to one or more variables

Other listings elsewhere can easily be consulted.[20] The above schema functions as follows with the numbers and letters being those in the previous paragraph:

1. I believe that person is honest.
2. I like that person.
3. I recommend this honest person to others.

a. Honesty is a significant human value.
b. He is always honest, with very few justifiable exceptions.
c. His striving to be honest reflects the values of his parents and to a lesser degree his religious faith.

It is neither anticipated nor assumed that anyone reviews those steps at a given moment or over time. You vote for that candidate because you consider him honest without delving into any of your other motives for doing so, without considering thoroughly why you consider him honest, and without preaching to yourself concerning the importance of honesty generally or especially in public office.

Psychologists, psychiatrists, and scholars or writers in other disciplines directly or remotely concerned with human beings investigate or express platitudes involving a wide range of topics ranging, for example, from anger and anxiety and ending the alphabet with weaning and work. These terms are variants on the above listing; thus anger plops into no. 2 and work into no. 3. Shame, guilt, embarrassment, and pride have been examined by an international group of scholars in a book directly related to the current chapter as its title clearly indicates: *Self-Conscious Emotions*.[21] Their orientation is also no. 2.

The explication of judgments concerning the self cannot be specified for all eternity since the social and psychological disciplines have not reached and probably can never reach even the wavering levels of agreement and approach of the natural sciences. Here some of the more demanding and promising topics and challenges may be reviewed. First of all, there are the *traits* to be examined. The numerous traits of the self and others used to designate and explain the self and others are scattered on many pages of any dictionary. Arbitrarily consider sensation seeking, "the need for varied, novel, and complex sensations and experiences and the willingness to take physical and social risks for the sake of such experience," which is one trait especially puzzling. The cited definition comes from a psychologist who eventually contrived a scale containing pairs of items with one alternative indicating approval, the other disapproval of the trait. His analysis, based on American, English, and Scottish students, suggests four components of that trait. The four seem to be clustered around preferences, each of which is illustrated here by alternating the approving and the disapproving alternative provided on the scale: thrill and adventure seeking ("I often wish I could be a mountain climber"); experience seeking ("I prefer a guide when I am in a place I don't know well"); disinhibition ("I feel best after taking a couple of drinks"); and boredom susceptibility ("I like the comfortable familiarity of everyday friends"). Inasmuch as almost all of the data in these studies come from only three societies, the investigator indicates that elsewhere the trait may be affected by cultural factors, with Asians perhaps being less sensation seeking; in addition, there is possibly (how possible?) a genetic basis for the trait.[22]

Traits and all aspects of behavior change with the passing of time, and hence *development* is another crucial attribute and variable to note. Conceptions of the good life vary conspicuously with age (G5). As people grow older, their self-image changes, and they have different experiences related in part to their own assets and liabilities.[23] They are likely to become less responsive and to react more slowly, yet they may perceive subtler aspects of their surroundings as a result of accumulated experiences. Cultural prescriptions regarding the stages of aging and the treatment of the aged affect their reactions and those of persons evaluating them.[24] Older persons establish different social contacts, as they and their friends and enemies assume different roles in society for themselves; their loyalty to various institutions and their theoretical and practical evaluations change.[25] But another psychologist, cited above, indicates that "people of all ages report similar feelings of well-being."[26] The "feelings" themselves at any age may be "similar," although obviously the events giving rise to them differ for preadolescents and the aging. Five thousand American writers were once interviewed concerning their reactions to their occupations and personal status; ten years later 3,500 of them were located and again interviewed. At the second time, "most" who had retired for reasons other than health claimed they were "quite happy in retirement" and would have done so again "at the same age." But 13 percent of the whites and 17 percent of the blacks stated that they now thought they should have retired later. To avoid such "regret," the editor of the study suggests, the retirement decision should be made "as reversible as possible."[27]

Over time people generally change their conception of themselves. They are no longer innocent, they are somewhat sophisticated and evaluate themselves somewhat differently; they do not keep pushing ahead. They imagine, and in later years they are likely to believe, that they can or should relax.[28] Indeed at any age they may have what has been a trifle sensationally called an "identity crisis."[29] Meliorists observing the self and others note that people seek goals that appear worth achieving but that may be achieved never or at a given time. They grope for substitutes or downplay the significance and importance of the goals eluding them. They cannot remain young, much as they once enjoyed or claim they enjoyed that period of their lives, and so they seek, perhaps find, "deeper" satisfactions.

At any stage of development, actually at any time, the self's goals are not attained; there is *frustration*. That self may be "primarily an active rather than a contemplative organic unity"[30] and cannot avoid knowing from time to time that people do not dwell in the kingdom of heaven, nor while alive do or can they enter paradise. Failures to achieve goals and other frustrations are unavoidable and inevitable. Eventually living itself, whether unified and satisfactory or not, is supplanted by death. Less cosmically, and almost daily, control is lost: on occasion "innocent" children and weary adults may wish to remain awake but doze off. It may be inconvenient, taboo, or impossible to eat, drink, exercise, relax, or copulate whenever one wishes. The magnificent plans of youth are not, cannot be realized, and there is sorrow. In their occupation and marriage (marriages), individuals are not as satisfied as they once hoped to be. Some frustration is inevitable, therefore, and somehow efforts are made to block the disappointment; the disappointments must be endured or substitutes are found.[31] A humanist who has attempted to help patients in medical institutions begins a comprehensive analysis by stating that pain is "as elemental as fire or ice," but eventually he claims there is "no conclusion to the study of pain." His examination of psychiatric and especially of literary sources, however, demonstrates vividly, again in his words, a "link among pain, pleasure, and death."[32] In *Coping with Negative Life Events*, to which twenty writers have contributed, there are occasional undocumentable statements ("Never before in human history have so many people had so many romantic/sexual involvements") and an excessive dependence on dingdong samples, but a quick glance at some of the beliefs and actions attempting to cope with adversity reminds one of the losing struggles at hand: seeking help from others, mobilizing energy, not dwelling on the self, hoping rather than denying, not underestimating personal vulnerability, retaining a sense of self-identity at all costs, escaping from social approval, making excuses.[33]

Frustration may lead to fear and anxiety about one's welfare, reactions of the self that are double-edged. On the one hand, some of such beliefs and feelings are realistic and productive: hazards experienced by pedestrians who cross streets in the middle of traffic, wild animals suddenly appearing in wilderness areas, a thief threatening with a gun. Others may even have, it has once been claimed by a psychologist, an "innate" component like the fear of the dark, of heights, and of snakes, although each may also spring from actual experience.[34] There is a distinction between a senseless coward and a courageous hero; somehow meliorists try to locate the boundary between them.

One way to cope with frustration in the future and also, it is hoped, to increase gratification later, is through *renunciation* of a momentary gratification. A simple but impressive illustration is saving in any form: you do not spend now but invest your figurative or literal money in an activity or organization from which you think you will be rewarded with greater future benefits.[35] Renunciation is difficult, but somehow the individual must anticipate a gain from doing so that justifies whatever risk or pain is involved in postponing present routines and joys. A serious danger that may accompany hesitation is signaled by the polite concept of procrastination, which suggests that a decision is avoided or postponed with the realistic or unrealistic hope that eventually the problem will or can be faced and possibly resolved.

Whether or not there is *transfer* of knowledge or experience gained in one situation depends not only on the actual similarity of the past and future situations but also on the self's perception of their similarity. The individual who has coped with a difficult problem in the past may or may not transfer that experience to similar or different situations in the future. If flattery has produced cooperation once, will it be effective again when another person is approached with the same or a different appeal?

At any moment, no matter which trait is being evaluated, no matter how the trait has developed, no matter whether frustration occurs in the course of development or now, no matter whether renunciation seems desirable, and no matter whether experience from the past is or must be transferred, the momentary state of the self, the *mood* may be yet another factor to be included in explication (G6). Do people, when they conceive they are happy generally or at a specific time, perceive or seek cheerful experiences, depressed people the reverse? What occurs may depend on a mood too: if happy, the future looks "bright"; if depressed, it may seem "gloomy." And what is remembered may be influenced by the similarity or dissimilarity of the mood during the initial learning and at the time of recall: if the moods coincide—if they are "congruent" as some writers prefer to say—individuals remember more precisely what they originally perceived or learned than if the moods had been incongruent. Research data gathered in experiments in the West, generally in the United States and usually in contrived experiments, overwhelmingly substantiate these commonsense observations and predictions.[36] Once those in a dingdong sample reported that, when momentarily "sad," they experienced distressing physical symptoms and they also believed that they were "more vulnerable to future illness" than when they were "happy."[37] Can one ever wait for a "neutral" mood before passing judgment so that realistically inputs of neither optimism nor pessimism then prevail? But moods may not always be crucial. A half dozen experiments testing the similarity between students' moods when learning and recalling verbal materials once produced "inconsistent results," which the saddened investigators admitted were "very disappointing."[38] Indeed, findings from other studies indicate that it has been the majority, and not everyone, who supported the hypotheses concerning moods;

exceptions occurred. When their participants were American university students who were "superior in intelligence and academic performance," two psychologists chose to employ no less than sixteen different scales to determine mood at a given moment, over time, and its relation to other psychological variables. These scales included "Fullness vs. Emptiness of Life," "Harmony vs. Anger," and "Present Work."[39] Whether or not the findings from such research are ever generalizable, at least they suggest the perplexing subtleties that may emerge in direct interviewing.

Individuals, when pressed by themselves or others, may disclaim the importance of their own moods, which of course fluctuate, and instead may claim that "normally" they are happy or unhappy in the midst of the admitted fluctuations. A tendency by the self to return to its own norms is so significant that recently psychologists and others have honored it and use a distinctive, if jargonistic term, "set-point."[40] Whether one accepts or rejects that concept as an academic attempt to appear original, its meaning has two implications for tentative findings regarding most values, especially happiness. First, even in a less imperfect world, people's subjective states are not likely to be stable at a given moment or over time; fluctuations in moods and feelings occur in favorable circumstances. Then, second, personal standards for positive feelings, the set-point, can perhaps be raised so that the fluctuations in either direction eventually move to more praiseworthy points. Conceivably more people can be happier more of the time—a platitude?

In spite of the intellectual equipment now outlined, the unexpected may occur on occasion or frequently. The unknown or unknowable factor may then be ascribed to *luck*, good or bad. Luck is invoked so frequently that it is expressed by means of a host of synonyms such as accident, coincidence, happenstance, chance, fortune, fate, destiny, and so on. Such a confession or admission of ignorance may be restricted by knowing or postulating a mathematical or pseudo-mathematical range indicating the probability of an event's occurrence. The probability, based on records from the past, is that rain would or will occur on a particular date near your home. If it then rains and the rain is considered desirable, then its occurrence may be considered lucky. Chance is thus a metaphorical way of signifying ignorance or the achievement or nonachievement by individuals or their society with respect to the occurrence or non-occurrence of events. The concept or its equivalents point not only to accuracy or certainty but also to moral challenges that have puzzled philosophers and others since ancient times: should lucky persons be praised for their actions; should an individual receive a lighter punishment when he or she "unluckily" or "by chance" injures another person than one who "deliberately" commits a dreadful deed?[41]

A significant concept that avoids luck or chance as the reason for many beliefs and actions is that of the *unconscious*. The self does seem to be affected by unconscious processes that in some senses are a substitute for attribution of behavior to a deity or other persons possessing hypnotic or supernatural powers. Meliorists forever seek to increase their comprehension of the unconscious and remain continually intrigued by Freud who, more than any other psychiatrist or investigator in recent times, has offered insight into unconscious processes; more careful if less inspired investigators are consulted who offer practical suggestions regarding "How to Discover Unconscious Motives" to therapists and patients.[42]

CULTURE AND PERSONALITY

Methodologists of all kinds, whether scholars, social scientists, the self, or others may be satisfied with efforts to explicate the validity of judgments concerning the self and human beings by means of concepts such as those now suggested here. Or they then also seek to organize those pieces around some central explanation. Via inheritance, genes certainly are important in determining, perhaps ultimately, the course of human behavior, but they do not affect directly or explicitly many actions, such as the choice of clothing to be worn on specific occasions or the conditions requiring self-sacrifice for the benefit of others. The organizing concepts of greatest interest and seemingly most promising are those of culture and personality.

Culture refers to "the configuration of learned behavior and results of behavior whose component elements are shared by the members of a particular society." In recent years this anthropological concept has been widely abused as a synonym for society, country, or almost any other group, each of which possesses a culture but includes more than a conventionalized, traditional configuration. The second concept, that of personality, has also been clearly defined by the anthropologist just quoted: "The organized aggregate of psychological process and states pertaining to the individuals,"[43] which is a configuration that refers to the self.

Locating and naming a theory of culture and personality is a first step for meliorists to take, if only to emphasize the dependence of the self on society and to be reminded that absolutely nobody is self-sufficient personally or culturally. But the constituents of the culture and personality must be specified, if the analysis is to be meaningful or an action is to be effective. A psychologist has illustrated the difficulties either concept entails as a result of "the thousand of dimensions proposed to guide our analysis of motivation and personality." He himself located ten "classes" of units then being used to describe that analysis, which are, in his own self-explanatory words, "intellectual capacities, syndromes on temperament, unconscious motives, social attitudes, ideational schemata, interests and values, expressive traits, stylistic traits, pathological trends, and factorial clusters not readily classifiable in the other nine categories."[44] Fashions in concepts perpetually change, however, as new and fruitful insights are obtained. The self's own concepts may provide easy, but not necessarily accurate, explications of behavior. A favorite word has formerly been "instinct," suggesting that behavior is determined by an inborn tendency, but the concept ignores the role of culture for particular persons. Similarly but reversed, behavior is sometimes attributed only to culture, an explanation that exaggerates its importance without specifying why one individual and not another accepts and probably modifies the behavior characteristic of many or most other persons in the society.

Whether the self is observed by the self or by others, either his or her uniqueness or similarity to all or other human beings may be a useful guide. Individuals fluctuate between the two characterizations. Perhaps a subjective bias leads one toward uniqueness because, let us repeat, only we have direct access to ourselves, at least on a conscious and semiconscious level; nobody understands you as you think you yourself do. An individual's own claim for uniqueness is likely to have more than a trace of validity when reference is made to personality, however that slippery concept in turn is defined or appraised.

Exploring the reasons for uniqueness and similarity with others requires knowledge about an individual's personality as well as his or her society and culture. At birth and immediately thereafter, a psychologist once pointed out, a person "is not even to the slightest degree a socialized being," but then slowly and later rapidly is able to learn from experience and especially from other persons. At any given moment the individual, though remaining "an idiom unto himself or herself," is stimulated by sources outside and inside the self, but "central to our sense of existence" are images of our own body and the "self" as well as strivings to reach goals now and in the future. Human beings, undoubtedly unlike animals, at times have regrets about the past and feelings of uncertainty about the risks they must take in the future; hence arise "guilt, doubt, and anxiety." Insight into the changes, doubts, and goals of a person may be obtainable from the answers to questions such as the following: "Where do you want to be five years from now?" or "What kind of a future are you bringing about?"[45]

DEATH, ETC.

Unlike our assumption about animals, human beings as they mature acquire "the knowledge about death," and hence for them usually "death becomes a problem."[46] Serious savants, no matter whether they be humanists or social scientists, modestly and immodestly reveal their own platitudes and the profundities of others about dying.[47] Even though in a Western society such as the United States, "very few of us actually witness the deaths of those we love," in our bodies we come to note changes "that are at first only biochemical and intracellular" but eventually "become manifest in the function of entire organs" such as the kidneys, heart, and brain.[48] A Greek psychoanalyst has suggested that "man's uncomfortable awareness of the passage of time and his wish to make it go faster, stop it, or somehow reverse it, or eliminate it from consciousness and with it the awareness of change, betrays the unconscious dread of failure, separation, and death."[49] As children become aware of their surroundings, they discover that plants, trees, animals, and human beings eventually die and, even though they imagine or hope they themselves differ from nonhuman and human beings, and even though they comfort themselves with some version of a rationale pertaining to existence, they nevertheless discover that the dead, including those who have managed to live beyond their estimated life expectancy, are now gone forever. The death of those others reminds the living of their own mortality and compels them to feel—sad, frightened, angry? Less drastic but often equally painful are the feelings of guilt that later may well up within survivors: we could have, we should have done otherwise and we did not do so. A practicing physician has suggested that the "fear of loneliness and dread of death" add to our suffering, which itself is "the core of the human condition in a world of imperfection"; one has no choice, suffering cannot be completely avoided.[50] And a sociologist believes that death and the fear of death are so universal and widespread that they provide the basis for the origin of culture in a strict anthropological sense: "There would probably be no culture were humans unaware of their mortality." Again he repeats: "Unlike other animals, we not only know, *we know that we know.*"[51]

The penalties of advancing age thus come to be appreciated. While younger persons may respect those euphemistically called mature or praised as senior citizens, individuals themselves must assume that death is coming closer; they have less energy, they suffer more illnesses, they may experience additional guilt when they recall what they should or should not have done, and they feel increasingly lonely as more of their associates die and as formal or informal obituaries record the deaths of many others. Some of them at any age may believe or be informed by others or medical authorities that they or others are suffering from an incurable disease leading soon or eventually to death.

Illustrative but not necessarily typical is the report of an anthropologist with medical training who once described in detail how the Akan-speaking peoples in rural Ghana usually cope with their personal problems and everyday existence. Some of them, even those with a personality judged to be "good," encounter depression during their "declining years." Then "their friends and relatives become fewer, the changing world more perplexing and their capacity for adaptation and effort less." As a result, "life takes on a menacing quality and they become, in the words of one of them, 'afraid of the world.' "[52]

A few persons have reported an unusual experience that, at least according to their claims, enables them perhaps to cope somewhat with death: they state that they have had a near-death experience. Through direct interviews and a questionnaire, one psychologist once conducted an intensive investigation of Americans who believed they had been "close to death" as a result of illness, accidents, and attempts at suicide. The experiences were said to have almost been "exceedingly pleasant," and after recovery the individuals reported profound changes in their lives ranging from a spiritual awakening and a greater appreciation of life to prophetic visions and a proclivity never "to fear death again."[53] Possibly persons who have never had such alleged near-death encounters require another kind of deep experience not involving complete death that induces them to act according to some positive values, to advocate similar values, and thus somehow to meet with equanimity the inevitable challenge and certainty of actual death.

Other unusual experiences not of death but concerned with overcoming some of the frustrations of living may be "altered states of consciousness" during which individuals report that they feel happy, relaxed, or at least different from their "normal" states. Such feelings may be induced by hypnosis, meditation, drugs, and ordinary or induced dreaming.[54] Also related are mental telepathy, clairvoyance, precognition, and the effects of "mental" states on physical matter. A dispassionate review of three decades of research starting in the 1920s in the United States reveals some deliberately and unwittingly fraudulent reports but also conscientious, scrupulously honest investigations suggesting the possibility that such phenomena may have been validated at least among a small number of persons or informants.[55] Nonbelievers also seek to anticipate the future, frequently to avoid frustrations; but they employ "scientific" methods as in weather forecasting by meteorologists or statistical trends by economists. Psychic research is so controversial and often concerned with intimate and personally significant phenomena that it is difficult to maintain a balanced view and to consider such efforts both important and inconclusive: must we keep our "minds" wide open? This writer once retained his skepticism about such phenomena during a year at an American university where a modern version of that research was beginning; he must say now that he thoroughly admired the investigators, he was sickened by the attacks of outsiders upon them, but he kept wondering and continues to do so even as, he timidly suggests, meliorists should do likewise. Sane and sagacious exposés from a scientific or human standpoint upon those extolling the unknowable validity of claims concerning visitors from outer space and various alleged miracles must also be at least tolerated in the interest of free speech.

PREJUDICE TOWARD PREJUDICE

Too often, meliorists realize, words or concepts acquire connotations that prevent those employing them from appreciating the real or valid problem at hand (G4). Like you, this writer can think of illustrations too numerous or embarrassing to categorize. Let us be restrained and latch on to only one word, that of prejudice. Of course prejudice is bad, isn't it? Good persons shout again and again that persons should not be prejudiced. The evils of prejudice in the United States have been and remain numerous; they include subtle insults to ethnic groups such as Afro-Americans and Hispanics as well as false arrests and criminal charges and (at least in decades past) lynchings. Frustrated persons who displace their aggression upon out-groups identify such groups on the basis of color, religion, language, class, ancestry, political actions or beliefs, or even clothing. Disapproving prejudices exist against pedophiles who molest children and against gangs who rob passersby. Prejudices may function unheralded and be less serious, such as feelings related toward adults who abuse the grammar and pronunciation of our language. As previously indicated and, as well as we know at least part of the time, no experience or impression can be completely described and no statement is likely to contain all possible details. With good reason, consequently, a psychologist has warned:

> To prejudge is not in itself necessarily wrong. No one ever knows enough, so all of us must sometimes either act on the basis of incomplete information and untested assumptions or not act at all. However, whenever we *claim* to know without really knowing, or whenever we refuse to accept what *is*

known and act as if it were not so, then we have gone beyond prejudging. Then we are behaving prejudiciously.[56]

Distinguishing between prejudgment and prejudice may be difficult, illustrated too easily by some Nazis in Hitler's Germany, sincere supporters of cold war governments in Europe after World War II, and Republicans as well as Democrats in the United States.

In combating some prejudices and evils, meliorists seek to consider all aspects of the problem. Thus anti-Semitism exists and persists in many countries of the West and the East: individuals there have unfavorable attitudes toward Jews and may treat them with overt hostility and unfair discrimination. It is both possible and necessary, however, as an American sociologist has indicated, to observe the opposite or favorable judgments and actions concerning Jews. Philo-Semitism—does the word sound strange?—can be located throughout historical time in societies as diverse as China and Turkey, and especially in the West. Non-Jews have been friendly and hospitable toward Jews for reasons ranging from their own economic and intellectual gains to deep and abiding democratic and humanistic convictions. "There can be no question," one author concludes, "that intense philo-Semitism, manifested at select and propitious moments, saved European Jewry from extinction."[57] Meliorists thus have had and do have the possibility of being "prejudiced" and hence feeling and acting in behalf of the good and against the bad.

Then the actual functioning of a prejudice must be carefully appraised by examining its effect upon individuals. The self considered by an observer may be unaware of the prejudice as judged by observers or later in retrospect. Women in most societies, including those in the West, have been the "victims" of a gender bias when seeking employment especially in prestigious or well-paying positions, but recently fewer have been considering themselves victims. Instead they have denied being deprived and have imagined their "real" function is to be "feminine" and to be concerned with their own families or with occupations traditionally assigned to women as dramatized by nurses or servants.[58] Hostile or discriminating prejudices may give rise to a sense of pride and to a respect for one's own traditions, beliefs, and actions.

Meliorists, therefore, know there are usually, as ever, no easy answers to eternal questions such as those arising when truth struggles with lying that is deliberate and not self-deceptive. Should she, he, they tell a lie? Of course not; lying must be avoided, truth must triumph. And yet when a boy of six states, "You don't want to show them that it hurts, because then they'll think you're a cry-baby,"[59] you do not condemn the lad, you consider him brave; he keeps his troubles to himself by concealing or trying to conceal the truth. You admire him, provided of course the trouble is minor and does not require medical attention. No wonder that the editors of *Lying and Deception in Everyday Life* assert at the outset of their book that the two phenomena are "universal human characteristics" and that "all cultures employ" them "to some extent."[60] A three-year-old child, this time a girl, is disappointed when her grandmother at Christmas gives her not the toy she had anticipated but a knitted sweater; she does not show her "disappointment and sadness, she smiles" and "announces how much she enjoys the gift"; allegedly she says, "I'm going to wear it right now."[61] The deliberate intention to deceive may thus serve a laudatory value, that of fortifying the self or pleasing someone else. Spies and practitioners of psychological warfare very deliberately lie in order to mislead enemies; surely then and now, righteous Americans would not object to efforts to mislead the Germans concerning exactly where and when British and American forces would land in France from England in the crucial and final drive to defeat the Axis countries in World War II. Lying thus may seem reasonable, necessary, and justified when it is believed that it serves higher values—*but* can we be certain that the values are now and forever higher?

And so meliorists are careful as they seek to express values that give the lie to or transcend their immediate surroundings. Transcend parents? Yes, parents may reflect "only" their own background which guides them in providing values to their children. Other socializers and educators? More certainly yes; they are likely to suffer, if less so, from similar shortsightedness. It is refreshing to note that Henry David Thoreau, that seminal offbeat New Englander, found in the classics of ancient Greece, as a result and in spite of his formal education, "corroboration or the extension of most of his favorite theories" as well as "an encouraging glimpse and a proof of the existence of a still greater and yet surely unattainable world."[62]

SELF-INVENTORY

On occasion individuals may or should deliberately compile and consult a self-inventory to understand their own assets and limitations and to guide or plan their actions. Such an inventory stems from past experiences, present and future estimates, and communications and assistance from others. The inventory is not likely to be a formal document written on parchment or recoverable on a computer screen but an informal reckoning of the self's own thoughts and musings.

The self's knowledge is of many kinds. Seemingly "objective" facts refer to age, height, weight, gender, marital status, occupation, citizenship, and society. Personal assessments pertain to the self's alleged or real assets and liabilities that range from health to appraisals of ability and talent. Other individuals are judged, whether they be neighbors, members of specific organizations, fellow citizens, strangers, and persons in near or distant countries. Eternal challenges and values appear. Significant achievements and failures are noted and related to life expectancy, religion, death, and afterlife.

The items on the inventory can be easily or arduously procured. After the very early years of childhood, age is immediately knowable; yet does one know the capabilities or responsibilities associated with each age? Others are difficult or almost impossible to include. The challenge is especially acute for both non-historians and historians regarding historical facts and tendencies: so much has occurred in the past that a selection must be made for an inventory. Persons cannot remember what happened to them when they were younger even while they realize that the effects of the past are affecting them now. In their publications, classrooms, and casual conversations, historians appreciate their own limited expertise: they know they cannot master all of history and that their expertise is confined to a particular historical period. To be successful in a profession it is not necessary to be a jack-of-all-trades; one or perhaps a few others must be quite sufficient. An inventory modestly accepts limitations, seeks tolerance, and avoids claiming to be omniscient.

Eventually each individual emerges with a view or him- or herself, of other persons, and of surroundings that include living organisms as well as all aspects of what is glibly or profoundly called the environment. The English language seems to have no single concept or phrase that embraces all these referents in the manner of the German word "Weltanschauung." The word "philosophy," however, suggests the role that the self has played, is playing, and should play in the future in reacting to events and determining them. "In a society in which there are few technical means of controlling the forces of nature or averting catastrophe," a sociologist once proclaimed before the start of World War II, "the prevailing philosophy of life will regard almost every event as the work of a blind fate."[63] Such a statement is one person's opinion based on his own formal observation of past records, his mode of synthesizing informal impressions, and the conditions in which he was forced to live in his own and then his adopted countries. The generalization, nevertheless, functions as a challenge to meliorists who would determine whether individuals are willing and able, according to their philosophy, to struggle in behalf of a "better" existence for themselves and others.

CHAPTER 6

Others

I am me, you are you, one states easily and glibly, as if the distinction were self-evident. Self-evident? What is self-evident or evident to the self may or may not be evident to others. More than verbal twistings are involved when the self is distinguished from those others. A link between the two appears when we judge others; are or are we not projecting ourselves and assuming they are like us? There is thus the peril of starting with the self and assuming that others are like us. Or the reverse: what others tell us about ourselves we accept because they are older or we believe them wiser and more "objective." Or what they say or, we guess, they believe about us we reject because again nobody knows us as well as we know ourselves. Nobody?

After early infancy it is probably impossible to perceive most objects and other human beings without some preconception of what to anticipate as well as having an enduring judgment about the anticipation (G6). Prejudices and stereotypes flourish. For groups there is likely to be "a rigid emotional attitude (favorable or unfavorable) . . . which results in an advance evaluation of any particular group member." A contrasting attribute is tolerance, "a neutral, disinterested attitude toward a category of people," which is difficult to achieve.[1]

Others, then, pervade the self. When present conditions are compared with the past and are "felt" or "reasoned" to be "more bleak, grim, wretched, ugly, deprivational, unfulfilling, frightening, and so forth," and when later they are accompanied by "the nagging sense of the absence of a future," individuals may evaluate their own past and present successes differently. An American sociologist once summarized his open-ended interviews with a dozen Americans in a paraphrase: "I mostly get nostalgic over the nice, pleasant, and fun things in my past. The unpleasant things I've either forgotten, or when someone reminds me of them I drive them out of mind. But I never feel nostalgic about them."[2] The "things" include relations with other persons. Thus we miss departed acquaintances, friends, relatives, and parents: those others have been part of the experience we now wish we could have again.

The same concepts employed by the self to comprehend the self can be utilized in the effort to understand and evaluate other persons. From a psychiatric, psychological, or the self's own standpoint, the self is another person and hence may be included in a similar conceptual framework. According to the editors and authors of *Self-Conscious Emotions*, emotions generally "are founded in social relationships, in which people not only interact but evaluate and judge themselves and each other."[3] You may lack perspective about your self and about them, they may lack perspective about themselves, and you may both be wrong.

Warning: this chapter's next two headings are misleading. They suggest a clear-cut distinction between misunderstanding and understanding others. Living would be simpler and pleasanter if meliorists could point to such a sharp line. No, the two are interrelated: there are cures for misunderstanding and perils of understanding. The squeaky difference between the headings, then, is only one of emphasis.

MISUNDERSTANDING

It is not necessary to be cynical to adopt the view that judgments of others are likely to be faulty to some extent for at least two reasons. Others do not or cannot reveal themselves completely or adequately. And the observer of others, the self, may make faulty judgments about them.

In the first place, information about others is obtained from observing them, or from listening to what they say about themselves or to what others relate about them. Above all it must be emphasized that others function like the self: their beliefs and judgments are known only intimately or privately to themselves and cannot be completely known to anyone else besides themselves. Observers may be or believe themselves to be more "objective" or accurate about others than they are about themselves; yet they may be wrong because obviously they cannot get inside those other persons.

Common words provide a conspicuous illustration of such misunder-standings because they may have private or distinctive connotations for the self and others. Thus "good" and "bad" are evaluative without specify-ing their precise referents. One person may consider her goodness wishy-washy (which means what?) and his badness courageous (which also means what?). In the late 1960s a Swedish anthropologist studied Afro-Americans living in a ghetto area of Washington, D.C. Those whose "way of life" tended to be "middle class" referred to themselves as "respectable," "good people," and as "model citizens"; those with whom they usually did not associate they labeled "undesirables," "no good," "the rowdy bunch," "bums," or "trash."[4] Decades later French-Canadian students were inclined to be favorably disposed, they reported on a questionnaire, toward Latin Americans, Eastern Europeans, Haitians, and Arabs when and if they at-tributed to these groups attributes they believed they themselves pos-sessed.[5]

Or do we have a "good" government right now? Two persons reply af-firmatively; both believe we have a magnificent government. Do we then know that they agree and are praising the government? Their attitudes seem to be the same, yet their praise may stem from different beliefs. One person thinks that government officials are honest and trying to do their very best; the other person praises the government because it keeps taxes low while not neglecting allegedly vital problems involved in education, transportation, and assistance to the indigent and disabled. These two per-sons differ concerning not only the content of their attitude toward the designated government but also its degree of goodness: one considers the government good, the other very good. The first person saying "good" uses an all-or-none distinction, governments are either good or bad; the second employs a wider range of judgments extending from very bad to very good, with gradations in between. Really to comprehend attitudes and beliefs, therefore, meliorists also probe detailed content and the actions to which the attributes lead.[6]

A more specific example: suppose another person calls himself or is called a Marxist. What do we then know about him? Even when the word is not being used as a positive or negative epithet, in a strict sense its meaning may be unclear, as the following pedantic analysis suggests, because Karl Marx himself used ideology, one of his key concepts, in four ways (as indi-cated by a modern sociologist) to refer to "men" generally, "real active men," "the ruling class," and "men" conscious of a "conflict" between eco-nomic conditions and nonscientific formulations.[7] Other scholarly com-plications arise when the meaning of Marxism itself is pursued. A psychiatrist argues that Marx "did not see that a better society could not be brought into life by people who had not undergone a moral change within themselves," and hence he "paid no attention, at least not explicitly, to the necessity of new moral orientation."[8] Then the goals Lenin pursued may have been derived from Marx, and he may have been convinced of his interpretation of their validity in his role of leader in overthrowing the czarist regime as well as the Mensheviks who were his immediate predecessors. After these meanderings, return to the original question: should another person be called a Marxist by anyone including himself?

Misunderstandings also may result from situations in which other persons deliberately conceal or try to conceal what they or still others believe to be true. Observers may try to determine such deception, clues to which are provided by the others in face-to-face situations by slips of the tongue, louder or more insistent than normal speech, gestures, postures, facial blushing or blanching, and probably other symptoms known in each instance by the observers. Then the rationale of the deception may be sought. For reasons that transcend the situation at hand, deceivers depart from truth in order to achieve a goal they consider desirable. Once again meliorists cannot forget that during wars one side hides its next maneuvers from the enemy or misleads them in order to attain a particular objective related to ultimate victory. Physicians may conceal diagnoses or prognoses from patients when convinced that hearing the truth or discouraging information would make their recovery more difficult or produce additional depression if the illness is serious or fatal. And defendants in criminal cases may conceal their role in a crime or deny facts connected with it in order to be acquitted or to receive a less severe sentence. In addition, those who lie or conceal information may do so unwittingly: they "honestly" forget the truth or repress what they once believed to be true.

Observable behavior, whether deceitful or not, cannot be ignored because it may provide, however tenuously, a clue to others. It has been indicated that "If you have (a) a habit of explosively accentuating various key words in your ordinary speech even when there is no real need for such accentuation and (b) a tendency to utter the last few words of your sentences far more rapidly than the opening words," and if also among other features of so-called Type A behavior "you *always* move, walk, and eat rapidly," you may be more likely to suffer a cardiac ailment than if you are a Type B and do not reveal such observable behavior.[9] From the individual's standpoint, such behavior, whether A or B, is not likely to be "intentional"; but from another standpoint, Type B may result from a motive to conceal inner thoughts and feelings or from a long-established tendency to be taciturn or reserved.[10]

At a given moment or over a period of time, others may be misunderstood when they change in significant or insignificant ways that are difficult to observe or record. They depart from ways of behaving that they have always or almost always displayed, such as being honest or dishonest, extroverted or introverted, confident or insecure. The changes may be temporary, as when persons are ill, lose their tempers, or suddenly encounter a compelling success or failure. Other changes may be more or less permanent and can be designated in many different ways. Transformation may occur: as a result of some event, a mood, or the deliberate action of someone else, as in politics and education, the same configuration in the environment is grasped differently. One perceives or is made to perceive that another individual is no longer attractive or unattractive but the reverse. Relocating from one location or environment to another induces or requires different behavior. He joins a religious order; she changes her residence after marriage. And there is conversion: the others become convinced they must change their central values if they are to be happy, survive, or achieve everlasting life.

What others say or do while being observed, in short, can be variously motivated and may not be an effort to increase understanding by observers. Direct contact with others does not immediately produce the "truth" about them. A useful, if platitudinous, guide for interviewing but applicable even to casual contact suggests that eliciting information from others "must be seen as a process of interaction between persons,"[11] at least between the self and the others.

Another principal reason for misunderstanding others resides not exclusively in the others but in the self or observer who seeks to understand them, or also in the relation between the observer and the observed. The sensitivity of observers in making their observation varies from person to person and depends, at least in part, on both their experience generally and the judgment or observation at hand. Meliorists, as must be repeated again and again, have the strong conviction that perfectly valid judgments and evaluations are likely to be elusive. Observed "facts" may give rise to varying interpretations. A philosopher once argued that comedy in the arts and everyday life makes "honest men laugh" by giving them "for the moment the gift of truth, of seeing things as they are"; tragedy may "make them weep through affording them a glimpse of cosmic justice and the relation between men's actions and the highest values."[12] Ah yes, but what inferences can be made about the personalities of individuals who do not laugh or weep during dramatic productions? Like the self, observers may be prone to make snap judgments concerning other persons and to cling to those judgments on later occasions; and they may or may not recall the bases for making their judgments initially.[13]

Changes in the others, those mentioned above, may be unnoticed by observers who remain stubbornly or unwittingly faithful to their original or initial views of the others. Coined as a phrase around the middle of this century and then inspiring considerable research and especially experimentation, the phrase "self-fulfilling prophecy" calls attention to a source of error in judging others and sometimes also the self: individuals anticipate specified action of any kind in the future and then their anticipation is validated when they perceive later only what they have anticipated or when they deliberately or unwittingly induce themselves or others to perform as they anticipated.[14] A teacher believes one of her classes will behave brilliantly, another class dismally; objectively an observer may note that both classes at the outset are very similar; but the teacher's expectations cause her, wittingly or unwittingly, to treat the two differently in accord with what she expects, and thus her prophecy is fulfilled.

Melioristically observers do not ignore the personal and anthropological context of the other person's actions or beliefs. Personally a French sociologist once contemplated that a jealous husband who strangles his wife, a burglar who stabs a person preventing him from escaping from the site of his crime, and the pilot of the plane who drops a bomb squarely on enemy soldiers or civilians have one action in common: all three have killed one or more persons.[15] Should they all be called murderers? Suppose further that the husband has been found to be psychotic, the burglar to be unemployed and homeless, the pilot to be enrolled in an air force defending a "noble" cause; what kind of murderer is each of them then?

The need to consider the anthropological context is suggested by a belief in reincarnation. A sociologist once concluded that, with few exceptions, the belief was "positively and significantly related to a settlement pattern of neighborhoods, nomadic bands, extended family compounds, and other small, but continuing units"; the settlement patterns were found in societies that differed "widely" with respect to population. And cannibalism? No clear association between that pleasant practice and other societal factors emerges in the same study, although it may possibly have been related to a belief in "exuvial magic" in which only the products of his or her body, such as nail parings, hair, blood, or semen, are used by a person to control another individual.[16] Although anthropological findings may be considered irrelevant and may or may not be subsequently confirmed, it is the search for them that enables meliorists to believe that all phenomena are not fortuitous or irrational but eventually have discoverable antecedents somewhere or some time.

The exciting climax to this section must be the awareness of another possibility to produce misunderstanding: a disagreement between two or more observers of the same person or persons so that one or more of them may be in error. Individual differences in perceiving others may be as numerous as judgments about art, poetry, and music that are labeled great or insignificant, original or trite, attractive or unattractive by different persons. She and he may agree on what another person has said but not concerning their interpretation thereof. The disagreement may be even more likely perhaps when the behavior rather than the verbal utterance of the other person is ascertained.

UNDERSTANDING

Understanding others is, or is thought to be, achievable by psychiatrists, psychologists, social scientists, and perhaps a few mortals when they guide themselves by principles of behavior presumably applicable, it is hoped, to all persons. The most significant principle is paradoxical and immediately self-evident: every individual is both similar to and different from other human beings. All persons are born, mature, and eventually die. Their bodies can be described in similar terms such as weight, height, gender, and health. Even when handicapped in some respect, they employ and respond to a language; and indeed "every language, without exception, is based on the same *universal principles* of semantics, syntax, and phonology," and "all languages have words for relations, objects, feelings, qualities, and the semantic differences between these denotata are minimal from a biological point of view."[17] People have hopes and values; they experience gratifications as well as frustrations. In some form they are in conflict with one another and have reasons for seeking to emerge as victors from minor or major struggles.[18]

While sharing attributes with others, each individual is also unique in some respect (G3). Understanding requires heavy emphasis on that uniqueness which in turn is facilitated by concentrating on some aspect of the person, such as his or her traits, a worthy concept mentioned in the previous chapter as characterizing a self. An individual is said to be honest or dishonest, conscientious or careless, brave or cowardly, ambitious or lackadaisical—other pairs are all too easy to supply and may have been offered and utilized by scholars and other observers.[19] Separate bits of behavior are observed and then joined together conceptually as a trait. Thereafter diverse actions are intelligible because they are thought to be expressing the trait's general tendency; slight or marked deviations are noted or ignored. A single or a few instances are observed, after which some trait is ascribed to that other person. Or individuals themselves claim or believe they are driven by a trait, or someone else provides them with the designation. In fact, few persons are so well integrated that they are completely consistent; they are generally honest or careless part or most of the time, but not always without exception. In addition, the referent of a postulated trait can be somewhat haphazardly extended to apply to all or most members of a group: they are Swedes and not Chinese, hence they must be XYZ and not ABC.

The naming of the other's trait or some overall designation of his or her personality or behavior may provide general insight and a clue to subsequent data. An English woman, who had been "gravely ill," later was able to "describe vivid and alarming experiences in the region where the unseen invades and takes over the normal world." Here are an arbitrary half dozen of the experiences she reported:

> I began at once to resume my direct relationship with God.
> Next day, under the guise and excuse of medical investigations, I was executed.
> God has missed me and wanted more of me because of my long absence.
> The most surprising thing that has happened was that I met the devil in a restaurant.
> My soul left my body through my eyes and shot straight through the sun.
> I came to life again in a mood of confidence, quite unperturbed by the fact that I had been dead.[20]

By themselves the musings provide only hints concerning that woman, but then they might be knit together by an overall diagnosis of schizophrenia.

Similarly, without dipping deeply into psychiatry, consider what has been said about a "normal" person: "If we see Mark Rogers from the outside, look at his life as he lived it but never really know what he felt or desired, it would appear that he had a quiet life." But then a psychologist weaves the reader through events in that individual's life, including data provided to psychiatrists, so that it becomes clear why Mark eventually murdered a person and then died "insane" as he was electrocuted for the crime.[21] Such detailed information is ordinarily not available, and so meliorists seek to probe beneath the superficial and respectable. In the account just cited, however, the author recklessly interweaves the account of Rogers' life with his own generalizations about human problems based no doubt on clinical experience but expressed in a manner as if they were eternally verified and applicable to human beings everywhere. A belief, a feeling, or an action of other persons may appear irrational and in fact may be irrational from the standpoint of the neutral or biased observer, yet what is observed can be made "understandable" when or if more information is obtained about them and linked by references to their mode of existence.[22]

It is unreasonable, nevertheless, to anticipate that every discussion of others, whether formal or informal, can be accompanied by a "scientific" explanation of the appraisal or diagnosis. The data may not be at hand, and the individual providing the characterization may have neither the time nor the competence to offer the explanation. What then can be done is to employ some overall, makeshift concept such as the search for security or prestige as the leading trait but without suggesting that the words are communicating eternally complete explanations.[23] Then current research findings may provide fruitful leads concerning factors associated with the behavior of others. It may be useful to note that students scoring higher on conventional intelligence tests were once less likely than those scoring lower to believe in superstitious statements as listed on a questionnaire.[24] This finding cannot be dismissed by noting that it stems only from a ding-dong sample or by alluding to all the evidence that intelligence as conventionally measured probably has no simple basis in the genes but may be related to environmental opportunities. In this instance, therefore, the more "intelligent" learned not only how to reply to conventional intelligence tests but also to appreciate some of the false bases for superstitions.

Even as the self may utilize group membership as one of the factors affecting self-appraisal, so the same attribute may be useful in understanding others. It may be inferred that in groups others derive "a sense of psychological security and well-being."[25] Obviously the most useful group to locate is that of the family. From this source meliorists can anticipate the language others will speak as well as many of their values and actions. Some of these values change as they mature and especially when women are pregnant or when they later become grandmothers. Younger children may be treated differently from their older siblings. The family itself may vary over time: the occupation of either parent or both may shift and encourage different living standards. In the West, perhaps everywhere, when homes are broken by desertion, divorce, death, or major disagreements, the immediate environments of the participants are likely to be drastically altered. Young children may be treated much more indulgently than older ones who are perhaps encouraged to lead more independent existences. It is not surprising that meliorists can find both consistency and inconsistency in children and adults as time passes.[26]

On an adult level, in 1958 political leaders in various countries, largely parliamentarians, were promised anonymity and confidentiality by an American researcher and his native assistant. Among other questions, they were asked: "please tell me about your aspiration for our country." "Higher standard of living" was mentioned spontaneously, among other aspirations, by 21 percent of these leaders in Italy, 24 percent in India, 41 percent in Japan, and in Great Britain by 43 percent of Labourites and 29 percent of Conservatives.[27] One need not have complete confidence in these specific numbers, yet they offer at least a clue, if not a guide, to some of the actions of the leaders and their followers (G1).

RIGHTS AND RESPONSIBILITIES

Somewhat universally, at least in democratic countries, the value of human rights is affirmed and lauded, a lofty statement of which follows.

> All human beings are born free and equal in dignity and rights. . . . Everyone is entitled to all the rights and freedom set forth in this Declaration, without distinction of any kind, such as race, colour, sex, language, religion, political or other opinion, national or social origin, property, birth or other status.

The two sentences are in the Universal Declaration of Human Rights proclaimed by the General Assembly of the United Nations in December 1948. Implied in the proclamation is the assumption that "everyone" has rights and freedom only when an authority assumes the responsibility for permitting and encouraging conditions for their existence and continuation. In the opinion of Jeremy Bentham a century earlier, "a man's happiness" depends on "his duty to himself" as well as on "his duty to others" or "his neighbor."[28] The others or the neighbors thus also have rights, so that the roles of both the self and others are interlocked.

Rights, then, imply responsibilities, and the two cannot be separated whenever values are appraised. Thus the demand for "social justice" subsumes the values of health, education, and the use of land and natural resources in behalf of persons in both dominant and subordinate positions in a society. As a result of social and political changes in their country, do Africans in South Africa, for example, have the right to deprive other ethnic groups there (Afrikaners, English, and Indians) of privileges they once enjoyed so that they themselves can now have those rights? Or should the new government treat all groups "equally" in that society? Rhetorical questions of that nature permeate the discussion of rights and responsibilities here for a clear-cut reason: solutions cannot be dictated, problems forever recur, we must keep groping, replies to the questions must be sought.

The list of specific and general rights ascribed to the self as well as others is long, there is little agreement concerning the ones to be included in any informal or formal affirmation, and hence rights cannot be phrased in absolute terms without qualifications (G4). The right to live and survive, yes, but also the right to execute anyone "justly" convicted of having committed murder? The right of an innocent bystander who has suddenly been attacked by a stranger to defend himself, inadvertently or deliberately causing the death of the assailant? The right to intervene in another country ("send in the Marines") when "innocent" and not-so-innocent persons there are victims of violence or when the so-called laws of war are being violated? The right to construct shabby or unconventional buildings that offend the "good" taste of neighbors or passersby whose own homes are conventional and modest and who are "offended" by what they consider to be the atrocious, insensitive taste of the others? The right of profit-seeking lumber companies to chop down trees rather than the rights of those who enjoy flourishing forests, who would protect endangered species therein, and who envision the possibility of discovering health-giving herbs now growing there? The right of the very wealthy and powerful to splurge their resources on land and sea when such "conspicuous waste" appalls the less fortunate; have they the right to do what they wish with their own wealth? Quickly: who has priority when the rights of individuals are in conflict; are some rights "higher" than others?

In a broad but not necessarily "idealistic" sense, meliorists know that so-called hermits, who believe they have the right to live alone and presumably have chosen to do so, actually subsist on some of the benefits, varying from language to clothes, that they have not rejected and for the creation of which others have had the responsibility. Most of us know and admit we are interdependent and deliberately interact with one another. We can and do occasionally perceive that we "share a mutual fate," that our "success is mutually caused" at least in part by factors beyond our own control, and that we are not always competing against one another "to achieve a goal that only one or a few can attain."[29] Everywhere, particularly in modern societies of the West, the right of privacy is sought and valued, the responsibility for which is assumed not only by legal and other authorities but also by individuals themselves.[30] For the self and others the range of actions considered private is considerable and extends from bodily functions and sexual activities to an individual's thoughts and the almost overwhelming desire at some point in the day, week, or month to be alone. Toilets have in-side locks; except in an emergency or with a prior agreement, friends are not telephoned at a late or "unreasonable" hour. A few persons wonder in stray moments whether animals and brooks and trees have rights not de-pendent on whether or not they affect human beings.[31]

Probably individuals anywhere experience a violation of what they con-sider their own rights. They then feel threatened or frustrated and seek or find an outlet. They may displace the feelings and assign responsibility to some target other than the one they know or believe to be the source of their trouble. Parents scold helpless children for a minor offense when they themselves have failed to obtain a goal unrelated to the family and home. The person or group thought to be responsible for the loss of rights may be attacked directly in ways ranging from grumbling and a display of dissent or fury to organized resistance with or without the use of violence.[32] In mod-ern societies, certainly in the West, most adults are frequently kept in-formed about their rights by the mass media, and they may consult scholarly treatises embodying or dissecting those rights and identifying re-sponsible agents.[33] They may be urged by friends or foes to promote and fa-miliarize themselves with their own private or "sacred" rights and those of others.

From another viewpoint, individuals may wonder whether they should exercise the rights granted them in their society. You are permitted to seek a position of prestige such as being a leader or director of an industry, but do you have the necessary talent or support from your peers, are you willing to forego extended periods of personal relaxation that such positions render unlikely? This issue arises when rights are assigned not to the self but to others. Perhaps "facts" are needed; thus the question may be asked by young people or their parents whether American adolescents have the right to seek remunerative employment part-time while still enrolled as students in secondary schools. A systematic exploration of the available facts related to that question in California and elsewhere in the United States once reported positive, negative, and neutral consequences when such labor was viewed in terms of its ultimate economic, social, and educa-tional gains and losses. School children did acquire new skills from work-ing, but these skills may or may not have been helpful later in life. The money being earned was employed to satisfy either essential or frivolous needs. The conclusion extracted from the report suggests that "the critical factor" affecting young workers was "the amount of time" spent working and "not simply whether they work."[34] This finding at least raises the problem but does not resolve the puzzle of how the time of youth can best be expended.

Inequality with respect to strength, age, sensitivity, "intelligence" however defined, and status is evident in every society; should those with the greater or lesser proclivities be given rights, respectively, to maintain or improve their existence? Should all people have "equal" rights? In countries whose officials are elected at specified intervals or occasions, should everyone have the right to vote? In the West and in treatises elsewhere, the reply to that last question is of course affirmative; but, may one ask, why? The thesis that only competent adults should be permitted to vote has been advocated by diverse and respected thinkers such as Aristotle, John Locke, and Thomas Jefferson. Meliorists guiltily but timidly wonder whether laypersons are able to pass sensible judgments on the views and policies of aspiring or actual leaders in democratic countries concerning details in proposed legislation involving complicated economic or political change. While more than 90 percent of persons once polled in the United States considered voting "a moral obligation," in almost all elections the turnout of those eligible to vote has been less than 50 percent, especially in local elections. In other places, such as Italy and Sweden, the turnout is always considerably higher; and in Australia, non-voting is fined. The American survey just mentioned found that non-voting was associated generally or dramatically not with the demographic attributes of economic status and gender but with the attitudes of non-voters concerning their own power and the importance they ascribe to voting.[35]

Conflicts between the rights of the self and others, according to religious and pietistic values, should be settled in favor of others and not the individual self. Otherwise the self is selfish, and selfishness is quickly deplored. Hypothetical exceptions have an emotional appeal, such as the "genius" who exploits his or her peers for benefits they or their descendants will eventually enjoy, if only in the future. Rights thus are accompanied explicitly or implicitly by references to responsibility.

Factual and ethical challenges arise in connection with the effects of individuals' actions upon others and also in turn with the effects of others' actions upon those individuals. From a deterministic viewpoint, it is usually not the self alone but previous actions by others who share a major or minor responsibility for the self's behavior. Responsibility is less likely to be ascribed to the self when the individual is young, under the influence of specified drugs, seriously physically or psychically ill, or driven by decidedly more powerful others. Those who claim responsibility for many of their own actions nevertheless may likewise wonder whether responsibility is also limited in circumstances in which they think they do not have complete control. If parents are responsible for many actions of their young children, should they also be held responsible for their adult offspring; are their later misdeeds then the consequences of earlier parental training? An addict is thought not to be responsible for damaging others because at the time he is being affected by a drug he has taken; but is he not responsible for taking the drug in the first place, and why did others not prevent him from having access to the drug or from being addicted to it? Responsibility, in short, may include more than the moment when an action occurs: no alternative may seem available, although one might have been in the past or could be in the future.[36]

Another and frequently employed and seemingly practical way to affix responsibility upon the self is to refer to his or her intention related to the action. A lawyer who once surveyed the problem of intention as viewed in various social systems and especially by justices and courts in the United States set the tone of his analysis by quoting at the outset an English judge in the late Middle Ages: "The thought of man shall not be tried, for the devil himself knoweth not the thought of man." He then outlined the difficulties and contradictions in legal systems that seek to make rational assumptions about the role of intention in legal affairs. To evaluate "the freedom and capacity of any individual to act on his choice," it is necessary to consider the "value systems" of the society as well as the "differing degrees of conscious control" over human actions and the effects of drugs and other unusual physiological conditions mentioned above. A positive if sometimes ambiguous conclusion emerges: "the question of intent should properly be considered not as an element of the offense but as a factor to be determined and considered in specifying the treatment to which convicted criminals are to be subjected."[37] And so, in the Anglo-Saxon legal tradition, those convicted of murder are considered to have premeditated their crime and are given heavier sentences than others guilty of manslaughter, who allegedly have not intended to kill their victim but did so on the spur of the moment without forethought but as a result of a momentary impulse provoked by the situation, a drug, or their alleged inability to foresee the consequences of the fatal act.

A very puzzling, almost metaphysical challenge likewise arises when one wonders whether individuals have responsibility for others who are momentarily or permanently not identifiable. He cheats in an important examination in his university; she steals a small object in a large shop unobtrusively when nobody is looking. Neither culprit will ever be discovered; but are they not thus avoiding their responsibility to be honest to others who advocate honesty and to the society that places a high value on honesty? Why be honest, or why be honest all of the time?

Codes of conduct allocate responsibility immediately or eventually to parents, neighbors, legal and religious authorities, and specified individuals and groups. Its Declaration cited above and the United Nations itself assign to governments the responsibility to promulgate and enforce human rights among its members and nonmembers. The rules, regulations, and customs in a society determine the situations in which to affix responsibility for the actions of individuals so that presumably other persons eventually benefit. Exceeding a posted or conventional speed limit when driving places responsibility upon drivers for accidents and other mishaps to other persons as well as to themselves. The age below which children are not punished or not punished severely for an illegal or "immoral" act is known informally by parents and formally by police and other members of a judicial system. Parents may require their own children to be polite or "behave" in specified ways: the children thus avoid punishment or receive praise, and the parents feel proud or satisfied. More generally, responsibility is placed upon leaders and officials to designate the rights and responsibilities of their constituents for the sake of themselves and, if not themselves, for others in the constituency. Citizens of a country are responsible for paying taxes or their equivalent in return for benefits they and others then receive. This responsibility cannot be avoided, even if they believe some taxes are "unjust" or that other persons are not paying their "fair" share. Are the less affluent responsible for paying the "unfair" taxes levied upon them? Should minorities or noncitizens living in a country be responsible for participating in military service for the benefit of the society in which they reside and from which they benefit?

Persons with "good" intentions from their own or some other viewpoint may engage in actions that violate the rights of those they affect. On occasion, they truly seek to help others, have "nothing" whatsoever to gain from doing so, even make sacrifices in behalf of the beneficiaries, but the others may resent outside interference, they may not wish assistance, and they would continue to behave as they have been behaving, or they simply favor the status quo. In short, they may appreciate the generosity of the intervener but prefer to be left alone. Such a conflict or misunderstanding often characterizes relations between interveners from the West and traditional people. Westerners believe that their way of life has notable advantages ranging from understanding the universe to increasing life expectancy; they cannot readily convince the "heathen" who would remain as they are, who believe they know all that is essential to know, and who are convinced that the prolongation of living depends not upon what they themselves do but upon the will of superior gods. Thus intentions of interveners, good or bad, may lead to actions affecting others favorably or unfavorably from the latter's viewpoint.

Perhaps the most perplexing challenge to the self's and others' rights concerns the distribution of the pie: in the pursuit of your rights, are you receiving more than your fair share? The question, as "fair" is defined, is yet another way of challenging responsibility. You merit a larger share, you think, because you are older and your need is greater than the others; but if you grab more because you are stronger or more powerful, is the basis for the distribution then fair? Within your country you wonder whether you should exploit its natural resources, however defined; are you thus depriving future generations of their due? Or do or should you consider other countries that do not have those resources, should they receive more of what you are now enjoying? Then there are disasters resulting from human error such as large oil spills: should the persons directly or indirectly responsible for them be punished; should compensation be given to people who suffer therefrom because their land has been damaged or because the cost of oil rises without their profiting from the increase?

CHAPTER 7

Society

The referent of the self is obviously a specific person, and others are persons who do, may, or can influence or be influenced by the self, one another, and other others. Usually the human beings being mentioned can be identified at least vaguely, but sometimes they seem to disappear, and their existence is only tacitly assumed. In the latter case, reference is made to no specific self or to others. "In the United States it is believed that . . ."—the statement presumably conveys a truth by assuming that in American society all, almost all, most, many, or at least some persons have the belief about to be unveiled. For the self, the responsible individuals may never be known: their identity may be concealed, they may have died long ago after contributing knowledge, beliefs, value, or actions that have become part of the group's cultural heritage; or they are not investigated because at the moment their contribution is accepted without tracking them down. And so there are useful if somewhat loose terms like society, community, organization, company, and group that are the proper concern not of the individualistic disciplines of psychiatry, psychology, and biography, but of the struggling social sciences of anthropology, sociology, economics, and political science.

The concept of society or its equivalent serves a useful function not neglected by meliorists. Consider two "normal" adults. No matter where or in what society they live, they both use a language as they communicate to others and to themselves. Her language is French, his is Luganda; that difference cannot be attributed to their genetic structures or their genders; they live in France and Uganda, where their own languages are spoken.

Meliorists who would change or improve existence note the similar, numerous functions performed in all societies, and then they also try to describe and account for the differences or similarities. In a study of five diverse American communities—two American-Indian, a Spanish-American, a Mormon, and a Texan-Oklahoman farming village—it was once noted that all five sought solutions to "five common problems" of "the nature of man himself, his relation to nature and supernature, his place in the flow of time, the modality of human activity, and the relationship man has to his fellow human beings."[1] In some of the communities, solutions to the problems were "permitted," in others "required." Each "cultural world," in short, "operated according to its own internal dynamic, its own principles, and its own laws—written and unwritten," but there are "some common threads that run through all cultures."[2] The distinction is so important that it has been honored by two attention-getting suffixes inspired by the study of linguistics: *etic* to refer to alleged universals prevalent at least in "many" societies, and *emic* to refer to particular cultures or societies[3] (G3).

SOCIETAL FUNCTIONS

Although probably every French woman must agree that her mother tongue is French and every man among the Baganda that his is Luganda, no detailed agreement exists among citizens or scholars concerning the precise list of functions performed in all societies. In modern times a valiant, impressive effort was once made to uncover "universal ethical principles" and hence the societal functions at the basis of those principles at least from "an anthropological view." Obviously there is "unlimited variety" in this respect and more generally when different cultures are examined; yet "when these patterns are analyzed in terms of their function and interrelations, certain general principles emerge" because every culture has to provide for the same basic physiological and psychological needs of individuals. Among the universals mentioned by this particular anthropologist are the family as the unit for production and consumption, marriage (with a few exceptions) and "lifelong union of spouses," prohibiting and punishing incest, caring for and training children, some personal property, the right of eminent domain, punishment for murder in some circumstances, obligations in the "exchange of goods and services," some provision for the poor and unfortunate, an ethical system, and values that insure "the perpetuation and successful functioning of the society."[4]

To that or any list, additions and amplifications are necessary or possible. In every society temporal judgments are made, if only as a result of natural phenomena like the seasons and the rising and setting of the sun. Coordinated activity, whether in industry, sports, or the home, requires participants to note time so that they may be prompt or at hand when they must act. We think in terms of the past and present, orienting ourselves accordingly.[5] Also living together in a society requires individuals to have a sense of responsibility, as indicated in the preceding chapter and here repeated with reluctant emphasis: no one can be completely "free" and not show some concern for others in immediate groups and perhaps eventually for the entire society. A bit of wisdom, perhaps obvious, comes again from Bentham: "The business of government is to promote the happiness of the society, by punishing and rewarding."[6] Details of course vary from society to society and from time to time. After suggesting that in the United States a "civil society" seems no longer to exist and that the "market" with its powerful and blind forces has become the substitute, a sociologist has argued that, to receive "benefits" from economic growth and the services rendered by government, its citizens must relinquish "pure" freedom or "the ability to do anything they want in any way at any time."[7] Individuals and organizations function to curb aggressive impulses and behavior resulting from frustrations of a personal sort or from the group or groups to which one belongs that cannot be assuaged by making a peaceful attempt to achieve another goal.[8] Aggression is regulated by government officials, including the police or their equivalent, as well as by parents and other peers. Hostility in behalf of a "good" cause, such as against an enemy in time of war or persons considered criminals, is sanctioned, even rewarded, and considered "respectable." By definition or custom, political parties in a society usually engage in regulated aggression against one another. On the basis of careful interviews and surveys in the 1950s, a social psychologist once offered this portrait of persons in France and Italy who at the time were not members of the Communist Party but who supported and voted for that party:

> The protest voter—like every other human being everywhere—wants to experience more frequently and in new ways what he senses is *potentially* available out there in the world around him to be experienced and enjoyed. What the protest voter, like all other people, believes *is* potentially out there is, of course, what he has learned are satisfactions that might some day be his and that constitute his own particular bundle of hopes and aspirations.[9]

"Of course," as the writer also indicated, details varied, but not the discontent.

"Religion invariably strives to subdue violence, to keep it from remaining wild," a scholarly account of *Violence and the Sacred* suggests: punishments now or in the hereafter are foreshadowed, human or nonhuman scapegoats are indicated, or rituals are institutionalized to diminish the tensions.[10] Religions specify actions that are acceptable or unacceptable as well as some rationale for guides thereto (G5). A rationale, according to the observation of one philosopher, responds to deep and profound "awareness" of "the fact that the world of empirical things includes the uncertain, the unpredictable, and the hazardous" and hence is "a precarious place in which to live and nothing in it has its survival guaranteed in advance," as death always looms.[11] In religious dogmas and treatises, these awarenesses are expressed simply and intelligibly.[12]

"Religious faith and philosophical thought, the most fundamental spiritual forms in human life," the same philosopher has suggested, however, "have always found themselves in the peculiar position of not being able to get along with each other and of not being able to remain permanently apart." Historically, he notes, at least in the West, one such thought has been dominant during various historical periods. Within "Western Christianity," both the strictly religious and the moralistic philosophy have been present, as here illustrated, respectively, by two citations from the Bible: "God is our refuge and strength, a very present help in trouble" (Psalm 46:1) and "Love your enemies, do good to them which hate you" (Luke 6:27). Religion and morality, according to this view, must be related: one cannot evaluate the morality of actions without alluding to some transcendental principle offered by religion, and moral principles require the "inspiration" (justification?) also supplied by religion. "Ultimately," therefore, our guide asserts in italics, "no view of the good life, no serious doctrine of what man ought to do, is ever possible apart from some view of his final destiny."[13]

Consider also an American rabbi's view concerning "The Ten Ethical Values Parents Need to Teach Their Children," listed here in alphabetical order: compassion, fairness, faith, friendship, gratitude, honesty, maturity, peace, respect, and responsibility.[14] Meliorists immediately agree that these are "good" values, but they wonder whether all ten are necessary, how the ten are related to one another, and which ones are considered more important or neglected especially in non-American societies. More significant, however, is the probability that, although Christians and adherents of other religions might not employ identical words concerning desirable values, they probably have no objection to these ten as guides for teaching and action. Do you agree?

In every society, traditional beliefs and actions bequeathed from the past serve to justify past, present, and anticipated actions. Traditionally there may also be the conviction that new beliefs and actions should not be rejected because they are new but must be evaluated with the view that one's ancestors, if they were alive, would counsel examining closely their merits and demerits. A calm if proud view of scholarly history has been quietly expressed by a member of that profession: history, he thinks, offers an "opportunity of a unique intellectual experience, a rigorous form of mental training which has high educational value, and a stimulus of imagination and understanding which can enrich a man's life by deeper insights into human behavior."[15] Attached explicitly or implicitly to propositions concerning the future are not only reasons for the anticipations but also beliefs or guesses concerning the probability of their occurrence (G6). Will that sliver of a moon we now see out there ever become full; how long will present economic conditions continue and why?

Efforts are made by citizens and scholars alike to account for the similarities in all societies. During the first third of this century one valiant social scientist collected and evaluated 136 "social laws" and referred to 32 others in footnotes. He classified them into five categories as follows, each of which is followed here by an arbitrarily selected illustration either in his own words or those of a writer he cited:

1. Teleological laws: Institutions flourish or decay according to their adaptation to the circumstances of life surrounding the people that possess them.
2. Aphorisms and methodological presuppositions: Each individual seeks the largest return for the least sacrifice.
3. Statistical laws: As population increases, the total productivity also may and does generally increase, though at progressively diminishing rates after a certain stage.
4. Near-causal laws: To every type of economy there corresponds a particular type of family.
5. Dialectical laws: Societies, like all other aggregates, pass from less to more coherence.

The analysis of these "laws," the writer states, "has yielded a negative result" and "no causal laws so precise or certain as those of physics." He concludes that "we should either give up the search for efficient causes in social phenomena or follow the lead of the causal psychologists"; social problems "are resolvable ultimately into problems about men: what they are, what they want, and how they get it." There are "some laws of a reasonable probability," and hence "science may help us to get what we want by presenting us with sets of facts."[16] Years later there are no grounds for feeling less pessimistic, in spite of the tons of data and the many theories that have become available. Societal differences and functions cannot be ignored; they must be explained at least tentatively.

SOCIETAL DIFFERENCES

Human traits may be universal, but their evaluation varies from society to society and from individual to individual.[17] Families exist, men and women interact in all societies; frequently, but not always, monogamy prevails. Every male has a penis that excretes semen and urine at different times; its size and shape may or may not be associated with virility and pride.[18] Drinking intoxicating beverages varies from being taboo to being obligatory in some ceremonies and situations, hence there is "no universal pattern of alcohol use," as illustrated in the United States by abstinence that is high among Mormons and low among Italian-Americans and Jews. Still, "the act of drinking is socially controlled for most people in most societies."[19] And food? People must eat, but the quantity, quality, and kind obviously varies between and within societies. Children's education? Yes, but only if education is broadly defined to include learning from parents and peers and not the details or the method. In the 1990s the grammar of Turkish youths between the ages of fourteen and fifteen who were living in Germany was less proficient in spoken and written German than a comparable group of German students.[20] Were the Turkish students "inferior" to the Germans; should second languages be taught in countries like Germany? In this instance the culprit was obviously not the second language but the additional time required to become proficient in a second language, an empirical fact calling for knowledge of that particular situation.

Likewise religion performs a similar function in every society, but religions worldwide obviously also differ with respect to their precise beliefs and recommended actions; and they change over time. Within recent years, especially in the West, religions have not provided many individuals with either a completely satisfying explanation of their current problems or recommendations for appropriate actions. Such persons do not reject all religious practices, rather they occasionally invoke religious beliefs, attend religious services especially on conventional holidays, and perhaps treasure sentimental recollections of how their parents or ancestors and they themselves as children were "religious." Substitute philosophies or worldviews then arise, the most recent being fascism and communism that have trumpeted the actions leading to earthly rewards and the enemies to be fought to obtain these rewards.

The neo-religious beliefs have been propagated by their adherents who make abundant use of the mass media. Marxism has employed an intellectual or scholarly approach, inspiring many social scientists to suggest or try to reveal its validity or futility. For non-scholars seeking enlightenment or inspiration from Marxism, it has been sufficient to consult not the profound and not always consistent writings of Marx himself, Engels, or Lenin but rather the brief, inspiring declaration of the Communist Manifesto of 1848. The formal if not the actual ending of fascism after World War II and of communism after the dissolution of the Soviet Union in the early 1990s did not lead to a complete eclipse of all believers. Decades ago a brilliant legal scholar who impressed students and university colleagues and later his colleagues in Washington argued as follows.

> As the comforts of the present world increased, the future life became less important and the church, the chief custodian of the blessings of that life, lost its influence. Reason displaced mysticism and the law became the great repository of the symbols of government. . . . Actually, of course, the reason for the existence of the jury is to absorb the criticism of the numerous unsatisfactory results in the trial of cases, and thus to deflect it against the judicial system itself. When [a well-known person] is acquitted, we blame the jury if we do not like the result. We cannot blame the law, because according to law there was a question of fact to be left to the jury which the law had no right to decide.[21]

Evaluated carefully from a melioristic standpoint must be explanations proposed to account for societal differences. In a broad perspective it is evident that races or ethnic groups, however defined, appear to prevail in some societies; do race and ethnicity account for a society's distinctiveness? That explanation must be rejected according to contemporary wisdom that ascribes societal attributes not to genetic but to environmental and historical factors of each society. Possibly the statement of the poetic philosopher who eventually became president of Senegal should be heeded: "Races are not equal but complementary, which is a superior form of equality."[22] "Complementary" means differences to be respected. Nevertheless, the competitive and aggressive behavior prevalent in the politics of societies containing different ethnic groups, as in many African and other countries,[23] is a fact to be recognized when seeking peace and unity.

Another sweeping concept calling attention to the distinctive attributes of a society is that of morale. The word can be used to characterize members of a society who possess courage and zeal in pursuing a more satisfactory existence. More than two dozen American psychologists once responded to what they considered to be a world crisis by publishing as their country entered World War II a book on what they called civilian morale. The first article therein illustrates the mode of analysis. Its author believed that "high national morale" could be attained when people were endowed "with abundant energy and confidence in facing the future"; when their efforts to cooperate with their government and one another were derived from their own "personal convictions and values"; and when they agreed with one another concerning the values and efforts to attain the "necessary objectives." Toward these ends he offered eleven "features of democratic morale" that are grouped here into two categories with some of their components quickly suggested in parentheses. First, for morale to be high, individuals must have certain feelings about other persons (social responsibility, tolerance of minorities, cooperation for the common good, confidence in leaders). Second, they are likely to have those feelings only under specified societal arrangements (equal rights to all, promotion of well-being, existence of security and fair treatment, rule of majority, freedom of speech, condemnation of violence and usually war, affording opportunity for persons to use full intellectual equipment).[24]

Either at the moment or over time the distinctive environmental or physical resources of each society vary and determine significant aspects of human behavior. An economic factor appears relevantly important when reference is made to fish in its waters, the oil and minerals embedded in its soil, and the prevailing climate and fluctuations in weather. In the politics and scholarship of the West, the classical or neoclassical doctrine of economic determinism has viewed "individuals as seeking to maximize *their* utility, rationally choosing the best means to serve their goals." This model has been criticized and supplanted by an approach that considers in greater detail the nature of the society and its culture as well as the persons who make the decisions. Thus it is argued that "the majority" of economic choices by individuals involve "little information processing or none at all," rather "they draw largely or exclusively on affective involvements and normative commitments"; hence it is misleading to label them economic men and women.[25] Market forces vary from society to society and are likewise only one of the crucial variables affecting beliefs and actions.

Within every established group of birds, chickens, or apes and within every human society is a distinctive "pecking order" organized around "some kind of dominance hierarchy" that is communicated in innumerable ways and allocated to individuals with varying attributes. Among persons, gestures of the body convey a sense of superiority or inferiority; by "turning our eyes away from someone who has been looking at us, we are declining any challenge they may be making."[26] Severe or moderate inequality exists everywhere, the privileges or deprivations of which are associated with a class, ethnic group, association, or specific persons. Those on top justify their position in ways ranging from the biological (genetically "superior") to the privileges the powerful allegedly merit. The justifications are at least partially false as judged by social scientists or observers from other societies or during other eras in the same society; they may be called "myths" that rationalize dominance during long or short periods of time.[27]

Many persons in the West and elsewhere who call themselves liberal or emancipated deplore inequality. Sometimes its condemnation leads to the wishful conviction that in sweet and innocent traditional societies outside the West equality doth reign or once did. Actually inequality, not equality, is to be found in every sub-Saharan African country, as anthropologists, political scientists, journalists, travelers, and the inhabitants themselves have suggested or experienced.[28]

Respect must be shown for the platitude that every society has its own history which, in the view of its contemporaries and as mentioned in the previous section, justifies many or some of its current practices and actions or can serve as a basis for condemning them. Generalizations or descriptions of societies during earlier periods appear easier to formulate and identify than in the present day, probably because evidence provided by documents, objects, buildings, and bones from the past was less plentiful and hence more tempting to inspire imperfect generalizations. A competent scholar who has carefully surveyed relevant sources provides the following summary of medieval English literature and beyond:

> Ultimately, they believed, all disease comes by the will of God, and the most common moral justification for disease is that God in his justice inflicts disease on the unrepentant sinner as a punishment. . . . For the Middle Ages sin was real madness; an unrepentant sinner is more truly mad than the most violent maniac, for he cares not in life that the devil's hounds will possess him horribly in death.[29]

Almost anyone reading those lines today is likely to assume their validity and not to be only tolerantly and sympathetically amused; see how far we have advanced, our beliefs are superior to those once held by people long ago. But how can we be sure that everyone living at the time held such views or codified them so clearly? When our present beliefs are neatly and similarly packaged centuries from now, will readers then be similarly enlightened or amused by what they are told about us?

An illustration of the need for acquiring specific information about the differences and their function in a society is a study conducted in Durban, South Africa, between 1978 and 1979 during the apartheid era. Its aim was to examine "the quality of life" there, a way of probing the values sought and occasionally achieved. Three samples were interviewed: 103 "Whites" or Europeans, 105 Indians, and 201 "Blacks" or Africans. The "social indicators" of the study were introduced during an interview that lasted from three to four hours with the following statement: "I will read you a list of things in people's lives. Listen to each one and tell me if you feel it is very important in your life." Offered were 148 "things"—yes, 148, but a few were omitted when not relevant to the participant. The first three items were "Owning a house in town," "Having cattle in the country," "Having a good education"; the last three, "Living among neighbours that you know," "Standing a chance of promotion at work," "Having close and loyal friends"; and three toward the middle, "Making progress in your work," "Being able to watch the sports you like," "Feeling respected by your superiors at work." With so many data, various indices were subsequently computed. "Overall life satisfaction" was reported by 93 percent of the Europeans, 81 percent of the Indians, and 41 percent of the Africans. Generally the Europeans and Indians were "more prone to consider the more subtle, non-material issues of life as high priorities," and the Africans "tended to regard the more basic material needs in life as particularly salient." The extremely forthright investigators admitted that their interviews did not enable informants to recognize and then report "intangible issues reflecting the more personal aims in life"; and their data could not be related to the informants' mood, or to their personalities and needs and other "personal background factors." Ignored, too, were "objective social indicators" such as "income, life-expectancy, disease rates, housing standards, available educational facilities, and the like."[30] Within the limited context of the interviews, however, the study clearly indicated that differences existed not only between but also within the three societies.

Every society has beliefs and practices that may or may not be unique (G6). Here are the first two lines from a work of fiction:

> My name is Kisimi Kamara.
> I was born at the height of a rainy season, in the village of Lokko in the British West African colony of Songhai.[31]

Without reading the rest of the story, what information is conveyed above by the African name, the dating of the birth through a reference to "a rainy season," and by the location of the birth? Are we supposed to be intrigued by the atmosphere thus created by this introduction to the character, are we puzzled or pleased, do we wonder why the author begins the tale in that manner, have we learned something unique about the society?

Personal statements may offer similar challenges. A Kwakiutl Indian born in 1910 reported:

> People would call me up when they had some problem or needed help and they still do that now. I had a number of people call me up, like when their baby had died and they didn't have enough money so they asked me if they could bury their child in our graveyard. So I just called up the undertaker and told him to get a little casket and take care of the child and charge it to me. I would just loan the money to those parents but I didn't expect that they would pay me back. I have helped people a lot of times when they needed money and often I would never get paid back, but I liked to help my people.[32]

After praising such a generous person, do we wonder whether his behavior springs from some attribute of his society or from his own experiences and uniqueness?

Differences between societies may be noted, but then their functioning may not be obvious and must be interpreted cautiously. Again during the years of apartheid in South Africa it seemed obvious that Africans there were being exploited by Europeans who had become their villains. Evidence: many Africans worked in mines in distressing conditions, others lost their lands which were occupied by Europeans and Afrikaners. An American anthropologist, however, who once spent two and a half years among the Twansa people in South Africa and Botswana, who learned their language, and who carefully and sensitively explored their self-identity, self-image, and self-concepts, reported that these people "in the main affirm their existence in terms of values and an image of the self that parries and overcomes the denigration inherent in the colonial political economy of southern Africa." The colonial "bondage," however, was not completely despised; thus in the Kalahari Desert almost all respondents were of the opinion that in addition "white people could be a positive resource, especially in hard times."[33]

Within the same society, differences probably attributable to individual citizens can easily be ignored. On the basis of his values and prejudices and also from experiences in Hitler's Third Reich, the present writer once believed that little or nothing praiseworthy could have been possible during the Nazi regime. Forty years after Hitler's death, an American historian convincingly documented the fact that psychotherapists in Nazi Germany had been able to function effectively, to contribute to the profession, and to provide psychiatric assistance to many Germans. Part of their success resulted from their nominal chief who was a cousin of the powerful Nazi leader Hermann Göring; of even greater importance was the determination of German therapists to continue to function fruitfully in spite of the government.[34] This observer thus had overlooked that laudable development because it was unanticipated and because news about the activities of German psychiatrists at the time was generally unavailable outside esoteric circles. Obviously the contribution of these psychiatrists did not and does not justify the Nazis; they provide only a whiff of grace about that period in Germany's history.

Although it is both tempting and necessary to specify the uniqueness of a society and its differences from other societies, valid supporting evidence is usually not immediately available, but must first be sought and then carefully evaluated. Do Americans live in "a self-centered society where the individual's responsibility and the individual's feelings are given priority over his concern about the social group"; do they feel "guilt rather than shame" when they do something "wrong or ridiculous" and hence are "controlled by internal conscience rather than by external group pressures," even though they also display a "considerable degree of individuality"? Those are some of the questions once modestly raised and deliberately not settled by two American sociologists after administering and analyzing data from a battery of psychological tests to 733 Midwestern American children and 904 Southwest American Indian children between the ages of six and eighteen.[35] The investigations of responsible, respectable social scientists may lead them to draw provocative conclusions that may or may not be valid when they are drawn or later. Toward the middle of this century a British physician, functioning as a psychiatrist in Kenya, believed that the ideal person must be a scientist and that Europeans who behaved well were responding to a sense of duty and responsibility, whereas "Africans" did so only when they feared the consequences of behaving otherwise.[36] True or false, then or now?

Faced with societies' similarities and differences, meliorists struggle to find summaries of current views as guides to action. Herewith a tentative, struggling effort:

1. People are affected by their society, but therein they belong to different groups having more or less distinctive attributes not only defined by ethnicity, status, origin, and/or location within the area, but also weighted or evaluated differently.

2. The history of the society or group affects the actions of its members, deliberately or not.

3. Societies and groups may be affected by the experiences of other societies and groups to which they do not belong. An analysis of the transitional Constitution of South Africa in 1994 indicated how past revolutions before and during apartheid affected many of its provisions, yet simultaneously solutions that had emerged elsewhere, especially in the United States, were known to its formulators who thus could critically evaluate the "lessons" of their own history; history from the inside and outside could function at this critical moment in South Africa.[37]

4. Peoples' experiences with one or more persons provide some kind of guide to their judgments and values. Scholarly research by psychiatrists and psychologists almost always leads to additional guides, which then may be accepted or rejected. In "literature," one psychologist once observed, "it is the single person, the 'particular truth' that stands revealed," and hence "whatever broader applications literature may have are merely implicit and are usually debatable."[38]

That "single person," nevertheless, whether in fiction or daily experience, can give rise to guides for other persons like him or her or even for human beings generally. Do Hamlet and Hitler tell us something about everybody?

PART III

ACTIONS

CHAPTER 8

Individual Actions

Meliorists, let the guiding platitude be repeated flamboyantly, seek happiness for themselves, for other individuals but not everyone, and for society generally. Usually happiness is not quickly or easily achieved; it is pursued through action. A sensational insight by the present writer a while back is herewith repeated because he and you must similarly sigh now and will do so in the future: "The search for means to achieve moral ends is everlasting and ever incomplete."[1] In addition, unlike our best guess concerning animals, the self recognizes consciously the need to plan and act.[2] Whether meliorists or not, we take heed and are baffled by a philosopher in this century who likewise disclosed that "nothing is strictly right or wrong except some possible activity or the manner of it, where in an equally strict sense anything under the sun can be good or bad."[3]

Actions of any kind appear and appeal to individuals who believe or imagine that their objective is related to happiness immediately or remotely. The success or failure of such an action in the past may lead to the belief that the same action will have similar consequences in the future. But of course the future may be different from the past, a possibility that may be anticipated before selecting the action (G4). Counterfactual reasoning, as defined previously in Chapter 2, may influence the decision not by projecting into the past but rather by imagining the consequence of inaction or a different action in the present. If you do not help that friend of yours who is in trouble, you will feel guilty later and he, poor fellow, will be miserable; hence you do what is necessary.

As meliorists view and evaluate themselves, usually, often, or in passing, they realize that they are not unique. They know their own gender cannot be altered or easily altered, and there are limits in the extent to which they can affect or regulate their height, weight, and strength; consequently they may characterize themselves by referring to such attributes. For subtler traits, like intelligence and achievements, the judgmental latitude is broader. Some estimates of the self are vital and important, others less so. A guess: the more confident or self-confident individuals are, the more likely they are to seek or acquire the kind of true or false knowledge about themselves they believe is related to action in relevant situations.[4] In any case, many but not all the criteria for selecting actions are also found in the self's society, illustrated especially by actions to be pursued in order to be healthy or avoid illness. One learns how to behave in specified circumstances or is forced to do so. A fierce or unrelenting critic can be the self: privately it is discovered that a goal has not been completely or honestly attained or that the self somehow has been misguided. The criticism of the self by the self can be painful and hence hypocritically avoided.[5]

The actions by the self can be viewed in terms of three different referents: actions in behalf of the self and by the self; similar actions and with help from others; and actions by the self in behalf of others. These divisions overlap but are considered separately in this chapter. Each of the three concerns the self in one, two, or three ways, illustrated by considering the reactions of two persons to a simple event, a threatening storm:

1. *knowledge*: Miss A and Mr. B both believe there will be a storm tomorrow, whether or not their knowledge comes from looking at the sky or from a forecast by a weather bureau relayed in the mass media.
2. *value*: A is happy at the prospect because she thinks her lawn needs watering, and a storm means rain; B is unhappy because the storm, if it comes, may prevent him from visiting a friend.
3. *action*: A does nothing, there is nothing she can or wishes to do about the storm; B telephones the friend, and they agree to postpone the visit because of the storm.

Both A and B may or may not be affected by a third person who has the same or different view of that storm and who also communicates the view convincingly or not either to A or B or both. Finally, it is essential to determine the person or persons from whose viewpoint the above trio is being analyzed: from that of the self about the self or from that of the self as viewed by another person? That other person is then called an observer meriting a capital O and may be a member of the self's family, a peer, a casual bystander, a psychiatrist, or some other so-called expert.

Noteworthy is the interrelation of knowledge, value, and action. Ordinarily the sequence is the one listed above: individuals engage in an action when they anticipate the result (knowledge) and approve of the anticipated result (value). The sequence, however, may be reversed: the outcome of an action differs from what has been anticipated, so that in the future, as a result of that action, the knowledge and perhaps also the value change. You dislike a group such as an ethnic group, you meet and interact with one or more members of the group, you react favorably to the contact; thereafter you change your attitude toward that group as a whole.

To the "objective" observer—a scholar, a social scientist, a psychiatrist, a cynic, obviously you—the self is seldom completely alone while searching for an appropriate act. The pronoun "I" generally means that the self is active, whereas "me" suggests passivity or the object of an influence outside the self.[6] On a winter's day you feel cold, and you go inside where it is warmer; your action is successful and appropriate, but of course the temperature of the room has been raised previously by you or another occupant of the house. Often, but certainly not always, more gratification is obtained from real or imagined self-initiated actions than from those of others or from an exterior circumstance, although assistance may itself be gratifying and require less effort. In any case, again unlike animals and also young children, individuals usually believe they deliberately plan some or most of their actions and evaluate their own contribution to the consequences: "Human behavior is purposefully biased toward improved control."[7]

How frequently must and should individuals engage in melioristic action and in a specific action toward a melioristic end? The self-imposed question is easier to raise than to supply a reply that is neither glib nor trite. Some melioristic action is always desirable, provided it remains satisfying when repeated. A medical drug to reduce pain is ingested repeatedly in accordance with a physician's suggestion ("use no more than three times a day"), is no longer taken when the pain ceases, but later may be used again when the pain recurs or at the physician's suggestion. In like manner, a religious or philosophical value is utilized only in "appropriate" situations. You do not try to be "honest" when you scratch an itchy part of your skin. Up to some point, repeating a melioristic action is desirable because its melioristic gain is thus repeated and because the action recurs with less effort and planning. But repetition can be boring, and boredom is negatively flavored. It all depends, it all depends; or, as the organization Gideons International suggests in its foreword to the New Testament distributed on the street to pedestrians willing to accept the gift, "We are pleased to present you with this copy of God's precious Word and trust that you will enjoy reading it daily." The critical word may be "enjoy"; is that why you read or do not read the Bible?

This chapter, concerned with actions by individuals in behalf of themselves, is organized around the concept of "help," help for the self, help from others for the self, and help to others by the self. The close and inevitable relation of the self to others and to the society in which the self and others dwell is thus indicated. Considerable and in this case impressive evidence suggests that the concept of self-help is meaningful to individuals in societies all over this world, but is usually employed to refer not only to efforts to improve the self but also to groups like those concerned with almost every conceivable goal (economic, political, social) to benefit its members and the individual self. Such groups might be called "selves-help groups," if our grammar would permit.

SELF-HELP: CONTROL

If "help" be defined broadly, it may appear clear that individuals help themselves when they act in ways that benefit themselves and perhaps others. Obviously yes, but an infinite regress appears when the individual self is operationally defined. A psychologist wonders whether the notion of self-control includes both the self and not-self.[8] Who or what is then exercising control over the individual self, another self that is patrolling the self so that action does or does not occur? A foolish question?

Without replying to the question, introspection reveals that the self, selfishly or not, can or does seek to satisfy or help that self achieve a variety of goals. But then avoiding one question is followed by another equally challenging, partially metaphysical issue of determinism vs. free will. It was once argued that "freedom and determinism cannot both be true"; people may assert they possess freedom, but "in reality what they believe for the most part is only that they are hypothetically free."[9] Or else they think themselves free only part of the time: they know they can control simple actions such as opening or closing their eyes but that they are unable to affect other actions such as stamping out many forms of evil (defined as you wish) with or without cooperation from others. Whether a belief in freedom is illusory in some or all situations, that belief, perhaps especially in the West, has "a definite and a positive role in sustaining life."[10] For this and other reasons, if the thought may be continued in the words of another savant, "in the study of moral behavior, it is essential to determine the actor's interpretation of the situation and the behavior since the moral quality of the behavior is itself determined by that interpretation."[11] Americans were once said to reveal a "curious discrepancy": they were thought to be "freer than ever before of the risk of premature death, yet they feel that things have been getting less safe." The discrepancy, it was guessed, reflected a decline in motor vehicle deaths but also a fear of possible accidents or calamities stemming from discharging of nuclear and other wastes.[12] Presumably most persons believe they control their driving habits but not the disposal of wastes by others.

Many actions of the self are not deliberately self-controlled and eventually become involuntary. Individuals blink reflexively when rays from a bright light suddenly strike their eyes, and they pull their hand away from a hot object they have inadvertently touched. But for most actions, whether of the face, the hands, or the rest of the body, the distance between oneself and another person or persons may also be as "deliberate" as speech: such actions communicate, they express what the self is feeling or wishes to emphasize, and they may be affected by the custom of the group or culture that encourages or discourages an overt display.[13] Movements of the hands accompanying speech are varied and have been so thoroughly learned and expressed that they occur without reflection and can communicate an emotion or its significance. Thus the self has once learned an action that later occurs without perceptible reflection.

Dreaming is covert behavior by the self that cannot be deliberately controlled, although it is a consequence of past actions by the self that may or may not have been previously deliberate. The rapid eye movements (REM) accompanying dreams reveal only their occurrence but not their content. After awakening, individuals who recall at least parts of the dream's content can consider them simple memories, reflections of unsolved problems, or mandates for or against future action. Trances and other dissociations, an anthropological survey once revealed, existed in 90 percent of a carefully selected sample of 488 societies; and these were "institutionalized" and "culturally patterned." Their function seemed to be to produce changes within individuals or the society; thus a decision favored in a trance could alter the belief of the person having the experience or, if he or she were important in a group, a small or large number of followers.[14] Psychiatrically, the interpretation remains, such phenomena reveal status-quo information about individuals and their society and can function as guides to themselves and others when the dreamers or those experiencing the trance believe in their credibility.

Self-initiated actions that have not been controlled or anticipated may eventually differ from what has been anticipated as a result of uncontrolled consequences (G6). "I didn't mean to hurt him, but I did." You agree to help a friend and later find it difficult or awkward to fulfill the promise: do you then try somehow to keep the promise, or are you "sensible" and disappoint the friend whose trust in you is thus violated? A term like "unintentional propaganda" refers to the far-reaching consequences of advertising, politics, psychological warfare, and education not anticipated or controlled by the original progenitors.[15] A dramatic and pervasive challenge has been subsumed under the almost neologistic title of "sunk cost." To save money, you respond to an enticing advertisement for something or other by making a deposit of $250 which, according to the terms set forth by the merchant, is "nonrefundable." Before you actually purchase the article, you discover another one that seems superior or a good friend tells you that the boast of the advertisement is exaggerated or false. What should you do, buy the product anyway and add good money to your deposit, or not buy the product and forfeit the deposit? Either way you feel uncomfortable: purchasing an inferior product or losing $250. "Throwing away good money after bad" can be a metaphor for nonmercenary situations in which the self apparently cannot favorably control the self's actions.

Self-actions occur after events uninitiated and uncontrollable by the self to which only "adjustments" can be made. Cyclones, hurricanes, earthquakes, thunderstorms, floods, and droughts cannot be cancelled, although measures can be taken to mitigate their effects, such as constructing or strengthening buildings to withstand the vagaries of weather. Above all, let it be endlessly repeated, dying cannot be eventually avoided; actions may only be taken in the meantime to achieve real or imaginary control. Without denying that some day they will die, individuals act in effect to postpone death by fighting disease and trying to avoid accidents. Some diseases can be sidestepped, and others can be controlled by drugs or physicians after their onset. The effects of aging can be mitigated, and perhaps dying can be delayed by leading a "sensible" life, whatever that means, at a given moment in time. Individuals may acquire a conviction that says of death, "We'll cross that bridge once we come to it," but not "right now."[16] Or they adhere to the credo of some existing religion that provides a rationale to overcome their fears of death. For this rational-emotional action, you might turn to Socrates who, according to Plato, stated as he was about to be executed that "there is great reason to hope that death is good." The "hope," according to the words ascribed to him in one translation, springs from two alternatives:

... either death is a state of nothingness and utter unconsciousness or, as men say, there is a change and migration of the soul from this world to another. Now if you suppose that there is no consciousness, but a sleep like the sleep of him who is undisturbed even by dreams, death will be an unspeakable gain ... if death be of such a nature, I say that to die is to gain; for eternity is then only a single night. But if death is the journey to another place and there, as men say, all the dead abide, what good, O my friends and judges, can be greater than this? ... What would not a man give if he might converse with Orpheus and Musaeus and Hesiod and Homer? Nay, if this be true, let me die again and again.[17]

Socrates, it may be noted, qualifies his hopes with "if's," which is seldom done in established religions; thus the Mohammedan Koran proclaims repeatedly:

What is the life of this world but play and amusement? Best is the Home in the Hereafter for those who are righteous. ... Here is a representation of the Paradise which the righteous have been promised: there shall flow in it rivers of incorruptible water, rivers of milk forever fresh, rivers of delectable wine, and rivers of clearest honey.[18]

And the New Testament of the Christian Bible: "Jesus said to her, 'I am the resurrection and the life. Whoever believes in Me, though he may die, he shall live.' "[19]

A desperate way to cope with death is to control its ocurrence by committing suicide. It was once reported that in the United States "relatively little information" was then available concerning youths who commit suicide; but one careful study did indicate that such persons revealed "a heterogeneity of personality characteristics."[20] An American philosopher, after examining sufficiently copious evidence, has observed that suicide "occurs in all cultures, nationalities, races, age-groups, and professions."[21] One requires no special talent or ability to end one's own life—different methods are available—rather what is needed is a decision to plunge into death, deliberately and quickly.

SELF-HELP: VALUES

Actions to achieve specified values are advocated by parents for their children, by leaders for their followers, and by educators for their pupils and students especially in societies whose values are many and changing. The ancient claim that schools should teach "moral values" and develop "good character" for the self was once made semi-concrete in a book with a two-word dedication ("for God") by providing "ten good reasons" for seeking that objective. The reasons begin with "a clear and urgent need" because young people are hurting themselves and are less concerned with the welfare of others and conclude with the assertion that such education is "a doable job." The principal values to be taught were thought to be, first, respect (for oneself, for others, and "for all forms of life and the environment that sustains us") and, second, responsibility for being oriented toward others and responding to their needs. Other recommended values were "honesty, fairness, tolerance, prudence, self-discipline, helpfulness, compassion, courage, and a host of democratic values." Good character thus consisted of knowing, feeling, and acting in behalf of such values. Individuals could also possess nonmoral values that carry no direct obligation but that please them personally, such as enjoying a meal or listening to music.[22]

Psychiatrists recommend actions to their patients and others; they are often not loath to suggest the value or values thus to be achieved. Casting modesty and caution aside, in a relatively brief paragraph one of them courageously summarized what he believed to be "a core of ideas and norms" common to "Lao-tse, Buddha, the Prophets, Socrates, Jesus, Spinosa, and the philosophers of the Enlightenment":

> . . . man must strive to recognize the truth and can be fully human only to the extent to which he succeeds in this task. He must be independent and free, an end in himself and not the means for any other person's purposes. He must relate himself to his fellow men lovingly. If he has no love, he is an empty shell even if his were all power, wealth, and intelligence. Man must know the difference between good and evil, he must learn to listen to the voice of his conscience and to be able to follow it.

"Analytic theory," therefore, he emphasized in italics, "is essentially an attempt to help the patient gain or regain his capacity for love."[23] Thus all peoples in every society crave love; united they stand, consciously or otherwise. Do you think so?

Direct questions to individuals concerning the causes of their happiness or unhappiness or the associations therewith provide preliminary clues to the actions they desire to retain or change in their present state. Herewith the examples selected quite randomly from the 7,838 "correlates of happiness" mentioned in Chapter 4:

"How do you feel things have worked out for you generally?"

"If I had the choice to make again, I would choose the same occupation or type of work I do now."

"How do you feel about the sleep you get?"[24]

Another illustration from the many studies available: in the 1970s adequate samples of adults in four communities in the state of Illinois were interviewed at some length concerning their views about the "quality of American life" and also how "happy" they felt when "taking all things together." Their marital status was a crucial factor, they thought, in leading to satisfaction; blacks and unemployed men tended to say they were less satisfied than, respectively, whites and men then employed.[25] Would the less satisfied and the less happy be more likely to perform actions in behalf of change in order to improve their present status?

Some action-oriented values of the self have important implications for actions regarding others and society (G5). Surveys were once conducted in the United States, supplemented by others in Japan, Germany, and Botswana, to determine the "essential needs" people believe give rise to values and may lead to self-serving actions. Nine values emerged; in the author's sweeping terminology they range from aesthetic and symbolic to humanistic and utilitarian. Significant statistical relations were found between informants' age, gender, urban-rural location, region of country, and the year the surveys were conducted on the one hand and the aforementioned values as well as with attitudes regarding fish, birds, whales, forests, and the costs of making appropriate changes on the other hand.[26]

Another valued activity, that of leisure, may be pursued by the self alone but involves other persons as well as the organization of society. Individuals in the West after they mature may or may not crave relaxation and the joys derived from the arts, sports, the media, and their own feelings or cogitations. Whether or not they have the "spare" time to devote to leisure depends on obligations to their immediate family and other associates and also on the time they devote to the necessities of existence. And the latter may be affected by legal regulations concerning the length of the working day, medical emergencies, and vacations. During available leisure time the activities may be either satisfactory or unsatisfactory from the self's viewpoint.[27] Both the pursuit and mode of leisure activity may also be affected by the location of the individual's residence. In what part of town do you live, do you prefer an urban to a rural area; do you support legal measures requiring factories to be at a distance from your home?

One value, a negative one, related to leisure is the avoidance of loneliness. A psychiatrist suggests that the feeling of "essential aloneness" affects people at some times more than at others; it probably reflects "the decline in vital energies which begins at first slowly and then proceeds more and more rapidly following their peak at the beginning of adult life." The inevitable consequence of feeling "remote from other people" may be depression and melancholia, the symptoms of which, according to the same source, plague all human beings on and off during their early existence, even though "many mental illnesses" in the more serious sense are "not related to depression at all."[28] Few if any persons, therefore, escape this "painful experience" that is likely to be associated with an individual's distinctive personality such as being "shy, introverted, and less willing to take social risks" and with "self-depreciation and low self-esteem." In addition, "cultural and situational factors" also play a role affecting the degree to which a person is dependent on others and hence whether he or she cooperates with them. Available physical arrangements for housing and recreation may likewise be relevant. Clinicians emphasize a "common association of loneliness and disruptive life changes, including widowhood, divorce, and moving."[29] In American society, perhaps elsewhere, loneliness may arise in the absence of "an intimate partner" or of "ties to a social community."[30] Among older Americans another study once revealed "a wide variety of factors" affecting loneliness to some degree but not without compelling exceptions, such as being male rather than female, without children and many friends, in poor health, in the lower economic or education bracket, and black rather than white.[31]

American college students have reported a large variety of devices they employ to overcome their loneliness. Cognitively, they have reminded themselves that they "actually do have good relations with other people" and they have "worked particularly hard to succeed at some activity" connected with their everyday existence.[32] The "cure" for loneliness is elusive: a psychiatrist, after examining case histories of lonely Americans, has admitted that "I can offer no method for ending loneliness other than the formation of new relationships that might repair the deficit responsible for the loneliness." That solution is "not easy"[33] and comes, if it does come, as a result of actions by the self or others—or by both.

The list of negative actions to be avoided by many, some, but not all persons is lengthy if only because values require prohibitions. Such actions include adultery, anger, divorce, "foul" language, hatred, intoxication, masturbation, murder, and revenge. You can easily add additional black marks. Do you include suicide under all conditions?

SELF-HELP: KNOWLEDGE

After or while selecting a value, the self somehow seeks to draw upon knowledge to achieve a goal implementing that value. The knowledge may come from previous experience in what is believed to have been a similar situation. You have known for years when the real or metaphorical fruit is ripe and harvesting can begin. Or knowledge may be obtained from experience transmitted directly or through traditions prevalent in a society. Whatever its source, the self must somehow appraise the knowledge related to the actions being proposed.[34]

Melioristically the appraisal involves three challenges: is such knowledge valid, is it available, and can it actually be utilized? The first challenge, that of validity or that of determining whether the knowledge is "true" or "false" (if seldom phrased so clearly), confronts individuals at almost every moment of existence when not reacting reflexively or from force of habit. Its broad outlines have been discussed previously in Chapters 2, 3, and 4. Meliorists seek to have knowledge that is valid on the same bases employed by scientists within their disciplines. Here a number of scientific ideals will be mentioned quickly, too quickly, in passing. Above all, a cause-and-effect sequence derived from experience or experimentation is valid when on a subsequent occasion it reappears or is repeated, provided all conditions in the future are the same (or almost the same?) as they were in the past.

Whatever criteria are obtained from pure science, meliorists suggest, are not likely to be completely or adequately achievable for planning many individual actions. A respected methodologist in psychology and his colleagues argue that even quantitative data derived from standardized tests may often seem "arbitrary and subjective, leading one to question" whether the conclusions are "trustworthy."[35] Similar doubts about knowledge from this standpoint are raised again and again in a struggle to achieve perfection. In a book appropriately titled *Rational Choice in an Uncertain World*, another psychologist has reviewed and criticized conclusions from well-designed experiments and real-life incidents. Well-intentioned individuals may note whether the knowledge could have occurred by chance for some reason overlooked by the investigator. They may thus count the hits and ignore the misses when associating an event with a desirable experience, but forget the need for a "control" to indicate whether similar or identical events could have occurred in the absence of that experience. They depend on "retrospection" (remembering only the pleasant or unpleasant aspects of events and forgetting or repressing other aspects). They claim they have learned to think or behave in a particular manner, yet the experience may be unique, like almost every experience, and what is lacking once again is a control: they believe it sufficient to note that they were happy at that time and hence they seek to restore and reexperience a similar event.[36]

Thus knowledge related to action may be not only untrustworthy totally or in part but may also be incomplete or even unavailable (G2). Perfect knowledge, especially about human beings, a philosophical Catholic priest has convincingly argued, is "impossible" for many reasons: all relevant facts may not have been available or taken into account; the individual's biases unwittingly may influence a formulation; and a later experience or additional data in the future may require a minor or major reformulation or a more inclusive or extensively valid principle may be formulated.[37] Differences between the present and the future, therefore, are likely; proclaiming "ceteribus paribus" (other things being equal) in Latin or any other language may be an unrealizable assumption. Individuals may be rereading a book decades later; although the words and sentences are the same, they may seem different as a result of "new" experiences or events that have transpired. Other components in the situation may be perceived or evaluated on later occasions.

When uncertain, it is difficult if not impossible to anticipate future events in detail and to act appropriately. You know you can walk to reach a specific place—unless, however, you are ill; unless you have broken your leg; unless you are barred by the police or gangsters from doing so. You expect to admire that person you meet for the first time and, sure enough, you ignore aspects of his or her behavior that ordinarily would induce you to judge and act otherwise. What would you do if you really won a substantial lottery? Perhaps the most important, elusive knowledge to obtain and retain is self-knowledge that differs from the assets or liabilities, the competencies or incompetencies assessed and provided by friends and foes about yourself. Absence of such insight is illustrated by a psychiatrist who recorded a "well-known joke": "A writer meets a friend and talks to him a long time about himself; he then says: 'I have talked so long about myself. Let us now talk about *you*. How did you like my latest book?' "[38]

The self who recognizes imperfections in knowledge related to action does not withdraw from existence, rather in the tritest and truest of aphorisms, he or she engages in the "best" possible action in the circumstances. The knowledge, though imperfect, can always be improved through science, systematic investigation, and experience. Formal or informal research may determine the reasons why the trees in a particular forest are drastically declining, why a species of insect is threatened with extinction, why the crime rate in an area of a city is increasing, why a candidate in a democratic election has been defeated, or why a person feels happy or insecure. Only the value not being sustained or violated is implied in such findings; perhaps even more important, the action or actions that may change the current tendencies in accordance with some value being presumed is not necessarily specified.

Admitted must be the fact that some compelling beliefs simply cannot be verified, conspicuously those related to death. Is there life after death on this earth; do the dead survive either in an attractive place (heaven) or in a hideous one (hell); through reincarnation after we die will we live at another time or place and again experience joys and sorrows? Replies to such questions cannot be proven in the manner of offering a reply to 1 + 1 = what?

Less metaphysical are other challenges to the self as an effort is made to determine the availability of knowledge. Here let us heed not a psychologist but an important, versatile mathematician who emphasizes that, "for effective action on the outer world," the world must be not only accurately and appropriately perceived, but the knowledge must also be "properly combined with the other information from the sense organs to produce a properly proportioned output to the effectors."[39] What this guide is emphasizing neologistically is that melioristic knowledge requires that feedback from other sources be related to the knowledge at hand, and it is not easy to put the relevant pieces of knowledge together, whether they come from past experience, the present situation, or anticipated consequences.

And then there is self-deception: we may believe what we wish to believe or how to act without checking its validity. According to the wisdom of one psychologist, there is no certain cure for such self-deception. He indicates, as might be anticipated from a member of his profession, twenty-three devices that may enable you, and me too, to "accept life's perspectives as a whole" which include competing with another person to achieve "more direct confrontation with reality," integrating "analytic thinking with feedback thinking," and seeking help from someone else (such as a therapist like him of course).[40] "Morally significant life," consequently, according to a similar source, "does require us to make a large commitment to being honest with ourselves, for only self-honesty can overcome our self-made obstacles to self-understanding."[41] It may be misleading, even dangerous, to believe in one's own conviction or the knowledge of predecessors because of the sharp increases in knowledge and technology in the interim. Perhaps one feels superior to Marx and other earlier economists and proselytizers only because one lives in a later era in which events in communist states like the former USSR and China have occurred and been reported. In fact, of course, the knowledge of every person is "limited and selective." Again meliorism cautions: individuals cannot absorb all available information whether in printed or mass media; their interest and the time allotted to learning are perforce limited.[42] Cause-and-effect sequences are valid only when all relevant variables are included, which in human affairs actions is seldom possible.

Then, third and last as well as first, adequate information is not available. We do not know how to prevent or control earthquakes and violent storms. Crimes occur, no matter what we do to "improve" a police force, a legal system, and educational and moral efforts that seek to have children and adults less prone to break the law or commit evil deeds. Most of us, perhaps not you, engage occasionally in temper tantrums that apparently cannot be curbed.

In these and other instances, adequate or complete knowledge is lacking but—and let us capitalize BUT—some existing knowledge is relevant if incomplete, and hence actions are possible. Natural disasters cannot be avoided, yet they usually can be forecast by specially trained professionals, so that either they can be avoided by living or moving elsewhere or their destructive consequences can be mitigated by building or strengthening the places in which people seek refuge.

Violent responses by the self, even when ostensibly merited, may be avoided and less violent or constructive actions substituted; the threat of punishment can diminish deplorable "crimes," if not always. People can come to terms with growing older, senior citizens can receive special treatment. The best available means at the time are employed; influenza cannot be eradicated, but for decades "flu shots" (inoculations likely to prevent succumbing to the ailment) have been advised and then accepted by the general population, especially by those at greatest risk from the latest virus.

Since no simple formula is usually either available or valid to forecast future events or the effects of action by the self for the self and others, perhaps hesitation is required to consider the relevance of available knowledge and its probable consequences leading to action that is necessary or desirable. Are decisions after hesitation "better" than those springing from impulses?[43] In comparison with animals and very young children, maturing and mature adults are less "stimulus bound" and therefore do not always respond immediately to the stimuli and opportunities at hand; yet they are also guided by past experience, even when apparently lacking the actual or potential ability to evaluate attitudes as being either prejudiced and false or valid and solidly based.[44] In "democratic" countries, proposals for new legislation may be carefully prepared and discussed before being submitted to debate; or at least they are supposed to be. Judges in court cases may call a recess or require deliberation during periods of varying length before reaching decisions. Hesitation, however, may discourage inspiration; quick decisions may sometimes be preferable. Individuals who value personal or political consistency may not hesitate when they believe they know the correct or appropriate action to be taken; for them hesitation then means rejecting their own significant values or intentions. On occasion, however, spontaneity rather than deliberation is desirable: suddenly, on the spur of the moment, the individual is inspired and acts upon the impulse; only later do the impulse and the act secure approval.

In reaching a decision to act, it is melioristically advisable to consider the sources of the knowledge on which the decision is based. Yes, this has been my own experience, but may I not have been affected, especially in the West, by the mass media that perhaps even unwittingly have affected my judgment? In Western countries, advertisers continually seek ways to increase sales or support for their clients by finding elusive slogans and memorable messages pointing to the actions being advocated. All organizations and governments forever wonder how they can improve their communications and function more "effectively."

Meliorists remain skeptical: no certain principle is ever available—always, without exception—to ensure or increase success. Even when the challenge is less general and attention is concentrated on the particular emotions in an audience to be aroused, the only valid generalization seems to be, "well, it all depends." Thus whether shame or guilt is the emotion to be tapped depends on the particular persons who are the targets as well as on modal tendencies within their society.[45] It may be known that repetition promotes learning but can be boring and disadvantageous. Consider likewise the ancient challenge of primacy vs. recency: which communication is likely to be more effective, the one reaching you first or last? No forever valid reply to that question is available; again it all depends, here on the action being advocated, the audience, and a host of other factors you can easily mention. Continually reinforced attitudes learned during childhood (primacy) are likely to remain unaffected by adult experiences (recency), yet not if the later experiences are dramatically different or arise when earlier views no longer seem true or satisfying. Elusive insight into one's own abilities and qualifications and deficiencies is required.

And finally—initially?—there is hope. After a disaster one hopes that soon or eventually conditions surrounding the self or the self itself will improve as a result of actions by the self or others. Without such cheer, existence is dismal. Hope, however, can be unrealistic: figuratively one imagines what one will do after some achievement or praise that may never occur. Hope can be difficult when realistic knowledge intrudes. Younger persons hope to recover from an illness and return to a "normal" existence, but for the elderly such hope may be delusional because for them health problems increase and never cease. Previously, one sadly recalls, it has been feasible to say "when I get better . . ." Other anticipations may be probable or certain: "when I am older . . . ," "when she reconsiders . . . ," "when economic conditions improve . . ." How is one to know whether a hope is realistic; without hope, can one stay alive or at least be reasonably happy? There is always the possibility of fortifying hope by appropriate action and by prayer or its equivalent. Hope, moreover, must eventually be linked to reality if the self or others are to benefit or be improved. Some appropriate knowledge must be "creative," whether connecting the past to the present or anticipated conditions or when striving to discover new and "better" ways to think and act. "Productive thinking" and action are not easy to achieve. An influential German psychologist, who once devised ingenious experiments that required his subjects to find new ways to resolve the perceptual problems at hand and who also studied the thinking of Galileo and informally and repeatedly interviewed Einstein at length, offered no foolproof formula to achieve creativity. He did suggest, nevertheless, that the initial step is to realize that hope involves the "requisitioning" of established principles and ways of thinking, to be followed anew by "investigation."[46] Amen?

HELP FROM OTHERS

Help is sought from or with others when the self feels that a goal cannot be achieved alone or without an effort by others or when that self is generally accustomed to depend on others to resolve a problem at hand. From whom should help for the self be obtained? Others are consulted with little or no hesitation by children who turn to their parents, by citizens who consult officials or leaders, by laymen who reach out to the clergy, and by you when you know literally or figuratively that more than one person is needed to lift that heavy object. In science there are recognized and respected helpers such as Newton, Einstein, and modern specialists, but in human affairs there may be no similar persons with competence and prestige. Who can supply definitive replies to questions whether interest rates should be raised or lowered, about the "best" way to administer medical facilities, or concerning the ideal mixture of diverse ethnic or social groups in schools? Self-help, as the concept appears in the scholarly literature, is obtained from others who also require assistance, as when minorities in a society band together to preserve their values or culture.[47]

When there is a choice, the self decides whether the others should be friends or strangers, persons with similar or dissimilar interests, a single individual or a few or many others. Other questions are raised. Should there be a single meeting with the helper or more than one to plan the action at scheduled or unscheduled intervals? Give-and-take sessions with others may have uncertain or unknown consequences. In the West, so-called parliamentary procedures are praised: individuals take turns in speaking after being recognized by the chair; decisions are reached by voting or some form of registering consensus. But orderliness can lead to rigidity; hence participants may react only conventionally and not realistically toward one another so that novel or bizarre ideas may not be advanced and creativity may be stifled. The interaction during the give-and-take of a meeting may also produce a promising or innovative proposal that leads somewhere only if provision has been or eventually is made for a follow-up in the real society or by scheduling one or more meetings of the same group or of some of its designated members. To end hesitation, a frequently proposed but not necessarily helpful bit of advice is to follow past experience. Sometimes the help consciously or unconsciously sought is only to find someone who will listen to the self in need or distress and whose very presence, whether or not sympathy is expressed or advice given or help offered, is believed to be helpful.[48]

Psychiatry is the formal discipline to which some, not many, persons in Western societies do or can turn for help when they or others believe their discomfort is too disturbing or overwhelming. Psychiatrists have been trained to provide professional advice; but, although too often their diagnoses and prognoses differ from those of their patients or other consultants, one may conceivably secure new insights from them. Thus in a standard textbook two psychiatrists once suggested how widespread aggressive behavior is: when they are aggressive, individuals engage in "destructive or hostile behavior," they have "a disposition to anger," and they are "more prone to approach, attack, and pursue than to avoid, retreat, and defend." In therapy it gradually may be made clear that such aggressive behavior "often stems from weakness and not from strength," but that this explanation must be suggested "without injury to the patient's self-esteem." Broken must be "the vicious circle of provocation and punishment,"[49] so that persons can become aware of their disruptive behavior.

Psychiatrists also grope to find the attributes conducive to mental health. Hints come from what their patients and other persons claim to seek, and these hints they attempt to transmit to those consulting them. What should persons do when they are momentarily or endlessly unsuccessful, when they are depressed and wonder whether suicide is the tempting solution? There is no overall panacea; therapies and cures are forever sought but remain elusive. In some circumstances and in some societies, those being consulted may suggest that the unhappy turn to alcohol and other drugs. Is alcohol really a drug, however defined? For drugs we must wait and see: on the basis of experience, competent and popular opinions change over time, as has been the case with the antidepressant drug known by its trade name, Prozac.[50] A psychiatrist interviewed and gathered information systematically in the 1970s from ninety-five American men, "a narrow spectrum of the population," thirty-five years after they had been initially examined as college students. They had employed eighteen different adaptive mechanisms to resolve or try to resolve their problems in the interim. The eighteen he divided into four different "levels." The first three are the following, with two of the mechanisms illustrating each: psychotic (denial of external reality, delusional projection), immature (projection, hypochondriasis), neurotic (repression, displacement). The fourth is called "mature" and is said to be "common in 'healthy' adults" and consists in his words of:

1. Altruism: Vicarious but constructive and instinctively gratifying to others.
2. Humor: Overt expression of ideas and feelings without individual discomfort or immobilization and without unpleasant effect on others.
3. Suppression: The conscious or semiconscious decision to postpone paying attention to a conscious impulse or conflict.
4. Anticipation: Realistic anticipation of or planning for future or inner discomfort.
5. Sublimation: Indirect or attenuated expression of instincts without either adverse consequences or marked loss of pleasure.[51]

Confusion may result from the fact that psychiatrists and others concerned professionally with mental health use different concepts and express themselves differently when they pursue their objectives. Compare the above five criteria of maturity with a report of an American "Joint Commission of Mental Illness and Health" which once proposed that "mental health is an individual and personal matter" and "is one of many human values; it should not be regarded as the ultimate good in itself."

Mental health may be "positive" with respect to one of six "major categories": attitude toward the self; degree of growth and self-actualization; integrating those two factors; autonomy; adequate perception of reality; or environmental mastery. The following pronouncement is thought to be "compatible" with all six: "an individual should be able to stand on his own feet without making undue demands or impositions on others."[52] Help then is required when such independence has not been attained or appears in jeopardy, at least in some Western societies.

Psychiatrists sometimes force themselves to admit, in the words of one of them who is both sensible and experienced, that "although proponents of every method offer persuasive reports of their successes, extensive and persistent research efforts have failed to produce conclusive evidence that any form of interview therapy with neurotics or schizophrenics is more helpful than a simple helping relationship."[53] A failure may occur, according to another psychiatrist, when "the positive gains made in any one therapeutic setting often are not generalized to other settings and systems in which the patient is involved."[54] That trite but profound insight comes from a book in which the advantages of play therapy for children are lauded and impressively documented; yet some children under conditions often difficult to specify do not benefit from play. Again and again instances are reported in which each child reacts beneficially if somewhat differently to help from others. A therapeutic or psychiatric technique must be adapted to the person at hand even when its broad outlines, as in psychoanalysis, are depicted in advance. For most persons, stress is said to be related to anxiety, depression, coping, "critical life events," lack of social support, and a host of other unpleasant experiences[55]; among the "elderly" it may be experienced after the death of a spouse, a serious disease of a "close person," conflicts, or even an eating problem.[56]

Uncertainty and disagreements among psychiatrists, however, do not lead to the negativistic conclusion that their discipline is useless or unreliable as a source of self-help. Evidence of the assistance they have offered to particular persons is overwhelming. One does not shun physicians because sometimes their diagnoses and prognoses are wrong and because they cannot cure all ailments. Psychiatric assistance, however, may be avoided for less lofty reasons. Individuals cannot afford the fees psychiatrists charge. Psychiatrists may not be available in the community. Seeking professional guidance from others may be viewed as humiliating or an admission of weakness that the consultant is disaster-prone or unable to solve his or her own personal problems. Resorting to drugs or alcohol is easier than finding a psychiatrist or some other person and may bring instant, if temporary, relief. The presence of professional and informal helpers throughout the ages in many societies reflects individuals' need for assistance from those who have prestige or are close at hand. In the United States, so-called "positive thinkers"—Henry Ford, Dale Carnegie, Norman Vincent Peale—have been more or less accessible, and painlessly or almost painlessly they have helped their audiences allegedly achieve "health and wealth."[57] And more recently the Internet offers pseudo-psychiatric help, whether it be valid, commonsensical, or commercially motivated.

Whether seeking and obtaining help from others when distressed is praiseworthy or effective, the conclusion must be, depends on the value thus obtained. The self may need the skill of a psychiatrist to be happier or of a physician to recover from an illness, that of a friend to enjoy a hike in the woods, that of a colleague to rob a bank, or that of a sophisticated person to commit suicide. The help may or may not achieve a value for the self.

It would be naively misleading to conclude this section on help from others without also suggesting again that the help being sought may be not a function of almost pathological distress but may have benefits for both parties. Two persons are lonely or in love; they "help" one another by means of what is euphemistically and occasionally called an affair or they marry. One scholar seeks out a colleague in another discipline to investigate a scientific problem; their ensuing collaboration turns out to be productive for them both and for their disciplines. Or you want to play a game or engage in some sport, and you find others eager or at least willing to participate. Such help is available to almost every person and in every society, and so "progress," however defined and minute, occurs.

HELPING OTHERS

Voluntarily or not, help is frequently extended to others as a result of the obvious and indisputable fact that contact between human beings is inevitable. During the contacts, some persons help others who in turn also anticipate, request, or demand help. The help includes almost all actions of which people are capable, ranging from providing cheer or entertainment to providing intellectual, financial, or practical assistance. The concern for others follows a direct perception of their needs, or it may be communicated by peers, by any of the media of communication, and by a self who is being helped by cooperating with others.

Helping those others may be involuntary when the motive is other than the ensuing assistance. A universal example of such help is parenting that begins with conception induced sexually and not always by a desire to produce offspring. Then after the actual birth and sometimes extending to their children's adulthood, parents function as models and thus, deliberately or not, offer help to their own future generation. They may not know precisely the goal they help children achieve: do I want him to pursue a career different from mine, do I want her to have a profession of her own and to be more than a housewife, should I leave the choice up to them? Parents may change their plans and action as children acquire knowledge and goals of their own. And they may be uncertain how and when to convey certain information, such as the idea of death, with or without help from some established doctrine in religion or biology.[58]

The motive to help may be quite "unselfish" when helpers believe—truthfully or not—that their actions spring from an altruistic motive to spread joy, to aid someone in need, or to give expression sincerely to moral or religious principles. On the other hand, the helping motive may be only incidental to the helper's "ability to get someone to carry out one's will despite resistance on their part"[59]—exerting power over a beneficiary—or to a recipient's desire not to be helped but to demonstrate a willingness to submit to another person. More than a touch of power seeking is to be found in many diverse persons such as witches, educators, hypnotists, therapists, clergymen, advertisers, drug peddlers, and even fairy godmothers. Power then means social control, the very idea of which may produce moral twitching when it is believed broadly that "freedom is the antithesis of control" and therefore warnings appear such as:

> In a complex society, where many kinds of individual regulation are unavoidable, and where social responsibility of some kind must be advocated as a positive value, it is easy even for lovers of freedom to forget that the idea of responsible freedom is a contradiction in terms and that the ultimate doctrine of social responsibility is "statism," a form of slavery, politically expressed in government by tyranny.[60]

A primary motive for helping others may thus be to help the self who is the helper. Candidates during political campaigns and advertisers in the mass media of the West seek actions ostensibly to assist or benefit their audiences, but obviously they also benefit from being elected or increasing their sales or patronage. Evidence for selfishness is easy, too easy perhaps, to come by. Decades ago one of the first efforts to evaluate the "effects" of the mass media was made by consulting scholars as well as the public opinions of notable communicators such as the propaganda minister in Nazi Germany. Generally, it was unsensationally concluded, those media function in conjunction with other "mediating factors and influences." Also they operate by "creating opinions on new issues" and affect "moods" in their audiences directly, or they initially influence the "elite" such as editors of newspapers when they advocate changes in values. In addition, they reinforce or change "attitudes on specific issues."[61] Not on its jacket but capitalized on the first page of another book appears the following sentence: "By fasting 2 days out of 7, the life of a mouse can be prolonged 50 or 60 percent." The book itself was part of a series on science and written seriously and competently by a medical gerontologist.[62] The sentence was snatched from a scholarly investigation. Did, would such a communication really promote dieting? Individuals may receive, interpret, and believe the statement and perhaps, perhaps, perhaps change their own eating habits. It is probably useful for parents and others at least to know or to guess, as indicated in yet another scholarly publication, that play, however operationally defined, and the heavily advertised toys and gadgets may possibly have educational, interpersonal, and therapeutic value for children experiencing minor or major problems or traumas.[63]

To be genuine or effectively helpful, the helper must possess at least some valid and relevant knowledge concerning the beneficiaries. In the words of a psychologist, a primary prerequisite is to have a "tolerance for diversity" and also not to employ others as "scapegoats" for one's own defects.[64] What is "good" for you may not be "good" for them; what you consider "good," they may consider "bad." Meliorists keep searching for ways to satisfy both you and them without abundant sacrifices or compromises. Helpers may run a risk when they consider their own values more compelling than those of beneficiaries: they are acting, they believe, for the good of others; but suppose those others don't agree? Helpers become especially self-confident when they believe or know their value is supported by "truth" or science. Are you helping other persons when you tell them the number 13 is not unlucky or that eating onions or some herb will not diminish the chances of ever being plagued by cancer? You may be "objectively" correct, but the recipients may be deriving real satisfaction from their erroneous beliefs. Non-Western people may be happier without scientific knowledge. Ah yes, but will they die sooner?

A helper's knowledge may come, deliberately or not, from many sources. Groups in which individuals participate or act may reveal their goals or values. Members of so-called "interactive groups" obtain information about one another, and, if the interaction persists over time, they may also "create opportunities to use a vocabulary that directs and controls problem-solving behavior."[65] Such groups, however, may be devoted to cooperation or competition, so that their values must be weighed before being accepted or rejected. It was once noted that the American Peace Corps "clearly" strengthens "the same ethical and humane impulses in men and women on which missionary movements for centuries have been built"[66]; if true, is the Corps tapping the same impulses in recruiting volunteers? Variables that can have dramatic effects on human beings and their actions, such as climate and economic conditions, may provide valuable information about their differences without, however, also precluding the possibility of uniformity; whether the weather is hot or cold, whether prosperity or a depression reigns, individuals so affected continue to derive satisfaction from achieving a goal or recovering from an illness.

Pollsters acquire knowledge about other persons which they subsequently communicate as a service to a general or special public or to sponsors or clients who use the information to promote their own political, commercial, or ideological objectives. Less formal but more restricted detailed information is obtained from face-to-face conversations or casual interviews in which the informants, with or without probing, reveal information that can be utilized later to affect them.

Helpers are likely to note, before, during, and after rendering help, whether the beneficiary will be, is, or has been helped by their assistance. Here, if ever, are diverse possibilities ranging from sincere or feigned gratitude to passing or enduring resentment. Resentment? Yes, receiving benefits from others may signify the loss of initiative or of self-respect. Individuals may feel alienated, it has been suggested by a psychologist, when "the prerogative for decision making is expropriated by others and they have little control over their own actions or outcomes."[67] Again that smiling baby does not feel alienated, but persons in a self-proclaiming society like the United States wish to believe they themselves are responsible at least somewhat for their joys and that they ought to be able to avoid at least some sorrows. Satisfaction from being helped may also be tempered by adults who then imagine or know they must eventually reciprocate and somehow help or please their benefactor.

Physicians in all modern and other societies serve or are supposed to serve the function of helping others obtain temporary or permanent relief from ailments or illnesses. Cast aside the fact that they themselves earn a living from their profession and that on occasion, if rarely, they promulgate a favorite technique to attract patients and increase their own revenue. Instead respectfully consider some of the moral challenges that confront the medical profession. Physicians conduct inquiries to determine the problem or ailment as perceived by their patients and/or to supplement what they can learn from their own impressions and objective measurements such as temperature, blood pressure, and bodily fluids. Aspects of this knowledge may not or cannot be communicated to untrained persons. Very extensively in the West physicians themselves follow rules prescribed in the Hippocratic Oath to which they symbolically subscribe after completing their training and before beginning their medical practice; one modern, abridged version includes the following:

> ... into whatsoever house you shall enter, it shall be for the good of the sick to the utmost of your power, you holding yourselves far aloof from wrong, from corruption, from the tempting of others to vice ... that whatsoever you shall see or hear of the lives of men which is not fitting to be spoken, you will keep inviolably secret.[68]

In fact, although opposed to spreading information about patients "abroad" (the word used in another version), the oath does not prevent physicians from actually revealing details to patients' relatives and friends, without previously obtaining their "informed consent" as usually required, in order to relieve distress or speed recovery thereby or when the patients themselves are "incompetent" or unconscious and hence assistance from these other persons seems necessary.[69] Also "trust" in the physician, especially the psychiatrist, is essential for the healing process.

Additional extensions of the oath may be helpful but must be cautiously employed. Physicians and other investigators conceal information about their research from experimental and control subjects when the knowledge, they believe, can affect the participants' reactions and spoil the attempt to determine the effect of the factor being investigated; then after completing the study, both groups may be given truthful details about the experiment, including the need to have used a placebo or its equivalent for the control group. Physicians and clinics that sometimes advertise in the mass media to attract patients or customers promise confidentiality. Information may be withheld from patients when it is believed that it will affect their morale adversely, damage or lessen their chances for recovery, or cause them to refuse or avoid a therapy that appears too painful or expensive.

A thorny problem confronting physicians and the rest of us arises from the fact that eventually all persons die. More again on death, hasn't enough been said about death in previous pages of this book? The response to this interruption must be: no, there is always more to say, and no response is ever sufficient. Continue, then: death at some point or always is feared but perhaps not when individuals are convinced through religion or traditional lore that an afterlife of varying bliss is to be anticipated in specified circumstances. The need for action to cope with actual dying is suggested by the title of two of the numerous books on the subject: *The Loneliness of Dying* and *To Die with Style*.[70] But what actions are physicians to take when patients do not know that their death is imminent but who, according to the best available evidence (perhaps confirmed by other qualified persons), know that they have an incurable disease and consequently will die? Are such persons helped by withholding the dreaded expectation, or should they be told the truth so that they can make plans for their loved ones and perhaps even prepare themselves for the end? One sensitive American physician has been confronted with these questions many times; she tries to anticipate patients' reactions to the prognosis of dying. For her the significant question is not "Do I tell my patient?" but "How do I share this knowledge" with him or her? Patients may be reassured that "everything possible will be done, that they will not be 'dropped,' " and that with available treatments there remains a "glimpse of hope—even in the most advanced cases."[71] A gifted surgeon and author of a notable book on death notes the "clearly defined limits to life" and that "dying is a messy business." Regarding help, he agrees with the other physician cited above: "I have always assured my dying patients that I would do everything possible to give them an easy death, but I have too often seen even that hope dashed in spite of everything I try."[72]

Especially challenging and baffling are both the similar and different problems posed by physician-assisted suicide. For the physician and anyone else assisting a patient or any other person to commit suicide, a series of questions must be posed.[73] Does the patient wish to die or claim to be suffering physical or "mental" pain from which he or she and/or the physician believes significant alleviation or recovery is probably or certainly impossible? Does the physician suppose that medical advances including new drugs are or are not likely to be available sufficiently soon to be of assistance? Does the therapist or the helper consult, respectively, other qualified persons to verify the patient's or his own diagnosis? Is the patient's wish to die a momentary impulse or one persisting over time? A written statement from the patient concerning the wish to die may remove some of the moral responsibility from helpers; yet how can one be certain that the individual has been in a "reasonable" or "normal" mood when issuing that statement?

Then there is euthanasia, the "easy" death, induced by another person. Under certain conditions the patient is allowed to die without at the moment providing his or her assent. Death is hastened and eventually occurs by removing some or all medical or other support. Commandment 6 in the

Old Testament (Exodus 20:1–17; "Thou shalt not kill") and its equivalent in many other treasured treatises issue a clear-cut warning that cannot be unheeded, especially when the patient, being unconscious or in dire pain, is unable to provide consent. By means of a "living will," however, an individual may previously grant permission to a physician or a trusted friend to facilitate death under specified conditions if and when he or she is unable to give consent and/or is unconscious, or likewise when and if some or all of the conditions mentioned above in connection with physician-assisted suicide have been satisfied. Euthanasia as well as any form of assisted suicide raise such challenging ethical questions that in some countries and in some American states the practice has been declared illegal. In any case, the physician or any helper who has succeeded in facilitating another person's death may or may not feel guilty or courageous for having played that challenging role.

Illness or consent aside, deliberately killing another human being, in almost all circumstances, also raises similar doubts. Enemies are shot or bombarded in wars, and the action is thought to be "just" or necessary by the slayers and others in their society. Strict pacifists, however, disagree: all killing is "bad." Otherwise in civil society those who kill another person may be executed, if legally permitted, or severely punished in part to prevent them from repeating the crime, to punish them for what they have done, and also to help others in the society feel more secure in the belief that they themselves may feel safer by believing that such deterrence actually functions to deter similar crimes in the future. Executions and severe punishments usually but not always occur when it is believed that the criminal has been given a "fair" trial; that he or she has been following self-centered interests in committing the crime, was not "insane," and was not incompetent in other respects as a result of low intelligence, age, or drugs. Even then the conviction must be made by the individual's "peers," and "reasonable" doubts concerning his or her guilt are supposed to be absent; thus providing gratifying revenge to relatives or friends of the victim is allegedly irrelevant and seldom even mentioned. Their reluctance to kill deliberately is also suggested by most persons' unwillingness usually even to view a real or fictional killing. In fact, only certain persons may be permitted or required to witness legal executions of a convicted criminal whose actual death, at least in Western societies, is rendered somewhat humane at the very end by extinguishing the individual's life rapidly and hence pain is continued only briefly. In the mass slaughter of wars, the enemy is dehumanized or deindividualized, as has been noted,[74] so that a good part of the time bombs and bullets appear to be directed against symbols and not against human beings, even those in an out-group.

Thus emerges a guide provided by this chapter: numerous are the actions individuals can take to improve themselves and many but not all others nearby or in their society, but killing is usually abhorrent, rationalized, or disguised.

CHAPTER 9

Societal Actions

A vague term like society is often evaluated as the source of happiness or unhappiness. Individuals praise some of the regulations that control them and condemn others that they say must be changed. Probably no society has ever been considered perfect by all its citizens; actions in behalf of "progress" or perfection are considered desirable and deliberately performed. Symptomatic of the need for change and action is the long series of utopias described by Plato and then later, for example, by H. G. Wells.[1] If only we could change what we have and convert imaginary societies into reality, perfection might be closer.

Meliorists remind themselves and others that social actions come not from a great, impersonal force designated as "society," "government," or a strange if unknown organization but from particular persons in such groups who plan and carry out the action. A "happy society" is a careless figure of speech; it must mean that the self, specified others, ancestors, or descendants have been, are, or will be happy. Societal actions face the same challenges as individual actions outlined in the last chapter, only usually more so as a result of the larger number of participants and beneficiaries. Nevertheless, it is often useful and necessary to plan or analyze actions in societal terms. Leaders or organizers of political campaigns, of companies that seek to increase sales or memberships, of associations that promote health or safety, and of schools and universities that would increase knowledge of any kind would affect some or many members of the relevant group for which their efforts are directed without necessarily caring or paying close attention to the particular persons being influenced therein.

Aside from eternal questions concerning the origin and purpose of life anywhere, another obvious, puzzling challenge involves the movements of the visible, ever-changing universe. Differences between day and night, the four seasons, and the visibility of stars and planets "up there" are ever perceived and then perhaps questioned by everyone whose senses function. Over the ages, means have been devised to note the passing of immediate time (watches, clocks, bells), the changing of the seasons (calendars, holidays, possibly Stonehenge in England), and the nature of outer space (telescopes, space stations with or without persons aboard). Originally the devices or sections thereof were inspired and created by individuals alone or in groups, but now they and the information and knowledge they provide are available to everyone in society.

Social actions occur or should occur when solutions to problems seem necessary. Research in the United States once revealed that minority groups, such as blacks and Mexican-Americans, more vulnerable though they may have been to disasters resulting from transportation of hazardous materials and the storage of nuclear wastes, were less likely than whites or the more affluent to seek and respond to warnings concerning disasters from such materials as well as from floods; their status and previous experience were said to induce them to be willing and able to endure greater risks.[2] Also it has been shown that a very small sample of Americans living in Alabama, where the death rate from tornadoes had been high, tended to be less attentive to such threats and generally to weather forecasts and to be less confident concerning their overall destiny than another equally small sample in Illinois where the natural disaster rate actually was much lower.[3] In these and other situations, individuals alone cannot plan and achieve complete solutions to punishing problems, although they may contribute their bits; social actions are required or are inescapable.

"NATURE" AND ENVIRONMENT

The quotation marks around "nature" suggest that the concept is often employed, romantically or not, as a synonym for some but not all environmental conditions affecting people. "Nature demands that . . ." "This is contrary to nature . . ." "We must respect nature." No matter how the natural referent is designated, the obvious assumption is that actions of human beings are influencing and are influenced by some aspect of the physical and social environment. Obvious? Yes, quite obvious when the broadly defined persons (their feelings or behavior) are affected by the area in which they live. And it is likewise similarly obvious, whether the environment is viewed as climate or weather, housing or clothing, politics or religion. Clearly we depend on "nature" for food and joy. Also the same all-embracing "nature" is affected by human beings who live on the planet and hence encourage or discourage certain animals from surviving and who decide to extract lumber from forests or allow trees, plants, animals, and microorganisms to interact and survive or perish.

It has been and remains tempting to become sentimental about the environment whenever the concept is "Mother Nature" and when her attributes are extolled: "she," the dear lady, nourishes and clothes us, she bestows bracing and stimulating weather that we enjoy, her attributes are beautiful and inviting to behold when unperturbed by Man or Woman. For the many reared in the Judeo-Christian tradition the metaphor of trees in Genesis, the first book of the Old Testament, may be dimly or vividly recalled and assigned a most venerable role in human existence:

> And the Lord God commanded the man [Adam], saying, Of every tree of the garden [of Eden] thou mayest freely eat;
> But of the tree of the knowledge of good and evil, thou shalt not eat of it; for in the day that thou eatest thereof thou shalt surely die.

Eve, after being created from a rib of Adam, repeated God's warning to the inquiring serpent:

> And the serpent said unto the woman, Ye shall not surely die; For God doth know that in the day ye eat thereof, then your eyes shall be opened, and ye shall be as gods, knowing good and evil.
> And when the woman saw that tree *was* good for food, and that it *was* pleasant to the eyes, and a tree to be desired to make *one* wise, she took of the fruit thereof, and did eat; and gave also unto her husband with her; and he did eat.

Eventually the Lord found Adam and Eve and learned of their disobedience:

> And the Lord God said, Behold, the man is become as one of us, to know good and evil; and now, lest he put forth his hand, and take also of the tree of life, and eat, and live forever;
> Therefore the Lord God sent him forth from the garden of Eden, to till the ground from whence he was taken.[4]

Even as trees in Eden contributed both positively and negatively to human existence, so the environment as a whole may be evaluated. A Polish sociologist has stated quite recently that "nature may be looked upon as an alien, threatening external world which must be subjected to human manipulation, control, and conquest" or "as a valuable good in its own right, an indispensable milieu of human life, which should be preserved and cultivated, existing in full harmony with human beings."[5] Likewise the venerable Adam Smith showed concern for human beings as they subdued their environments. In the third paragraph of his influential *Wealth of Nations*, he proclaimed without reservation and ethnocentrically: "Whatever be the soil, climate, or extent of territory of any particular nation, the abundance or scantness of its annual supply must . . . depend upon" the following "circumstances": "the skill, dexterity, and judgment with which its labour is generally applied" and "the proportion between those who are employed in useful labour, and that of those who are not so employed."[6] An unimportant incident can illustrate "environmental ethics." A large hole was once cut through the center of a giant sequoia tree in California to amuse tourists who could drive through the artificial aperture. After the tree was blown down during a storm, some not so demure Americans cried out to "cut us another drive-through sequoia." The reply of those with ethical feelings about nature could have been, "No. You ought not to mutilate majestic sequoias for amusement. Respect their life."[7] Such respect, it often is said, should be extended to all living matter, meaning animals and plants, and priority must not be given to only one species, human beings.

Environmental and human factors interact. American physicians with clinical experience in various countries once indicated the numerous man- or woman-made conditions that do or can affect "human health" adversely. The conditions include some probably recognized almost everywhere: polluted drinking water, contaminated food, the devastation of war. Others have come to be gradually noted: possible occupational hazards, nuclear radiation, depletion of the ozone layer, changes in population size and composition over long periods of time. Less known or publicized perhaps are possible consequences from the loss of endangered species of plants and animals and also of microbes from which beneficial physical and medical products might eventually be obtained and also on the basis of which biological principles have been, will be, and could be learned and improved.[8]

Above all, according to one philosopher, "before one pontificates how human beings ought to behave toward other human beings, or how they ought to flourish, one should at least have some understanding of how the world of Nature works and the roles human agency plays, both as constituent of that world and as a potential bringer of change to it, through our intervention in the way it works."[9] If individuals are to "flourish" and achieve their values and especially those leading close to what may be considered perfection, they must adapt themselves somehow to an existing environment and, yes, also to "nature" with or without those quotation marks. They cannot abolish seasonal fluctuations, they dare not exhaust mineral and other resources on which they partially depend, they must devise or invent new ways to survive. The potentialities and variations of some immediate surroundings perforce are directly and inevitably appreciated—for example, the rising and setting of the sun—and other natural phenomena beyond the immediate senses are or can also be anticipated. All persons are not biochemists or conservationists, but they can learn enough about the physical environment to be cautious; they recognize that they may err and that in the future improved knowledge may enable them to utilize some natural resources now disdained.

Let a final prayer come from a distinguished architect and planner who once began his long and undocumented "loose and yet linked cycle of writ · ings collected over almost a lifetime" with a preface declaring that "the designing of structures, if we take it 'not in the abstract,' concerns, above all, labor for human beings and with them." And the first sentence of his text suggested that "nature has too long been outraged by design of nose rings, corsets, and foul-aired subways." Throughout the book the reader can stumble upon or be inspired by statements like these: "Irregularity is a space in the Platonic dish"; "Habits interconnect into a tough network"; "No personality is so plastic that it can learn and again unlearn things in a crazily checkered row"; "Design, never a harmless play with forms and colors, changes outer life as well as our inner balances."[10] Well-trained, skillful meliorists may smile when confronted with these assertions and consider them the relaxed thoughts of a gifted man who designed dwellings, buildings, college campuses, community centers, and other structures, but the contentions are real and compelling when combined with specific plans to utilize, yet protect the environment (G3). Thus the design of the locations where children live, play, attend schools, and hence are socialized, raises challenges for political leaders, parents, and likewise architects. A report on four urban areas including those in Argentina and Australia once indicated, among other findings, the extent to which children "are able to do what they propose to do; how their activities are interrupted or blocked, how they adapt and 'make do,' what conflicts arise, what environmental dangers and discomforts they endure, what they have access to."[11] Here the reach is not to utopia and beyond one's grasp but to the everyday lives of children during critical ages. Adults as well as children, moreover, can derive joy and wisdom from the music, drama, poetry, novels, and all forms of

art that, though not a part of "nature," exist or subsist generally or informally in surrounding environments.

A very competent forester and planner once suggested that for a well-
grounded life, many, maybe most, persons should and must have access to
three kinds of environments to which he gave the self-evident, appropriate
labels of primeval, rural, and urban.[12] In fact, he had no systematic basis for
this appealing classification and assertion other than his own sensitive intuition and the unreflective consent among his personal friends and associates, including the present writer. Immediately to be noted in evaluating
this contention is the growth of cities throughout the world and of suburbs
in Western countries, the decline of the rural areas in which crops are
grown, and the encroachment of wilderness areas or "nature" and especially forests by those suburbs. In addition, many persons do not have or do
not wish to have access to wildernesses. May planners advocate actions
contrary to trends and the wisdom of various individuals? Is their task, in
the words of our primeval-rural-urban friend, that of "the remodeling of an
unshapen and cacophonous environment into a humanized and well-
ordered one"?[13]

An aspect of wilderness and nature is the wildlife therein. Over the years
human "dependence" on wild animals, principally for food, has varied. In
the present, Americans' attitudes toward animals have included values
such as strong feelings for pets and concern for their welfare, satisfaction
from hunting them, and simple appreciation of their appearance and habits. Whether animals belong in one's general philosophy has also varied, although they have recently been included when efforts are made to regulate
or protect all of existence.[14] Among reasons vegetarians exclude meat from
their diets is that animals, unlike plants generally, are presumably sentient
beings and should not be raised, often inhumanely, and then slaughtered
for human-centered purposes.

Like responses to nature, other problems in this chapter are outlined in
three stages: factors instigating action, followed by planning and sometimes ending in action. These stages are especially important to note when
"society" is the actor. If, as previously emphasized, society from a melioristic
standpoint is considered to be only a convenient but ambiguous abstrac-
tion to refer to persons in a neighborhood, town, city, or country, or on the
entire planet, the identity of those who do or should act is either known or,
when not known, can be ascertained or somehow assumed. Then evidence
is sought to determine whether those so identified also identify themselves
with the posited group. You wish to help your self; you wish to help your
family; you wish to help your neighbor; you wish to help your neighbor-

hood; you wish to help your community; and eventually you would help faraway peoples you have never met. Meliorists recognize the interdependence of people in many if not all social situations: their actions do not affect everyone, yet ultimately what they do may have repercussions on an unanticipated number of other persons.

INSTIGATION

The initial step regarding action in or for a society is to discover whether there exists a need for change and, if so, what kind of change seems promising and possible (G6). A perplexing challenge is to note whether an aspect of a cultural heritage appears faulty. That heritage is usually transmitted and acquired unwittingly without a clear-cut realization of its implication for everyday thought and action. We must be good citizens, we must love our country; but do these beliefs and values mean that we should support the foreign policies of government or that we should enthusiastically and uncritically cooperate with leaders when they propose higher taxes or declare war? "The breaking of a family through divorce or desertion" seems to have been "an area of greater moral sensitivity a century ago than in our own time,"[15] so that with a change of general attitudes, at least in the West, divorce and desertion rates have increased. The decision by some persons to disrupt a family may have become less difficult when or if some additional change is sought.

How far into the future must and can we look to determine a course of action? Consider not quickly but slowly and thoroughly the following sufficiently well-documented statement: "it is just now becoming conceivable that within several generations the human species may face threats to its survival because of its disruption of Earth's life-supporting ecosystems."[16] Do we as a species really wish to survive? You and I obviously do and will; but our distant descendants? Both individuals and government agencies may be inspired at the moment, but only at the moment, to act in behalf of us and endangered plants and animals; are such actions sufficiently farsighted?

Some, maybe only a few, persons recognize that ordinary, even mundane actions of the self and others may require change for the benefit of the society more or less as a whole through minor or major sacrifices by themselves or others. Thus it may be tempting to place a higher value on the convenience than on the consequences of actions. Is it dreadful to waste a trivial amount of electricity when one is preoccupied and forgets to turn off the light in an unoccupied room? Patient investigation may be necessary to determine whether the manufacture of this or that product creates more environmental pollution. Also, is consideration given to the working conditions and the overall treatment of those who manufacture very similar products; are some of the profits of one company and not of the other donated to help the unfortunate? Whew, how deep must or can one go?

Without preaching, meliorists explore the ultimate consequences of social actions. By encouraging the spread of Western education in developing or non-Western societies, the children there allegedly become better equipped to deal with their own problems, to have access to the cultural and other achievements of distant lands, and eventually to find satisfactory and satisfying positions in their own society. But those desirable positions are more likely to be reserved for the well-educated and not for the children of the poor or dispossessed whose parents cannot afford or are less aware of the benefits therefrom. Increasing or "improving" such education for the few, therefore, may not lead to "advantages" for the great majority of people and may result in instability within the society. Should "higher" education be restricted to the few?

Recognizing that a value is being abused does not necessarily lead to advocating a remedial change. In ancient times some Greeks who owned slaves spent "time discussing with great intellectual freedom" and with "fellow slaveowners whether slavery is or is not justified."[17] Similarly people may appreciate the demerits of their own beliefs and actions without changing them. Whether or not it is taboo legally or socially, however, a discussion may be the first step toward change, if only or because the discussants thus may become aware of the inconsistency of not practicing what they preach. Recognition may or may not lead to action that effectively solves or resolves the problem at hand. Examples of failed actions are so numerous that no illustration, including the one about to be mentioned, can be called typical. During the last century, disenchantment with current society sometimes led to the establishment of so-called utopian communities. Groups of Americans removed themselves from everyday life and created their own "society" in which the inhabitants of some of these communes also "abstained from alcoholic consumption and even sexual activity."[18] While there the utopianists may have remained converted and enthusiastic, but eventually and often relatively quickly the communities perished. The good people could not remain isolated from a "normal" society, and their own needs did not appear to be satisfactorily fulfilled in their brave, new, impractical worlds.

Once again the challenge of death either in an immediate or ultimate sense is especially difficult or impossible to meet. In the United States, so-called experts have indicated various interventions available to reduce the incidence of suicide among younger persons: restricting access to firearms, medications, and areas where suicide is tempting; identifying "high-risk youths"; improving treatment and the use of "crisis center and hot lines"; "affective education" and "school-based screening."[19] Details of each action must be and even have been adapted to the young people at hand and to available facilities, yet obviously suicides continue. Within a society and an individual's own social groups, hope and consolation regarding death are offered by the clergy and by persons such as Socrates cited in the last chapter, so that the beliefs are transmitted impressively during socialization and more or less voluntarily adopted by adults. Another writer who, according to the jacket's blurb, has "served as a distinguished judge in the criminal courts of England and has written over 30 books," begins a new book by being "forthcoming": "I favour the death penalty for two reasons, firstly because it is far the most effective and dreadful deterrent to all murder, and secondly because . . ."[20] Should one read on and discover the second reason, should one read this book or any of the judge's previous books? The reply, nevertheless, must be affirmative if for some good reason the evidence and arguments therein are to be evaluated; otherwise they are rejected only on the basis of personal bias, which of course you and meliorists never, never do.

In many situations the instigation to produce and realize change exists, but the precise goal remains unclear or uncertain. An especially challenging problem of late is the overall direction in which societies everywhere on the globe are heading: are they leaning toward unification or diversity? The elusive facts at hand lead in either direction. The English language as the lingua franca is almost everywhere useful, while speakers of indigenous languages continue to utilize and treasure the nuances of their native tongues. The unknowables that all religions seek to fathom are explained differently by the major religions of Christianity and Islam. Everywhere people seek "modern" ways to cope with the environment, the economy, health, and happiness, but the "core elements" of their cultures remain and are treasured. A so-called "world community" has its advantages and disadvantages, its advocates and opponents.[21] Everlasting solutions and salvation will not come in this or any other generation; trials-and-errors, and especially errors-and-trials, remain and can inspire advocates of change only to keep trying while remaining puzzled.

PLANNING

After recognizing and advocating the need for change, some planning is required to designate subsequent action. Again challenges are overwhelmingly numerous. Certainly eugenic programs are to be encouraged, especially in combating ostensibly genetic diseases and psychiatric disabilities. But are there plans to prevent persons with such tendencies, genetic or otherwise, from "breeding"; actually how can anyone be forced to be continent or—whether male or female—to use contraceptive devices? In another sphere, most persons on the planet may agree that the violence involved in many actions, ranging from rape to war, is to be avoided, indeed "the atmosphere of violence is not only immensely destructive to many individuals and communities, but is also brutalizing and alienating many vulnerable young people, citizens of the future."[22] Perhaps sports like boxing and football (soccer) are to be encouraged in which violence during a contest is desirable and essential but regulated by rules enforced by referees and umpires. Still, are the participants or even the spectators consequently more or less aggressive in their normal lives: or rather are aggressive persons initially attracted to such competitive activities? Planning by governments specifies police and courts that would settle disputes and conflicts before violence results, but how and when can they be more effective?

More generally, established laws and customs indicate the nature of some conflicts and ways to settle them. Certain individuals—police, attorneys, judges, clergy, arbitrators—are designated or designate themselves to aid clients in settling disputes in a manner favorable to themselves and their point of view.[23] Alas, it is too easy to assume that arresting young persons guilty of crimes, trying them before a justice or in a court, determining the damage they cause, and then punishing those "fairly" found guilty reduce or eliminate criminal activity in the future by them or by others. Studies examining this wishful sequence, however, indicate that "subsequent offending" does not necessarily decline.[24] After being released, convicted individuals may be "free" again to be homeless or unemployed, and to suffer a discrimination that had originally led to their criminal actions.

Information about the relation of the quality of life or happiness as ascertained in surveys to other variables can or must be cautiously utilized in planning. It may be important to be reminded, as was once determined in a nonrandom sample of Americans, that their evaluation of the "overall quality" of life for themselves as well as their "enjoyment of life," successes, and self-evaluation were influenced by what they reported concerning their depressions, anxiety, stress, internal control, control by others, and overall performance. In statistical terms the correlation varied from strong to "modest."[25] Conceivably meliorists might thus obtain a preliminary guide to therapeutic actions: try to remove or help remove reasons for feeling depressed, anxious, and all the rest. Another report in the same scholarly tradition, however, suggests that immediate inferences from demographic or survey data to society may be perilous. Intuitively it could be reasonable to believe that countries with a high gross national product or with sufficient general satisfaction as reported in polls would have a relatively low suicide rate: secure or happy people do not take their own lives. Actual data once indicated that, among eighteen modern countries, Finland and Denmark had the highest suicide rates, and Italy and Greece were among the lowest. Denmark received the highest rating for "satisfaction with one's life as a whole," Finland also had a high if slightly lower rating, whereas Italy and Greece reported the lowest rating in this respect. These contradictions, the investigators feel, were not due to differences in the connotations of the words employed in the survey; thus the findings were similar in the three areas of Switzerland that have different languages and also in both sections of Belgium predominantly Flemish and French. Possibly countries differ in their permissibility to "express unhappiness and dissatisfaction with one's life."[26] In yet another survey, no relation was once found between the reported well-being of American blacks and various socioeconomic factors; rather, general living arrangements and interpersonal relations were the statistically significant variables. Since blacks have suffered discrimination, the authors question whether "subjective well-being measures" are useful as "social indicators of individual or group progress" among these Afro-Americans.[27]

Plans for action may seek to resolve conflicts between individuals or groups. At the outset of a detailed analysis of conflicts, readers are reminded that individuals experience conflicts within themselves when they must choose between alternatives, such as attractive offerings on a restaurant menu. Conflicts also occur when there is disagreement concerning the way to achieve a common goal typified by disputes between management and labor or between nations concerning only the precise location of their boundaries and not their overall sovereignty.[28] On a simpler level, shortages of water or electricity can be alleviated by increasing their supply or by inducing specific groups of persons to cease "wasting" them: which approach is more feasible or practical, should both approaches be employed? Answers to such questions require an assessment of relevant facts and opinion, which usually or eventually must be made by experts; but who are the experts—consumers, producers, or both?[29]

The procedure for achieving creative solutions may often not be fore-seen and hence cannot or may not be planned (G2). It is easier to raise sig-nificant but unresolved or unresolvable questions than to supply relevant replies. Should there be "no legal impediments to migration" from one country to another or, similarly, regulations regarding "the transfer of money" between countries?[30] Should specific groups with different objec-tives be regulated or controlled by a master plan, or is any master plan an obstacle to "freedom"? It has been noted "with dismay" that those demo-graphic factors (income, employment, "marriage and family") affected di-rectly by societal actions, and perhaps other attributes (gender, ethnicity) affected indirectly, in fact account for only a "small proportion of vari-ances" related to subjective well-being in a sample of Americans.[31]

Factories and automobiles, we now know, pollute the air, especially in urban areas. Such knowledge has been acquired and supplemented after recognizing the dangers from pollution; the new knowledge then has led to recommenda-tions concerning the actions to be taken by government and by individuals in order to diminish the hazard. The desire for fresh air is basic; the value of good health justifies the instigation to initiate new policies. Merely determining "the degree of well-being experienced by individuals or aggregates of people under prevailing social and economic conditions"[32] is important but only as a first step: expert knowledge is needed also to establish reasons for their well-being and for those less fortunate within the same society. The need must lead to action, some kind of remedial action. Potentially controllable factors re-lated to a plan, however, may not induce success to emerge.

Perforce the content of planned negotiations and interventions vary. The precise procedure may stem from prior agreements of the contending parties or be initiated by outsiders; in either case they believe that a peace-ful solution is possible and feasible. Participants from both sides of the con-flict come together and interact according to a formal or informal procedure on which they agree; eventually they may arrive at a solution or favor a proposal to achieve a solution. Unsettled and subject also to nego-tiation are many issues including the nature of the participants (officials and policymakers or laypersons who may have access to those in power); screening of those required or invited to participate in order possibly to avoid persons with self-seeking motives or likely to disrupt ongoing ses-sions; the number of sessions; the frequency of meetings; and overall public relations. Steps may be taken to prevent participants from perfunctorily agreeing with the interacting group at hand when in fact they also know that their decision will not be acceptable to leaders or the relevantly pow-erful persons. Members of the group may be encouraged to raise objections, "experts" may be invited to participate in some of the discussions, the entire group may occasionally be divided into subgroups, tentative decisions may be approved not immediately but at subsequent meetings at which members are encouraged to raise "residual doubts and to rethink the entire issue,"[33] and so on, on and on, because interactions cannot be neatly codified. Organizers of workshops are likely to be enthusiastic about particular ways through which in the past they attempted to solve problems, but as ever in actual practice there is no absolutely certain way to achieve the objectives at hand. Past experience in similar or even dissimilar situations, moreover, may even suggest that it is fruitless to intervene in a new crisis.

ASSESSMENT

Immediately or eventually social actions are assessed. Quite subjectively participants wish to glow with satisfaction after success or to ward off at least part of the gloom after failure. More important is the conviction that assessing the experience should or can be a guide for similar or even dissimilar problems in the future. And then the oft-repeated warning guide reappears: beware of ascribing a cause-and-effect explanation to the sequence of events following any program of action. This challenge begins on a simple level.[34] It was hot and muggy last Wednesday and—therefore?—all or most of the persons we met were disagreeable, at least unfriendly or not as cordial as usual; should "therefore" be inserted between the words "and" and "all" in that sentence? Most social actions face a similar challenge. During the late 1990s in the United States, efforts were made to reduce the number of crimes committed by juveniles or younger people. One action toward that end was to set a curfew, such as 11 at night, after which designated persons and their parents would be punished if the youths were on the street and not at home or at least inside somewhere. But obviously the crime rate also depended on socioeconomic and psychological factors other than the greater ease with which trivial or serious misdemeanors could be committed after dark.

In addition, quivers of doubt remain concerning the validity of social actions claimed to be motivated by eternal human values. Recommendations even from brilliant thinkers require similarly skeptical evaluation. H. G. Wells considered that "the almost world-wide insistence upon two legislative chambers [e.g., the Senate and the House of Representatives in the United States], devised to check and thwart each other" were in fact "superstitions" and often unfounded in practice[35]; all other institutions within a society can be similarly questioned before relevant action is taken. Do you agree with Wells?

Even a precise audit of past actions provides only a clue but not a certain recommendation for future actions. The general advantages and disadvantages of learning under competitive and cooperative conditions, especially in schools, may be carefully noted[36]; yet educators, parents, and citizens generally somehow decide which experiences in the past really affect children and themselves. Clearly, the most significant or vital challenge for action is that of education. In schools and thereafter individuals may learn not only that knowledge and values are likely to be imperfect but also that the limitations may be stimulating. You cannot be a versatile mathematician, yet you can appreciate that forecasting pleasant or dismal weather requires admirable persons who possess adequate knowledge. What you know and believe may originate and be reinforced by the language you have unwittingly learned as a child, but you can come to appreciate the possibility, the probability, that persons with other languages think and act differently. You break no records when in a sport you run from here to there, and either you are bored by chess or you have not learned to play the game; yet you respect, perhaps even praise, those who break racing records or who win chess games in international tournaments. You are not a genius, yet you accord real geniuses the respect and honor they merit, neither more nor less. Social action through education reveals and advocates such an appreciation of yourself and others. Educators thus have the responsibility to transmit both knowledge and values in some kind of meaningful if limited perspective (G4).

Planning and acting on the basis of historical analogies is risky and tempting. In 1938 Neville Chamberlain, the British prime minister, "chose to appease Adolf Hitler by acceding to Germany's demands for a chunk of Czechoslovakia"; later, then, counterfactual thinking suggested that "if Britain had confronted Hitler with the threat of war" at Munich, he would have "backed down" and not attacked Poland so that "World War II might have been avoided."[37] Eschewing another Munich, as Chamberlain's action came to be labeled, may have played a role in decisions by American policymakers regarding their country's intervention in North Korea's invasion of South Korea, in the Vietnam War, and in the fighting in Bosnia in the 1990s. Another counterfactual thought: suppose there had been no counterfactual analogy and the United States had not intervened?

As ever, that last rhetorical question is unanswerable. Unlike changes introduced by competent scientists, skillful technicians, and respected chefs, social actions cannot be definitively assessed. We can only pursue perfection in human affairs; nevertheless—and that adverb must be the appropriate title for the final chapter of this book.

PART IV

EPILOGUE

EPILOGUE

CHAPTER 10

Nevertheless

The pursuit of perfection occurs endlessly, then at some point an effort is made to try to assess its status. As the present effort hurries toward an end, such an appraisal is in order. Throughout these pages seven guides have sought to point the way. They offer reasons to be both somewhat discouraged and encouraged. Little cheer may be evoked by three of them—Imperfection, Searching, and Surprise—which point to uncertainty and hence imperfect perfection. Nevertheless, the existence and utility of these and other guides offered by the competent and the helpful imply the possibility of more successful pursuits now and later. A last, deliberately and necessarily brief chapter swings first to the less and then to the more encouraging clues to perfection.

Perhaps the worst blast comes from being reminded that appropriate actions may be elusive even when individuals are highly motivated and eager to act. A child does not receive the birthday gift he or she has anticipated and sought. It looks as if after all these years a marriage is cracking; how can reconciliation be achieved, is divorce possible or desirable? For the nth time in human experience—and also unabashedly in this book—the hazards of wars furnish the gravest illustration: can wars be prevented, can the tragic wastes involved in preparing for possible conflict with potential enemies somehow be decreased, mitigated, cease?

The selection of actions or of one action rather than another depends in part on the guiding principles of the participants; but available principles, as reviewed and appraised by competent scholars, may be too numerous, difficult, and hence impossible to evaluate.[1] Measures promoting international unity usually, at least at first glance, are praised beyond the heavens because it is believed that people having contact with one another are likely to achieve some mutual "understanding" and hence are less reluctant to go to war, to compete economically or culturally, or to threaten the quality of the other's environment. Is it desirable to have a United Europe or at least a common currency in many European or other countries? Should migrants from foreign lands, especially from Mexico and the Caribbean, be welcomed in the United States even as most of the ancestors of many American citizens from distant countries have been received? Whose happiness is promoted by internationalism, do only multinational corporations realize gains when they utilize workers abroad whose wages are lower than in the United States? When grain, fruit, meat, clothing, fixtures, and other products are exported from a country to reap the advantage of higher prices overseas, will the local population eventually or immediately have sufficient supplies for themselves? Does interest in and loyalty to an international organization symbolically diminish the warm, meaningful feelings resulting from actually participating in a community? Questions, questions, questions, but no definitive, everlasting answers because perfection is and must ever be pursued without being totally achieved.

When actions and principles are uncertain, individuals are unable to avoid some risk to achieve their objectives. That person knows he likes and then eats a particular food; the possibility of being displeased is minimal, yet in fact the tidbit at hand may be stale, contain traces of poison or too much cholesterol. Trivial, yes, and of course risks are greater for actions involving not only the self but also small or large groups of others. Two social scientists once indicated how American mass media reported almost three hundred hazardous activities involving some risk, beginning with natural disasters, including actions with benefits as well as costs (biking, swimming), and concluding with chronic and acute illnesses. The media, they demonstrate, usually tended to report newsworthy events and accidents without indicating adequately the risks, the responsible reasons for those risks, and ways to avoid or endure them for the sake of an alleged gain or delight in the future.[2]

After running a risk or expending energy to achieve a goal, participants may not appreciate accurately what they have accomplished. Thus consumers conscientiously recycle trash, allegedly for the good of the planet; they put aside paper, glass, and metals for that purpose. But what happens to those materials after they have been collected, are they actually recycled (G7)? Volunteers who help the unfortunate, the homeless, the ill, the drug-addicted, the lonely, or the maltreated may or may not accomplish their laudable objective as they themselves acquire a more sympathetic understanding of how their society malfunctions. In a very praiseworthy manner they are concentrating only on the victims and not on the underlying causes of their misery.[3]

Finally, it is usually both difficult and challenging to relate the attainment or nonattainment of an objective to some basic value such as happiness or the quality of life for the self, others, or society. You may believe and have evidence that one proposal or regulation increases individuals' wealth, that another provides jobs for some persons, and a third lowers taxes. Such judgments assume that wealth, jobs, and lower taxes are praiseworthy as such, which may be true within some frame of reference including yours and mine. The basic question, however, remains and requires an answer: is there greater happiness, has the quality of life been improved for whom? A platitude? No, let us produce happy children who then are a bit more likely, other conditions being equal as they never are, to grow up to be happy adults. But ever again: what is a happy person? And will not such a person eventually die, so that—so that what?

Nevertheless, in spite of such perpetual difficulties and challenges, there are overwhelming reasons to keep trying to improve "our lot," as human beings have always tried to do and still do. Look backwards for an infinite period of time, imagine how those ancestors of ours fought and negotiated to exchange food and services. Eventually number systems evolved so that there could be simple counting and later mathematics. Instead of depending completely on one's own memory, standardized sounds and other linguistic nuances developed so that with vocabularies and grammar communication between human beings improved without being perfected. The past and present could be preserved in conventionalized script; and musical notation became standardized.[4] The development continues with expanding computers and the Internet, which have increased the ready availability of knowledge if not also some confusion resulting from such easy access to the best and worst of that knowledge.

Nevertheless, differences remain and should remain if the gains from diversity are to be retained. Some international misunderstandings are avoidable, however, if only because as human beings we are all "basically" similar. Careful research, rather than guessing or resorting to dramatic or journalistic anecdotes, has punctured the view that the "primitive mentality" of traditional peoples differs markedly and importantly from so-called civilized people; the rejected view is now thought to have been derived "from weaknesses in both theory and empirical investigation." The cognitive processes of people living in "the bush" have been found to differ markedly from their own peers who have attended Western-type schools and from Westerners. It seems "unambiguous" that "schooling (and only schooling) contributes to the way in which people describe and explain their own mental operations."[5] Also, "localized changes in cognitive skills manifested in relatively esoteric experimental settings" may be affected by literacy anywhere.[6] All peoples, regardless of present culture and society, have had contact with Western ways in school. Differences, however evaluated, can thus be diminished or erased by education, although, fortunately or not, some persist within the same society. Even in the vaunted West, individuals with no special interest in colors may have difficulty in describing shades of colors for which artists and fashion experts have distinctive terms; and the terms distinguishing colors vary from society to society. Again education can rescue almost anyone from such an innocuous peculiarity.

Nevertheless, rays of hope and encouragement spring from apparent successes, however partial, even in international affairs. An American political scientist has surveyed the effects of economic and other aid provided to developing countries by the more powerful countries whose leaders have been motivated in part by "a sense of justice and compassion" and have therefore shown and expressed "concern for the welfare and empowerment of the poor and for human solidarity across national borders." Evidence indicates, he thinks, that "sometimes" these efforts can make "a big difference." The donor country may itself also be strengthened as its own citizens come to appreciate the expression of these values.[7] Not incompatible with such efforts can be eventual economic gains for the donors, and also steps, however minute, can be taken to discourage international conflicts and wars.

Nevertheless, someone, whether an individual or groups, may be always able and eager to puncture glittering generalizations with pungent questions that point to challenging modes of thinking and evaluation. Two American historians once sought to indicate how members of their profession have analyzed and hence explained both wars and related phenomena. The approaches, they suggested, can be designated as conservative, liberal, or radical, each of which leads to different generalizations. As scholars they forced themselves to adopt "an inclination toward eclecticism": "over a period of time societies tend to pass through" six periods beginning with "relative satisfaction/confidence," followed by "disappointment/anxiety" leading to "dissatisfaction/aggression" on the domestic front and then on the foreign front (including war), in turn resulting in "exhaustion/anxiety" (unless the foreign venture is successful and brief), and finally ending with "relaxation/adjustment."[8] Ah yes, but specific questions remain to be and in fact are asked: counterfactually, what would have happened in 1961 if the invasion of Cuba by Cuban exiles and supported by the United States had not failed but had been cancelled at the last moment for the good reasons that later turned out to be valid?[9]

Nevertheless, the unknown and the unknowable, the uncertain and the certain, the unimportant and the important can utilize general guides, even such as the seven in the present book, but also guides specifically adapted to a particular problem at hand (G6). For illustrative purposes are offered only timidly—really timidly—six additional, more specific guides in the pursuit of understanding conflicts between individuals and groups. People, it is surmised, accept a change readily:

1. When it appears to embody or is not in conflict with traditional beliefs and values apparently proving satisfactory at present.
2. When it is introduced by persons or leaders whom they consider important, competent, and trustworthy and who have adequately consulted or understood them or their leaders.
3. When it seems to have advantages that can be meaningfully demonstrated in the present or anticipated in the future.
4. When it makes demands they consider reasonable or tolerable and when they have already learned its components or feel confident they can do so.
5. When it seems to be in accord with their own modal personality traits or the goals they have been seeking.
6. When the risks appear surmountable or worth taking.

Yes, other pseudo-profundities emerge in the social sciences and in real life; the above schema is only one illustration of what is needed or, though phrased differently, employed by the self and others.

Nevertheless, although its expression takes many different forms especially in translations, all peoples at some time both advocate and seek to achieve a "Golden Rule" as expressed in the New Testament: "whatsoever you want men to do to you, do you also to them." Elaboration is unnecessary, except to note—as phrased by a psychoanalyst—that, although some "moral rules of conduct" also stem from a "fear of threats to be forestalled," the Rule itself prods human beings "to strive consciously for a highest good and to avoid mutual harm with a sharpened awareness" even when trembling with "destructive rage."[10] This rule of "mutuality between the doer and the other" is both a guide and a challenge but admittedly does not provide specific guidance in all situations. What action should be followed when threatened by a reckless assailant? Often assistance is also given by commandments proclaimed in the Book of Exodus in the Old Testament. A distinction there and elsewhere can be made generally between concrete and abstract commandments. Concrete ones recommend rules that prohibit killing, damaging others, employing force, and interference per se. The more abstract ones point to avoiding the violation of an esteemed principle, of "truth," of human rights, of not securing the assent of those affected by an action, of not ignoring future consequences, of inaction when action is desirable or feasible.[11] Is there any reason to believe that the concrete rules are remembered more readily than the abstract ones and hence are more likely to affect action when learned by children or heard passively on Sundays or from some other source?

Nevertheless, every person possesses personal or semi-original self-guides providing some help or encouragement as challenging problems arise (G1). The source of such guides, tempered and transmitted by tradition, is the self's own experience or that of others. Aristotle suggests how to reason from premises we have been given, St. Paul points out ways to deal with peers, a boxer indicates how we may be able to defend ourselves against an opponent attacking us with fists but not with a gun, a mathematician provides ways to calculate the area of an irregular polygon, your daughter tells you the name of her teacher at school, you know approximately how long it takes to walk from there to there, unwittingly or deliberately you have discovered persons or books telling you how to improve your life and solve absolutely all or almost all of your problems. The experts being consulted often do not agree with one another, but one or more of them provides at least encouragement or a possible if temporary solution. In spite of differences in society and changes in knowledge, individuals cling to their own beliefs for long periods of time. Otherwise there would be chaos: they could not plan, they could not predict, they would sit almost still and grow older while being buffeted by surprises within and outside themselves. Like it or not, it is repeated here once more, people are different from plants and other animals; they know or think they know what has happened, what is happening, what may or can happen later; they can at least pursue a version of perfection.

Nevertheless, everywhere you and the rest of us are bombarded with too many guides obtained from other persons and themselves. That gadget is "guaranteed" to last for ten years, provided it is utilized correctly as indicated in the attached instructions; do you believe that so-called guarantee? After death there is an afterlife for those who have not strayed from the prescribed rules; do you believe that, why do you believe or disbelieve it?

When you wake up tomorrow, will you be hungry and thirsty? Is there going to be another war between the superpowers, whoever they turn out to be?

Nevertheless, the safest guide is to remind oneself that almost all guides are perilous (G2). Past experience may suggest that a given procedure has always been successful and that its goal has been achieved. But then suddenly or gradually there is a change in the conditions for which the procedure has been employed or in the people who have previously been affected by that procedure; modification of the guide becomes necessary. The last qualification is important: some guides permit no exception—you cannot jump off a steep cliff and expect to fly safely into the air or to survive a direct fall. Self-deception, however, may enable you haphazardly to ignore the reality of the self or the actual and natural environment. For truly good reasons, individuals wish privately to believe that actions and beliefs are praiseworthy. To sustain the belief other evaluations must be denied or overlooked; they tell themselves that they are helping others or benefiting the community and that they really are not seeking their own ends. Unless precautions are taken, they may actually come to believe their own hypocrisy and find invalid reasons to sustain such beliefs.[12]

Nevertheless, we are not content, we use our discontent with a plaguing but encouraging question: have we done enough? Enough of what? Enough of what we once and even now believe "worthwhile." Enough in an effort to follow some golden rule in dealing with the others we love or unavoidably hate? Enough to try, however vainly, to rectify blunders in the past? Enough while seeking to overcome or remedy our own imperfections? Enough to preserve our chunk of the earth? Enough for the immediate future or our successors? A tiny bit, nevertheless, very, very, tiny? Nevertheless, nevertheless, there is so much more to say, think, and do.

Notes

CHAPTER 1: THE PURSUIT

1. William Little et al. (1955). *The Oxford Universal Dictionary on Historical Principles*, p. 1230. Oxford: Clarendon Press.

2. William James (1968). *Pragmatism*, pp. 84–85, 184–185. Cleveland: Meridian Books.

3. Frank Thilly (1957). *A History of Philosophy*, p. 642. New York: Holt, Rinehart and Winston.

4. Gerald Sparrow (1972). *Vintage Victorian Murder*, p. 399. New York: Hart Publishing.

5. Michael Billig (1987). *Arguing and Thinking*, pp. 119, 255–256. Cambridge: Cambridge University Press.

6. Leon Festinger (1983). *The Human Legacy*, p. 163. New York: Columbia University Press.

7. Wendell R. Garner (1962). *Uncertainty and Structure as Psychological Concepts*, pp. 7, 39. New York: Wiley.

8. Isaiah Berlin (1996). *The Sense of Reality*, p. 53. London: Chatto & Windus.

9. Harry Collins and Trevor Pinch (1993). *The Golem*, p. 142. Cambridge: Cambridge University Press.

10. Cf. Herbert Fensterheim (1971). *Help without Psychoanalysis*, chaps. 1, 6. New York: Stein and Day. Arnold A. Lazarus (1981). *The Practice of Multi-Modal Therapy*. New York: McGraw-Hill.

11. Robyn M. Dawes (1988). *Rational Choice in an Uncertain World*, pp. 115–119. New York: Harcourt, Brace.

12. A. R. Louch (1969). *Explanation and Human Action*, chap. 10. Berkeley: University of California Press.

13. Irving L. Janis (1972). *Victims of Groupthink*, p. 9, chap. 6. Boston: Houghton Mifflin.

14. Bertrand de Jouvenel (1963). *The Pure Theory of Politics*, pp. 33, 78. New Haven: Yale University Press.

15. H. G. Wells (1931). *The Work, Wealth, and Happiness of Mankind*, p. 895. Garden City, N.Y.: Doubleday, Doran.

16. Alexander H. Leighton et al. (1963). *Psychiatric Disorder among the Yoruba*, p. 278. Ithaca, N.Y.: Cornell University Press.

17. Thomas M. Ostrom and Harry S. Upshaw (1968). "Psychological Perspective and Attitude Change." In Anthony Greenwell et al., eds., *Psychological Foundations of Attitudes*, pp. 217–242. New York: Academic Press.

18. Keith Lehrer (1990). *Metamind*, pp. 2, 95. Oxford: Clarendon Press.

19. Cf. Thomas Szasz (1977). *Psychiatric Slavery*, chap. 1. New York: Free Press.

20. John Dewey (1922). *Human Nature and Conduct*, p. 238. New York: Henry Holt.

21. Ibid., p. 239.

22. Karl Marx and Frederick Engels (1970). *The German Ideology*, p. 53. New York: International Publishers. Cf. Wolf Lepenies (1992). *Melancholy and Society*, p. 227. Cambridge, Mass.: Harvard University Press.

23. A. C. Jordan (1973). *Towards an African Literature*, pp. viii, 83. Berkeley: University of California Press.

24. David Ferry (1992). *Gilgamesh England*, p. 50. New York: Farrar, Straus & Giroux.

25. J. David Singer (1979). "From a Study of War to Peace Research." In J. David Singer et al., eds., *Explaining War*, chap. 1. Beverly Hills: Sage.

26. Leonard Oeland (1975). *Prisons*. New York: Free Press.

27. Horst Petri and Matthias Lauterbach (1975). *Gewalt in der Erziehung*, p. 124. Frankfurt: Athenäum Fischer Taschenbuch.

28. Robert G. L. Waite (1977). *The Psychopathic God*, pp. xi, 234. New York: Basic Books.

CHAPTER 2: NATURE OF KNOWLEDGE

1. Juan R. Garcia (1980). *Operation Wetback*, pp. xii, 12. Westport, Conn.: Greenwood.

2. Philip Brickman et al. (1978). "Lottery Winners and Accident Victims." *Journal of Personality and Social Psychology* 36: 917–927.

3. Piotr Sztompka (1991). *Society in Action*, p. 13, chap. 2. Chicago: University of Chicago Press.

4. Bill McKibben (1992). *The Age of Missing Information*, pp. 8–36. New York: Random House.

5. Panayotes Kannelopoulos (1963). "Neutrality—Utopia or Reality," p. xiii. In Kurt London, ed., *New Nations in a Divided World*, pp. xiii–xv. New York: Praeger.

6. *New York Times*, October 6, 1995, p. B10.

7. Cf. Eugene Webb et al. (1966). *Unobtrusive Measures*. Chicago: Rand McNally.

8. Alexander K. Luria (1971). "Towards the Problem of the Historical Nature of Psychological Processes." *International Journal of Psychology* 6: 259–272.

9. Edna St. Vincent Millay (1956). *Collected Poems*, p. 571. New York: Harper and Brothers.

10. C. V. Wedgwood (1960). *The Senses of the Past*, pp. 99–100. New York: Collier Books.

11. Joseph Schwartz (1992). *The Creative Moment*, pp. 76–83. New York: HarperCollins.

12. Robert L. Heilbroner (1961). *The Future as History*, p. 175. New York: Grove Press.

13. Fiona Mackie (1985). *The Status of Everyday Life*, p. 140. London: Routledge and Kegan Paul.

14. Martha Wolfenstein and Gilbert Kliman, eds. (1965). *Children and the Death of a President*, pp. 193–194. New York: Doubleday.

15. Jacob Cohen (1994). "The Earth Is Round." *American Psychologist* 49: 997–1003.

16. Harold M. Schroder et al. (1967). *Human Information Processing*, p. 123. New York: Holt, Rinehart and Winston.

17. Philip F. Tetlock and Aaron Belkin (1996). *Counterfactual Thought Experiments in World Politics*, pp. 30, 36–37. Princeton: Princeton University Press.

18. Harry Collins and Trevor Pinch (1993). *The Golem*, pp. x, 78, 106, 142, 145. Cambridge: Cambridge University Press. Cf. Bruno Latour (1987). *Science and Action*, chap 2. Cambridge, Mass.: Harvard University Press.

19. Gerald James Holton (1993). *Science and Anti-Science*, pp. 126–127, 139. Cambridge, Mass.: Harvard University Press.

20. Richard E. Petty (1993). "Conceptual and Methodological Issues in the Likelihood Model of Persuasion." *Communication Theory* 3: 336–362.

21. Frank L. Schmidt (1992). "What Do Data Really Mean?" *American Psychologist* 47: 1173–1181.

22. Gene V. Glass et al. (1981). *Meta-Analysis in Social Research*. Beverly Hills: Sage. John U. Farley and Daniel R. Lehmann (1986). *Meta-Analysis in Marketing*. Lexington, Mass.: D.C. Heath.

23. Carl Sagan (1973). *The Cosmic Connection*, pp. 24, 27, 28. Garden City, N.Y.: Anchor.

CHAPTER 3: FUNCTIONS OF KNOWLEDGE

1. Robert D. Kaplan (1996). *The Ends of the Earth*, p. xi. New York: Random House.

2. Nathan Glazer (1988). *The Limits of Social Policy*, p. 143. Cambridge, Mass.: Harvard University Press.

3. Cf. Harold D. Lasswell (1950). *World Politics and Personal Insecurity*, pp. 132–133. Glencoe, Ill.: Free Press.

4. Johathan Baron (1988). *Thinking and Deciding*, p. 256. Cambridge: Cambridge University Press.

5. Peter Loewenberg (1985). *Decoding the Past*, pp. 214, 237. Berkeley: University of California Press.

6. Mortimer Ostow (1970). *The Psychology of Melancholy*, p. 3, chap. 7. New York: Harper & Row.

7. Cf. Valene L. Smith (1977). *Hosts and Guests*. Philadelphia: University of Pennsylvania Press.

8. T.F.H. Allen and Thomas W. Hoekstra (1992). *Toward a Unified Ecology*, p. 284. New York: Columbia University Press.

9. William G. Sumner (1906). *Folkways*, p. 7. Boston: Ginn.

10. Stephen Viederman (1995). "Knowledge for Sustainable Development." In Thaddeus C. Trzyna, ed., *A Sustainable World*, pp. 27–43. Sacramento: California Institute of Public Affairs.

11. Cf. Alan Garfinkel (1981). *Forms of Explanation*, pp. 159–163. New Haven: Yale University Press.

12. Thomas F. Jordan (1993). *The Democracy Crisis and Victorian Youth*, chaps. 1, 8. Albany: State University of New York.

13. Cf. Holmes Rolston III (1991). "Environmental Ethics." In F. Herbert Bormann and Stephen R. Kellert, eds., *Ecology, Economics, Ethics*, chap. 3. New Haven: Yale University Press.

14. Joel E. Cohen (1995). *How Many People Can the Earth Support?* pp. 109, 134, 386; italics his. New York: Norton.

15. Sally J. Goerner (1995). "Chaos and Deep Ecology." In Frederick D. Abraham and Albert R. Gilgen, eds., *Chaos Theory in Psychology*, chap. 1. Westport, Conn.: Greenwood.

16. Karl Pribram (1995). In Abraham and Gilgen, op. cit., chap. 22.

17. Frederick J. Teggart (1960). *Theory and Processes of History*, p. 234. Berkeley: University of California Press.

18. David Middleton and Derek Edwards, eds. (1990). *Collective Remembering*, p. 7. London: Sage.

19. Barry Schwartz (1990). "The Reconstruction of Abraham Lincoln." In Middleton and Edwards, op. cit., chap. 5.

20. Thomas J. Cottle (1976). *Perceiving Time*, p. 174, chaps. 6, 8. New York: Wiley.

21. Leonard W. Doob (1971). *Patterning of Time*, pp. 209–210. New Haven: Yale University Press.

22. Bennett A. Shaywitz (1995). "Sex Differences in the Functional Organization of the Basis for Language." *Nature* 373: 607–610.

23. Marlis G. Steinert (1977). *Hitler's War and the Germans.*, chap. 4. Athens: Ohio University Press.

24. Tracy Laquey (1993). *The Internet Companion*, p. 10. Reading, Mass.: Addison Wesley.

25. Joshua Meyrowitz (1985). *No Sense of Place*, p. 33. New York: Oxford University Press.

26. Mortimer J. Adler (1992). *The Great Ideas*. New York: Macmillan.

27. David W. Johnson and Roger T. Johnson (1992). "Positive Interdependence." In Rachel Hertz-Lazarowitz and Norman Miller, eds., *Interaction in Cooperative Groups*, chap. 8. Cambridge: Cambridge University Press.

28. Robert Rosenthal and Ralph Rosnow (1984). *Essentials of Behavioral Research*, pp. 182, 184. New York: McGraw-Hill.

29. Peter Duesberg (1996). *Inventing the AIDS Virus*. Washington, D.C.: Regnery.

30. George Gerbner et al. (1969). *The Analysis of Communication Content*, p. x, chap. 18. New York: Wiley.

31. Stephen Viederman, op. cit.

32. William S. Burroughs (1997). "Last Words." *New Yorker* 73, no. 24: 36–37.

CHAPTER 4: LANGUAGE AND VALUES

1. Alan Garfinkel (1981). *Forms of Explanation*, p. 137. New Haven: Yale University Press.

2. Norman Myers (1979). *The Sinking Ark*, p. ix. Oxford: Pergamon.

3. Lorraine Harner (1982). "Talking about the Past and the Future." In William J. Friedman, ed., *The Developmental Psychology of Time*, chap. 6. New York: Academic Press.

4. Paula Menyuk (1969). *Sentences Children Use*, p. 138. Cambridge, Mass.: MIT Press.

5. Frans de Waal (1996). *Good Natured*, chaps. 2–5. Cambridge, Mass.: Harvard University Press.

6. Wolfgang Köhler (1938). *The Place of Value in a World of Facts*, pp. 35, 55, 72. New York: Liveright.

7. Cf. Leonard W. Doob (1978). *Panorama of Evil*, pp. 19–21. Westport, Conn.: Greenwood.

8. Thomas More (1989). *Utopia*, pp. 65, 71, 80–81, 87, 510. Cambridge: Cambridge University Press.

9. William P. Alston (1964). *Philosophy of Language*, p. 90. Englewood Cliffs, N.J.: Prentice-Hall.

10. David O. Moberg (1979). *Spiritual Well-Being*. Washington, D.C.: University Press of America.

11. Psalm 131.

12. Harry L. Hollingworth (1949). *Psychology and Ethics*, chap. 2. New York: Ronald Press.

13. Wayne Meeks (1986). *The Moral World of the First Christians*, p. 43. Philadelphia: Westminster Press.

14. Desmond Bowen (1970). *Souperism*, pp. 15–30. Cork: Mercier Press.

15. Rick Osborn (1987). "The Whorfian Hypothesis Today." In Asher Cashdan and Martin Jordan, eds., *Studies in Communication*, chap. 4. Oxford: Basil Blackwell.

16. Casey Miller and Kate Swift (1977). *Words and Women*, p. 18. Garden City, N.Y.: Anchor.

17. Colin M. Turbayne (1962). *The Myth of Metaphor*, pp. 14–15. New Haven: Yale University Press.

18. Samuel Novey (1968). *The Second Look*, pp. 65–66. Baltimore: Johns Hopkins University Press.

19. Alan Garfinkel op. cit., pp. 21, 144.

20. G. Nigel Gilbert and Michael Mulkay (1984). *Opening Pandora's Box*, p. 188. Cambridge: Cambridge University Press.

21. Alexander J. Rothman et al. (1993). "The Influence of Message Framing on Intentions to Perform Health Behaviors." *Journal of Experimental Social Psychology* 29: 408–433.

22. Richard E. Petty (1993). "Conceptual and Methodological Issues in the Likelihood Model of Persuasion." *Communication Theory* 3: 336–362.

23. Bruno Bettelheim (1983). *Freud and Man's Soul*, pp. 74–75, 82–83. New York: Knopf.

24. Willis D. Ellis (1938). *A Source Book of Gestalt Psychology*, p. 109. London: Routledge & Kegan Paul.

25. Leonard W. Doob (1960). "The Effect of Codability upon the Efferent Functioning of Language." *Journal of Social Psychology* 52: 3–15. Leonard W. Doob (1960). *Becoming More Civilized*, p. 198. New Haven: Yale University Press.

26. Patricia Greenfield and Jerome S. Bruner (1969). "Culture and Cognitive Growth." In David A. Goslin, ed., *Handbook of Socialization Theory and Research*, chap. 12. Chicago: Rand McNally.

27. Peggy Rosenthal (1984). *Words and Values*, p. 118. New York: Oxford University Press.

28. Noam Chomsky (1972). *Language and Mind*, p. 116. New York: Harcourt Brace Jovanovich.

29. Cf. Sylvia Scribner and Michael Cole (1981). *The Psychology of Literacy*, chap. 14. Cambridge, Mass.: Harvard University Press.

30. Jane M. Healy (1990). *Endangered Minds*, pp. 22, 345. New York: Simon & Schuster.

31. E. D. Hirsch, Jr. (1987). *What Every American Needs to Know*, pp. 6, 19, 101–102, 152–215. Boston: Houghton Mifflin.

32. Frans de Waal, op. cit., pp. 12, 140.

33. Eduard Spranger (1928). *Types of Men*, Part 2, pp. 252, 290, 294, 301. Halle: Max Niemeyer.

34. Richard I. Evans (1970). *Gordon Allport*, p. 85. New York: E. P. Dutton.

35. M. Brewster Smith (1969). *Social Psychology and Human Values*, p. 112. Chicago: Aldine Publishing.

36. Milton Rokeach (1973). *The Nature of Human Values*, pp. 7, 174, 176, 358–361, Part 4. New York: Free Press.

37. Donald D. Searing (1979). "A Study of Values in the British House of Commons." In Milton Rokeach, ed., *Understanding Human Values*, chap. 9. New York: Free Press.

38. Angus Campbell et al. (1976). *The Quality of Human Life*, p. 19. New York: Russell Sage.

39. Nathan M. Szajnberg (1992). "Secrecy and Privacy in a Psychodynamic Milieu." In Nathan M. Szajnberg, ed., *Educating the Emotions*, pp. 193–213. New York: Plenum.

40. Bernard J. F. Lonergan (1956). *Insight*, p. 396. New York: Philosophical Library.

41. Gordon L. Paul (1966). *Insight vs. Desensitization in Psychotherapy*, pp. 31–70. Stanford, Calif.: Stanford University Press.

42. Dawn Publications (1995). *God's Plan*. New York: promotion folder.

43. Jacques Cousteau (1977). Cited in *New York Times*, June 26, p. B7.

44. Julia Annas (1993). "Women and the Quality of Life." In Martha Nussbaum and Amartya Sen, eds., *The Quality of Life*, pp. 279–302. Oxford: Clarendon Press.

45. James MacKaye (1915). *Happiness of Nations*, p. 29. New York: H. W. Huebsch.

46. James MacKaye (1924). *The Logic of Conduct*, p. 284. New York: Boni & Liveright.

47. Mihaly Csikszentmihalyi (1996). *Creativity*, pp. 110–124. New York: HarperCollins.

48. Hadley Cantril (1950). *The "Why" of Man's Existence*, pp. 25–32. New York: Macmillan. Hadley Cantril (1965). *Pattern of Human Concerns*, p. 316. New Brunswick, N.J.: Rutgers University Press. Albert H. Cantril, ed. (1988). *Psychology, Humanism, and Scientific Inquiry*, pp. 58, 124. New Brunswick, N.J.: Transaction Inc.

49. John M. Mecklin (1920). *An Introduction to Social Ethics*, p. 3. New York: Harcourt, Brace, and Howe.

50. Ruut Veenhoven et al. (1994). *Correlates of Happiness*. Rotterdam: Erasmus University.

51. Michael Argyle (1987). *The Psychology of Happiness*, pp. 3, 8. London: Methuen.

52. Johathan L. Freedman (1978). *Happy People*, pp. 5–6, 10–27, 203, 210. New York: Harcourt Brace Jovanovich.

53. Carol D. Ryff (1989). "Happiness Is Everything; Or Is It?" *Journal of Personality and Social Psychology* 57: 1069–1081.

54. Veenhoven et al., op. cit.

55. David G. Myers (1992). *The Pursuit of Happiness*, chaps. 8, 9; p. 206. New York: Morrow.

56. Charles Morris (1950). *Varieties of Human Value*, chaps. 1, 2. Chicago: University of Chicago Press.

57. Frank M. Andrews (1976). *Social Indicators of Well-Being*, p. 376. New York: Plenum.

58. Lewis M. Terman (1938). *Psychological Functions of Marital Happiness*, pp. v, 41, 53, 369, 430–438. New York: McGraw-Hill.

59. Harsha N. Mookherjee (1992). "Perceptions of Well-Being by Metropolitan and Nonmetropolitan Populations in the United States." *Journal of Social Psychology* 132: 513–524. Harsha N. Mookherjee (1994). "Effect of Religiosity and Selected Variables on the Perception of Well-Being." *Journal of Social Psychology* 134: 403–405.

60. Gene Sharp (1980). *Social Power and Political Freedom*, pp. 311, 410. Boston: Porter Sargent.

61. Frank M. Andrews, ed. (1986). *Research on the Quality of Life*. Ann Arbor: Institutes for Social Research, University of Michigan. Nussbaum and Sen, eds., op. cit. Alden Wessman (1966). *Mood and Personality*. New York: Holt, Rinehart and Winston.

62. Cf. Frank M. Andrews (1991). "Stability and Change in Levels and Structure of Subjective Well-Being." *Social Indicators Research* 25: 1–31. Cf. Ed Diener and Carol Diener (1996). "Most People Are Happy." *Psychological Science* 7: 181–188.

63. Cf. T. W. Adorno et al. (1969). *The Authoritarian Personality*. New York: Norton. Cf. Ann P. Bowling (1989). "Loneliness, Mobility, Well-Being, and Social Support in a Sample of 85 Year Olds." *Personality and Individual Differences* 10: 1189–1192.

64. Cf. Leonard W. Doob (1987). *Slightly beyond Skepticism*, p. 278. New Haven: Yale University Press.

65. Roger Brown (1958). "How Shall a Thing Be Called?" *Psychological Review* 65: 14–21.

66. Lawrence Kohlberg (1984). *The Psychology of Moral Development*, p. 44. New York: Harper & Row.

67. Jane Fritsch (1996). "Friend or Foe?" *New York Times*, March 25, pp. 1, 12.

68. Cf. Margaret Read (1960). *Children of Their Fathers*. New Haven: Yale University Press.

69. Cf. Michael J. Harner (1973). *Hallucinogens and Shamanism*. New York: Oxford University Press.

70. John S. Mbiti (1969). *African Religions and Philosophy*, chap. 20. New York: Praeger.

71. Paul Grosser and Edwin G. Halperin (1983). *Anti-Semitism*, pp. 1, 351. New York: Philosophical Library.

72. Ellis Freeman (1940). *Conquering the Man in the Street*, p. 21. New York: Vanguard Press.

73. Plato (1982). *Republic* (translated by G.M.A. Grube and C.D.C. Reeve), pp. 369b&d, 372a, 421d. Indianapolis: Hackett Publishing.

74. Aristotle (1957). *Politics* (translated by Ernest Barker), pp. 326–329 (Book VII). Oxford: Clarendon Press.

75. W. Evans-Wentz (1935). *Tibetan Yoga and Secret Doctrines*, pp. 67–79. London: Oxford University Press.

76. Albert Schweitzer (1969). *Reverence for Life*, pp. 67–79. New York: Harper & Row.

CHAPTER 5: SELF

1. Reinhold Niebuhr (1955). *The Self and the Dramas of History*, pp. 4–5, 6, 13, 30, 62–63. New York: Scribner's.

2. Gerald E. Myers (1969). *Self*, pp. 23, 25, 65, 149. New York: Pegasus.

3. D. L. Forrest-Pressley et al., eds. (1985). *Metacognition, Cognition, and Human Performance*, p. 1. Orlando: Academic Press.

4. James W. Pennebaker (1982). *The Psychology of Physical Symptoms*, pp. 4–10. New York: Springer-Verlag.

5. Wolfgang Köhler (1924). *Die physischen Gestalten im Ruhe und im stationären Zustand*. Erlangen: Verlag der philosophischen Akademie.

6. Gérard Genette (1988). *Narrative Discourse Revisited*. Ithaca, N.Y.: Cornell University Press. Anthony P. Kerby (1991). *Narrative and the Self*. Bloomington: Indiana University Press.

7. Marilyn Gist and Terrence R. Mitchele (1992). "Self-Efficacy." *Academy of Management Review* 17, 183–211.

8. John E. Mathieu (1993). "Individual and Situational Influences on the Development of Self-Efficacy." *Personnel Journal* 46: 125–147.

9. Christopher Baglet et al. (1979). *Personality, Self-Esteem, and Prejudice*, p. 9, chap. 6. Westmead: Saxon House.

10. Morris Rosenberg (1965). *Society and the Adolescent Self-Image*, chaps. 1, 2; pp. 208, 264. Princeton: Princeton University Press.

11. William J. McGuire (1984). "Search for the Self." In Robert A. Zucker et al., *Personality and the Prediction of Behavior*, chap. 3. Orlando: Academic Press.

12. Cf. John Hattie (1992). *Self-Concept*. Hillsdale, N.J.: Erlbaum. John O'Neill, ed. (1973). *Modes of Individualism and Collectivism*. London: Heinemann.

13. F. Clark Power et al. (1989). *Lawrence Kohlberg's Approach to Moral Education*, chaps. 1, 5. New York: Columbia University Press.

14. David Dunning et al. (1989). "Ambiguity and Self-Evaluation." *Journal of Personality and Social Psychology* 57: 1082–1089.

15. Roy F. Baumeister (1993). "Lying to Yourself." In Michael Lewis and Carolyn Saarni, eds., *Lying and Deception in Everyday Life*, chap. 8. New York: Guilford.

16. Lloyd H. Steffen (1986). *Self-Deception and the Common Life*, pp. 376–384. New York: Peter Lang.

17. Cf. Michael Jackson and Ivan Karp, eds. (1990). *Personhood and Agency*. Uppsala: Smithsonian Institution Press. Eleanor C. Irwin (1983). "The Diagnostic and Therapeutic Use of Pretend Play." In Charles E. Schaefer and Kevin J. O'Connor, eds., *Handbook of Play Therapy*, pp. 144–173. New York: Wiley.

18. Robyn M. Dawes (1993). "Prediction and the Future versus Understanding of the Past." *American Journal of Psychology* 106: 1–24.

19. Cf. Brenda Major et al. (1994). "Attributional Ambiguity of Affirmative Action." *Basic and Applied Social Psychology* 15: 113–141. Karen M. Ruggiero (1995). "Coping with Discrimination." *Journal of Personality and Social Psychology* 68: 826–838.

20. Cf. Icek Ajzen and Martin Fishbein (1980). *Understanding Attitudes and Predicting Social Behavior*, chaps. 2–4. Englewood Cliffs, N.J.: Prentice-Hall.

21. June P. Tangney and Kurt W. Fischer, eds. (1995). *Self-Conscious Emotions*. New York: Guilford Press.

22. Marvin Zuckerman (1979). *Sensation Seeking*, pp. 10, 107–109, 127–130, 378–379, 388–393. Hillsdale, N.J.: Lawrence Erlbaum.

23. Cf. John Hattie, op. cit., pp. 10, 113. Jerome Kagan (1989). *Unstable Ideas*, pp. 220–221. Cambridge, Mass.: Harvard University Press.

24. Cf. Kurt W. Back and Kenneth Gergen (1966). "Cognitive and Motivational Factors in Aging and Disengagement." In Ida H. Simpson and John C. McKinney, eds., *Social Aspects of Aging*, pp. 289–296. Durham, N.C.: Duke University Press.

25. Anselm L. Strauss (1959). *Mirrors and Masks*, chap. 4. Glencoe: Free Press.

26. David G. Myers (1992). *The Pursuit of Happiness*, p. 69. New York: Morrow.

27. Herbert S. Parnes, ed. (1981). *Work and Retirement*, pp. 4, 266. Cambridge: Cambridge University Press.

28. Cf. Arnold Modell (1993). *The Private Self*, pp. 3, 10, 169, 179. Cambridge, Mass.: Harvard University Press.

29. Erik H. Erikson (1968). *Identity*, chap. 1. New York: Norton.

30. Reinhold Niebuhr (1949). *The Nature and Destiny of Man*, pp. 1, 75. New York: Scribner's.

31. John Dollard et al. (1939). *Frustration and Aggression*. New Haven: Yale University Press.

32. David B. Morris (1991). *The Culture of Pain*, pp. 1, 209, 267. Berkeley: University of California Press.

33. C. R. Snyder and Carol E. Ford, eds. (1987). *Coping with Negative Life Events*. New York: Plenum Press.

34. Jeffrey A. Gray (1971). *The Psychology of Fear and Stress*, pp. 8–14. Cambridge: Cambridge University Press.

35. Leonard W. Doob (1987). *Slightly beyond Skepticism*, pp. 94–95. New Haven: Yale University Press.

36. Cf. C. Wegman (1988). "Emotion and Argumentation." In Vernon Hamilton et al., eds., *Cognitive Perspectives on Emotion and Motivation*, pp. 239–264. Dordrecht: Kluever Academic Publishers. Rolf Pfeifer (1988). "Artificial Intelligence Models of Emotion." In Hamilton et al., op. cit., pp. 287–320.

37. Gordon H. Bower (1991). "Mood Congruity of Social Judgments." In Joseph P. Forgas, *Emotion and Social Judgments*, pp. 31–53. Oxford: Pergamon Press. Peter Salovey (1991). "Influence of Mood on Judgments about Health and Illness." In Joseph P. Forgas, op. cit., pp. 241–262.

38. Gordon Bower and John D. Moyer (1989). "In Search of Mood-dependent Retrieval." *Journal of Social Behavior and Personality* 4(2): 121–156.

39. Alden Wessman and David Ricks (1966). *Mood and Personality*, p. 30, Appendix 1. New York: Holt, Rinehart and Winston.

40. Robert M. Schwartz (1992). "States of Mind Model and Personnel Construct Theory." *International Journal of Personal Construct Theory* 5: 123–143.

41. Cf. Daniel Statman, ed. (1993). *Moral Luck*. Albany: State University of New York.

42. John Dollard and Frank Auld, Jr. (1959). *Scoring Human Motives*, pp. 38–43. New Haven: Yale University Press.

43. Ralph Linton (1945). *The Cultural Background of Personality*, pp. 32, 84. New York: Appleton-Century.

44. Gordon W. Allport (1958). "What Units Shall We Employ?" In Gardner Lindzey, ed., *Assessment of Human Motives*, chap. 8. New York: Holt, Rinehart and Winston.

45. Gordon W. Allport (1955). *Becoming*, pp. 19, 28, 40, 79, 90. New Haven: Yale University Press.

46. Norbert Elias (1985). *The Loneliness of Dying*, p. 3. Oxford: Basil Blackwell.

47. Cf. Arien Mack (1973). *Death in American Experience*. New York: Schocken Books.

48. Sherwin B. Nuland (1995). *How We Die*, pp. 8, 54, 142, 242. New York: Vintage Books.

49. Peter Hartocollis (1983). *Time and Timelessness*, p. 209. New York: International Universities Press.

50. Adrian C. Moulyn (1982). *The Meaning of Suffering*, pp. 4, 7, 222. Westport, Conn.: Greenwood.

51. Zygmunt Bauman (1992). *Mortality, Immortality, and Other Life Strategies*, pp. 12, 31. Stanford, Calif.: Stanford University Press.

52. M. J. Field (1960). *Search for Security*, p. 187. Evanston, Ill.: Northwestern University Press.

53. Kenneth Ring (1984). *Heading toward Omega*, pp. 10, 44, 268. New York: Morrow.

54. Charles T. Tart, ed. (1969). *Altered States of Consciousness*. Garden City, N.Y.: Doubleday.

55. Seymour H. Mauskopf and Michael R. McVaugh (1980). *The Elusive Science*. Baltimore: Johns Hopkins University Press.

56. Marshall H. Segall (1976). *Human Behavior and Public Policy*, p. 113. New York: Pergamon.

57. Alan Edelstein (1982). *An Unacknowledged Harmony*, chaps. 2, 7; p. 201. Westport, Conn.: Greenwood.

58. Cf. Faye J. Crosby (1982). *Relative Deprivation and Working Women*, chap. 5. New York: Oxford University Press.

59. Carolyn Saarni and Maria von Salisch (1993). "The Socialization of Emotional Dissemblance." In Lewis and Saarni, op. cit., chap. 5.

60. Lewis and Saarni, op. cit., p. 15.

61. Michael Lewis (1993). "The Development of Deception." In Lewis and Saarni, op. cit., p. 90.

62. Ethel Seybold (1951). *Thoreau*, p. 85. New Haven: Yale University Press.

63. Karl Mannheim (1940). *Man and Society in an Age of Reconstruction*, p. 240. New York: Harcourt, Brace.

CHAPTER 6: OTHERS

1. James G. Martin (1964). *The Tolerant Personality*, pp. 10, 45. Detroit: Wayne State University Press.

2. Fred Davis (1979). *Yearning for Yesterday*, p. 14. New York: Free Press.

3. June P. Tangney and Kurt W. Fischer, eds. (1995). *Self-Conscious Emotions*, pp. 3–4. New York: Guilford Press.

4. Ulf Hannerz (1969). *Soulside*, pp. 34–35. New York: Columbia University Press.

5. Nicole Chiasson et al. (1996). "Ingroup-Outgroup Similar Information as a Determinant of Attraction toward Members of Minority Groups." *Journal of Social Psychology* 16: 233–241.

6. Donald R. Kinder et al. (1976). "The Attitude-Labelling Process outside of the Laboratory." *Journal of Personality and Social Psychology* 33: 480–491.

7. Michèle Barrett (1991). *The Politics of Truth*, chap. 1. Stanford, Calif.: Stanford University Press.

8. Erich Fromm (1955). *The Sane Society*, p. 264. New York: Holt, Rinehart and Winston.

9. Meyer Friedman and Ray H. Rosenmann (1974). *Type A Behavior and Your Heart*, p. 100. Greenwich, Conn.: Fawcett. Cf. Howard S. Friedman et al.

"Non Verbal Expression of Emotion." In Craig Van Dyke et al., eds., *Emotions in Health and Illness*, chap. 10. Orlando: Grune & Stratton.

10. Cf. Wilhelm Weischedel (1976). *Skeptische Ethik*, pp. 190–191. Frankfurt: Suhrkamp.

11. Walter Bingham and Bruce V. Moore (1959). *How to Interview*, p. 265. New York: Harper and Brothers.

12. Marie Collins Swabey (1961). *Cosmic Laughter*, p. 187. New Haven: Yale University Press.

13. James S. Uleman et al. (1993). "Tacit, Manifest, and Intentional Reference." *Social Cognition* 11: 321–351.

14. Robert T. Tauber (1997). *Self-Fulfilling Prophecy*. Westport, Conn.: Praeger.

15. Cf. Bruno Latour (1987). *Science in Action*, pp. 192–194. Cambridge, Mass.: Harvard University Press.

16. Guy E. Swanson (1960). *The Birth of the Gods*, pp. 34–36, 122–123. Ann Arbor: University of Michigan Press.

17. Eric H. Lenneberg (1964). "A Biological Perspective of Language." In Eric H. Lenneberg, ed., *New Directions in the Study of Language*, pp. 65–88. Cambridge, Mass.: MIT Press.

18. Cf. Morton Deutsch (1973). *The Resolution of Conflict*, p. 352. New Haven: Yale University Press.

19. Cf. Gordon W. Allport and Henry S. Odbert (1936). "Trait Names." *Psychology Monographs* 47: 3–32.

20. Morag Coate (1965). *Beyond All Reason*, pp. 1, 41, 81, 91, 92, 103. Philadelphia: Lippincott.

21. Edward Bennett (1959). *The Search for Emotional Security*, chap. 1. New York: Ronald Press.

22. Bruno Latour, op. cit., p. 86.

23. Leonard W. Doob (1940). *Plans of Men*, pp. 132–133. New Haven: Yale University Press.

24. Pat Killen and Robert W. Wildman II (1974). "Superstitiousness and Intelligence." *Psychological Reports* 34: 1158.

25. William Bloom (1990). *Personal Identity, National Identity, and International Relations*, p. 50. Cambridge: Cambridge University Press.

26. Leon J. Yarrow and Marian R. Yarrow (1964). "Personality Continuity and Change in the Family Context." In Philip Worchel and Donn Byrne, eds., *Personality Change*, pp. 489–523. New York: Wiley.

27. Lloyd A. Free (1959). *Six Allies and a Neutral*, pp. 9, 34, 76, 114. Glencoe: Free Press.

28. Jeremy Bentham (1948). *An Introduction to the Principles of Morals and Legislation*, p. 312. New York: Hafner.

29. Cf. David W. Johnson and Roger T. Johnson (1992). "Positive Interdependence." In Rachel Hertz-Lazarowitz and Norman Miller, eds., *Interaction in Cooperative Groups*, pp. 174–199. Cambridge: Cambridge University Press.

30. Cf. Eviatar Zerubavel (1981). *Hidden Rhythms*, chap. 5. Chicago: University of Chicago Press.

31. Cf. Anthony Giddens (1991). *Modernity and Self-Identity*, p. 227. Cambridge: Polity Press.

32. Cf. Charles E. Merriam (1934). *Political Power*, chap. 6. New York: McGraw-Hill.

33. Cf. Vernon Van Dyke (1985). *Human Rights, Ethnicity, and Discrimination*. Westport, Conn.: Greenwood.

34. Ellen Greenberger and Lawrence Steinberg (1986). *When Teenagers Work*, pp. 52, 226. New York: Basic Books.

35. Arthur Hadley (1978). *The Empty Polling Booth*, pp. 38–41. Englewood Cliffs, N.J.: Prentice-Hall.

36. Cf. James S. Coleman (1982). *The Asymmetric Society*, chap. 3. Syracuse, N.Y.: Syracuse University Press.

37. James Marshall (1968). *Intention in Law and Society*, pp. 12, 187–188. New York: Funk & Wagnalls.

CHAPTER 7: SOCIETY

1. Florence R. Kluckholm and Fred L. Strodtbeck (1961). *Variations in Value Orientations*, pp. 341–342. Evanston, Ill.: Row, Peterson.

2. Edward T. Hall and Mildred R. Hall (1990). *Understanding Cultural Differences*, p. 3. Yarmouth: Intercultural Press.

3. Cf. John W. Berry et al. (1992). *Cross-Cultural Psychology*, pp. 232–236. Cambridge: Cambridge University Press.

4. Ralph Linton (1952). "Universal Ethical Principles." In Ruth Anshen, ed., *Moral Principles of Action*, chap. 32. New York: Harper.

5. Leonard W. Doob (1978). "Time." In Tommy Carstein et al., *Making Sense of Time*, chap. 5. London: Edward Arnold.

6. Jeremy Bentham (1948). *An Introduction to the Principles of Morals and Legislation*, p. 70. New York: Hafner.

7. Alan Wolfe (1989). *Whose Keeper?*, pp. 76, 261. Berkeley: University of California Press.

8. John Dollard et al. (1939). *Frustration and Aggression*, chaps. 2, 3. New Haven: Yale University Press.

9. Hadley Cantril (1950). *The "Why" of Man's Existence*, p. 206. New York: Macmillan.

10. René Girard (1977). *Violence and the Sacred*, pp. 10, 20, 90, 302. Baltimore: Johns Hopkins University Press.

11. John E. Smith (1963). *The Spirit of American Philosophy*, p. 124. New York: Oxford University Press.

12. John E. Smith (1995). *Experience and God*, chap. 2. New York: Fordham University Press.

13. John E. Smith (1961). *Reason and God*, pp. ix, 188, 200. New Haven: Yale University Press.

14. Wayne Dosick (1995). *Golden Rules*. San Francisco: Harper.

15. David Thomson (1969). *The Aims of History*, p. 11. London: Thames and Hudson.

16. Kyung Durk Har (1930). *Social Laws*, pp. 3, 57, 79, 107, 119, 201, 239. Chapel Hill: University of North Carolina Press.

17. Cf. Marshall Sahlins (1976). *Culture and Practical Reason*, chaps. 2, 5. Chicago: University of Chicago Press.

18. Cf. Herant A. Katchadourian (1972). *Fundamentals of Human Sexuality*, pp. 27–28. New York: Holt, Rinehart and Winston.

19. Joseph R. Gusfield (1963). *Symbolic Crusade*, pp. 24–25. Urbana: University of Illinois Press.

20. Ulrich Steinmüller (1994). "Migration and Bilingualism." In Carol A. Blackshire, ed., *The German Mosaic*, chap. 11. Westport, Conn.: Greenwood.

21. Thurman W. Arnold (1935). *The Symbols of Government*, pp. 73, 144–145. New York: Harcourt, Brace.

22. Léopold Sédar Senghor (1964). *On African Socialism*, p. 13. New York: Praeger.

23. Cf. Leo Kuper and M. G. Smith, eds. (1969). *Pluralism in Africa*. Berkeley: University of California Press.

24. Gordan W. Allport (1942). "The Nature of Democratic Morale." In Goodwin Watson, ed., *Civilian Morale*, chap 1. Boston: Houghton Mifflin.

25. Cf. Amitai Etzioni (1988). *The Moral Dimension*, p. 95. New York: Free Press.

26. George Maclay and Humphry Knipe (1972). *The Dominant Man*, pp. 2, 57. New York: Delacorte Press.

27. Cf. Philip Mason (1970). *Patterns of Dominance*, pp. 7, 31. London: Oxford University Press.

28. Cf. Leo Kuper (1969). "Ethics and Racial Pluralism." In Kuper and Smith, op. cit., chap. 14.

29. Penelope B. R. Doob (1974). *Nebuchadnezzar's Children*, pp. 3, 53. New Haven: Yale University Press.

30. Valerie Møller and Lawrence Schlemmer (1983). "Quality of Life in South Africa." *Social Indicators Research* 12: 225–279.

31. William Conton (1960). *The African*, p. 1. London: Heinemann.

32. James O. Spradley, ed. (1969). *Guests Never Leave Hungry*, p. 177. New Haven: Yale University Press.

33. Hoyt Alverson (1978). *Mind in the Heart of Darkness*, pp. 3–6, 182, 270. New Haven: Yale University Press.

34. Cf. Geoffrey Cocks (1985). *Psychotherapy in the Third Reich*, pp. 13, 110–114. New York: Oxford University Press.

35. Robert J. Havighurst and Bernice L. Neugarten (1955). *American Indian and White Children*, pp. 20, 198; chap. 9. Chicago: University of Chicago Press.

36. Jock McCulloch (1995). *Colonial Psychiatry and "the African Mind,"* pp. 71, 74. Cambridge: Cambridge University Press.

37. Stephen Ellmann (1994). "The New South African Constitution and Ethnic Division." *Columbia Human Rights Law Review* 26: 5–44.

38. Gordon W. Allport (1937). *Personality*, p. 61. New York: Henry Holt.

CHAPTER 8: INDIVIDUAL ACTIONS

1. Leonard W. Doob (1987). *Slightly beyond Skepticism*, p. 255. New Haven: Yale University Press.

2. Cf. Carl E. Thoresen and Michael J. Mahoney (1974). *Behavioral Self-Control*, chaps 1, 7. New York: Holt, Rinehart and Winston.

3. Clarence I. Lewis (1955). *The Ground and Nature of the Right*, p. 59. New York: Columbia University Press.

4. Mervin D. Lynch et al., eds. (1981). *Self-Concept*, chaps. 2, 3. Cambridge: Ballinger.

5. Cf. C. Fred Alford (1991). *The Self in Social Theory*, p. 121. New Haven: Yale University Press.

6. Cf. Glynis M. Breakwell, ed. (1983). *Threatened Identities*, p. 7. New York: Wiley.

7. Myles E. Friedman and George H. Lackey, Jr. (1991). *The Psychology of Human Control*, p. 233. New York: Praeger.

8. Roy Schafer (1978). *Language and Insight*, pp. 79–86. New Haven: Yale University Press.

9. James W. Lamb (1977). "On a Proof of Incompatibilism." *Philosophical Review* 86: 20–35.

10. Herbert M. Lefcourt (1973). "The Function of the Illusions of Control and Freedom." *American Psychologist* 28: 417–425.

11. Anne Colby and Lawrence Kohlberg (1987). *The Measurement of Moral Judgment*, vol. 1, p. 2. Cambridge: Cambridge University Press.

12. James S. Coleman (1982). *The Asymmetric Society*, p. 88. Syracuse, N.Y.: Syracuse University Press.

13. Cf. Albert E. Scheften (1972). *Body Language and the Social Order*, chaps. 1–3. Englewood Cliffs, N.J.: Prentice-Hall.

14. Erika Bourguignon, ed. (1973). *Religion, States of Consciousness, and Social Change*, pp. 9–11. Columbus: Ohio State University Press.

15. Leonard W. Doob (1935). *Propaganda*, pp. 77–79. New York: Henry Holt.

16. Zygmunt Bauman (1992). *Mortality, Immortality, and Other Life Strategies*, pp. 152, 173. Stanford, Calif.: Stanford University Press.

17. B. Jowett (1931). *The Dialogues of Plato*, vol. 2, pp. 133–134. London: Oxford University Press.

18. Faruq Sherif (1995). *A Guide to the Contents of the Qur'an*. Reading: Garnet Publishing.

19. John 11:15.

20. Harry M. Hoberman and Barry D. Garfinkel (1989). "Completed Suicide in Youth." In Cynthia Pfeffer, ed., *Suicide among Youth*, chap. 2. Washington, D.C.: American Psychiatric Press.

21. John Donnelly, ed. (1990). *Suicide*, p. 7. Buffalo: Prometheus Books.

22. Thomas Lickona (1991). *Educating for Character*, pp. 20–22, 43–47, 53. New York: Bantam Books.

23. Erich Fromm (1950). *Psychoanalysis and Religion*, pp. 62, 87. New Haven: Yale University Press.

24. Ruut Veenhoven et al. (1994). *Correlates of Happiness*, vol. 2, p. 821; vol. 3, pp. 1480, 1817. Rotterdam: Erasmus University.

25. Willard L. Rodgers and Jerold G. Bachman (1988). *The Subjective Well-Being of Young Adults*, pp. 5, 15, 70–71, 155–157. Ann Arbor: University of Michigan Press.

26. Stephen R. Kellert (1996). *The Value of Life*, p. 38; chaps. 3–5. Washington, D.C.: Island Press.

27. Horst W. Opaschowski (1988). *Psychologie und Soziologie der Freizeit*, chap. 1. Opladen: Leske und Budrich.

28. Mortimer Ostow (1970). *The Psychology of Melancholy*, pp. 3, 92. New York: Harper & Row.

29. Letitia A. Peplau and Daniel Perlman (1982). "Perspectives on Loneliness." In Letitia A. Peplau and Daniel Perlman, eds., *Loneliness*, chap. 1. New York: Wiley.

30. Karen S. Rock and Letitia A. Peplau (1982). "Perspectives on Helping the Lonely." In Peplau and Perlman, op. cit., chap. 21.

31. Larry C. Mullins et al. (1996). "Social Determinants of Loneliness among Older Americans." *Genetic, Social, and General Psychology* 122: 453–473.

32. Rock and Peplau, op. cit.

33. Robert S. Weiss (1973). *Loneliness*, p. 231. Cambridge, Mass.: MIT Press.

34. Susan T. Fiske (1989). " Examining the Role of Intent." In James S. Uleman and John A. Barh, eds., *Unintended Thought*, chap. 8. New York: Guilford Press.

35. Lee J. Cronbach and Goldine C. Glaser (1965). *Psychological Tests and Personnel Decisions*, p. 121; chaps. 2, 3, 10. Urbana: University of Illinois Press.

36. Cf. Robyn M. Dawes (1988). *Rational Choice in an Uncertain World*, chaps. 6–8. New York: Harcourt, Brace.

37. Bernard J. F. Lonergan (1956). *Insight*, p. 651. New York: Philosophical Library.

38. Erich Fromm (1964). *The Heart of Man*, p. 69. New York: Harper & Row.

39. Norbert Wiener (1948). *Cybernetics*, p. 114. New York: Wiley.

40. Gardner Murphy (1975). *Outgrowing Self-Deception*, pp. 101–110. New York: Basic Books.

41. Mike W. Martin (1986). *Self-Deception and Morality*, p. 132. Lawrence: University Press of Kansas.

42. Cf. Charles R. Wright (1959). *Mass Communication*, pp. 75–76. New York: Random House.

43. Leonard W. Doob (1990). *Hesitation*, chap. 7. Westport, Conn.: Greenwood.

44. Cf. Harold M. Schroder et al. (1967). *Human Information Processing*, chap. 1. New York: Holt, Rinehart and Winston.

45. June P. Tangney and Kurt W. Fischer, eds. (1995). *Self-Conscious Emotions*, chaps. 2, 19. New York: Guilford Press.

46. Max Wertheimer (1959). *Productive Thinking*, p. 212. New York: Harper.

47. Cf. Elsa Abreu (1982). *The Role of Self-Help in the Development of Education in Kenya 1900–1973*. Nairobi: Kenya Literature Bureau. Thomas J. Powell, ed. (1990). *Working with Self-Help*. Silver Spring, Md.: NASW Press.

48. Niall Bolger and John Eckenrode (1991). "Social Relationships, Personality, and Anxiety during a Major Stressful Event." *Journal of Personality and Social Psychology* 6: 440–449.

49. Frederick Redlich and Daniel X. Freedman (1966). *The Theory and Practice of Psychiatry*, pp. 378–379. New York: Basic Books.

50. Francis Mondimore (1993). *Depression*, pp. 216–221. Baltimore: Johns Hopkins University Press.

51. George E. Vaillant (1977). *Adaptation to Life*, pp. 80, 383–386. Boston: Little, Brown.

52. Marie Jahoda (1958). *Current Concepts of Positive Mental Health*, pp. x, xi, 23, 80. New York: Basic Books.

53. Jerome D. Frank (1974). *Persuasion and Healing*, p. 19. New York: Schocken Books.

54. Charles E. Schaefer and Kevin J. O'Connor, eds. (1983). *Handbook of Play Therapy*, pp. 1–2. New York: Wiley.

55. Ralf Schwarzer (1984). "Introduction." In Ralf Schwarzer, ed., *The Self in Anxiety, Stress, and Depression*, pp. 1–16. Amsterdam: Elsevier.

56. Christine Schwarzer (1984). "Stressful Life Events and Emotions in the Elderly." In Schwarzer, op. cit., pp. 209–215.

57. Cf. Donald Meyer (1965). *The Positive Thinkers*. Garden City, N.Y.: Doubleday.

58. Leonard W. Doob (1940). *The Plans of Men*, pp. 178–181. New Haven: Yale University Press.

59. John M. Rich (1982). *Discipline and Authority in School and Family*, p. 40. Lexington, Mass.: Heath.

60. Perry London (1969). *Behavior Control*, pp. 204, 207. New York: Harper & Row.

61. Joseph T. Klapper (1960). *The Effects of Mass Communication*, chaps. 1, 10. Glencoe: Free Press.

62. Alex Comfort (1964). *The Process of Aging*. New York: Signet Science Library.

63. Schaefer and O'Connor, op. cit., pp. 1–10.

64. John Edwards (1992). "Language in Group and Individual Identity." In Glynis M. Breakwell, ed., *Social Psychology of Identity and the Self Concept*, chap. 5. London: Surrey University Press.

65. Barbara Bershon (1992). "Cooperative Problem Solving." In Rachel Hertz-Lazarowitz and Norman Miller, eds., *Interaction in Cooperative Groups*, chap. 2. New York: Cambridge University Press.

66. Howard E. Wilson (1963). "Education, Foreign Policy, and International Relations." In Robert Blum, ed., *Cultural Affairs and Foreign Relations*, chap. 3. Englewood Cliffs, N.J.: Prentice-Hall.

67. Breakwell, op. cit., p. 37.

68. Willkiam H. Harris and Judith S. Levey (1975). *The New Columbia Encyclopedia*, p. 1246. New York: Columbia University Press.

69. Allen R. Dyer (1988). *Ethics and Psychiatry*, p. 41; chaps. 4, 6. Washington, D.C.: American Psychiatric Association.

70. Norbert Elias (1985). *The Loneliness of Dying*. Oxford: Basil Blackwell. Marjorie C. McCoy (1974). *To Die with Style*. Nashville, Tenn.: Abingdon Press.

71. Elisabeth Kübler-Ross. (1969). *On Death and Dying*, pp. 32–33. New York: Macmillan.

72. Sherwin B. Nuland (1995). *How We Die*, pp. 8, 54, 87, 142, 242. New York: Vintage Books.

73. Cf. James Rachels (1986). *The End of Life*, chaps. 7, 9. Oxford: Oxford University Press.

74. Cf. Leonard W. Doob (1978). *Panorama of Evil*, p. 97. Westport, Conn.: Greenwood.

CHAPTER 9: SOCIETAL ACTIONS

1. Elisabeth Hansot (1974). *Perfection and Progress*, chaps. 1, 6. Cambridge, Mass.: MIT Press.

2. Ronald W. Perry and Alvin N. Mushkatel (1984). *Disaster Management*, chaps. 2, 4, 8. Westport, Conn.: Quorum Books.

3. John Sims and Duane D. Baumann (1972). "The Tornado Threat." *Science* 176: 1386–1392.

4. Genesis 2:16–17, 3:4–6, 22–23.

5. Piotr Sztompka (1991). *Society in Action*, p. 143. Chicago: University of Chicago Press.

6. Adam Smith (1937). *An Inquiry into the Nature and Causes of the Wealth of Nations*, p. lvii. New York: Modern Library.

7. Holmes Rolston III (1991). "Environmental Ethics." In F. Herbert Bormann and Stephen R. Kellert, eds., *Ecology, Economics, Ethics,* chap. 3. New Haven: Yale University Press.

8. Eric Chivian et al., eds. (1993). *Critical Condition.* Cambridge, Mass.: MIT Press.

9. Keekok Lee (1989). *Social Philosophy and Ecological Scarcity,* p. 14. London: Routledge.

10. Richard Neutra (1954). *Survival through Design,* pp. viii, 3, 125, 143, 156, 226, 228, 314. New York: Oxford University Press.

11. Kevin Lynch, ed. (1977). *Growing Up in Cities,* p. 98. Cambridge, Mass.: MIT Press.

12. Benton MacKaye (1928). *The New Exploration,* chaps. 4–6. New York: Harcourt, Brace.

13. MacKaye, op. cit., p. 214.

14. Cf. Gary C. Gray (1993). *Wildlife and People,* chaps. 1, 3, 5. Urbana: University of Illinois Press. Max Oelschlaeger (1991). *The Idea of Wilderness.* New Haven: Yale University Press.

15. Richard Sennett (1970). *Families against the City,* p. 113. Cambridge, Mass.: Harvard University Press.

16. Anthony J. McMichael (1993). *Planetary Overload and Human Health,* p. 1. New York: Cambridge University Press.

17. Hilary Putnam (1987). *The Many Faces of Realism,* pp. 54–55. La Salle, Ill.: Open Court.

18. Jerold S. Auerbach (1983). *Justice without Law?,* chap. 2. Oxford: Oxford University Press.

19. Mark L. Rosenberg et al. (1989). "Developing Strategies to Prevent Youth Suicide." In Cynthia Pfeffer, ed., *Suicide among Youth,* chap. 11. Washington, D.C.: American Psychiatric Press.

20. Gerald Sparrow (1972). *Vintage Victorian Murder,* p. 17. New York: Hart Publishing.

21. Samuel P. Huntington (1996). *The Clash of Civilizations and the Remaking of World Order,* chaps. 3–5, 8. New York: Simon & Schuster.

22. J. Martin Ramírez, ed. (1994). *Violence,* p. 15. Madrid: Centreur.

23. James A. Schellenberg (1982). *The Science of Conflict,* pp. 9–10, 235. New York: Oxford University Press. Cf. Auerbach, op. cit., chaps. 1, 2.

24. Anthony Doob et al. (1995). *Youth Crime and the Youth Justice System in Canada,* pp. 88–89. Toronto: University of Toronto Press.

25. Antonia Abbey and Frank M. Andrews (1986). "Modeling the Psychological Determinants of Life Quality." In Frank M. Andrews, ed., *Research on the Quality of Life,* chap. 3. Ann Arbor: Institute for Social Research, University of Michigan.

26. Ronald Inglehart and Jacques Rabier (1986). "Aspirations Adapt to Situations." In Andrews, ed., op. cit., chap. 1.

27. James Jackson (1986). "The Subjective Life Quality of Black Americans." In Andrews, ed., op. cit., chap. 7.

28. Clyde H. Coombs and George S. Avrunin (1988). *The Structure of Conflict*, pp. i–iii, part III. Hillsdale, N.J.: Lawrence Erlbaum.

29. Cf. Joel E. Cohen (1995). *How Many People Can the Earth Support?*, chaps. 7, 17. New York: Norton.

30. Brian Barry (1992). "The Quest for Consistency." In Brian Barry and Robert E. Gordin, eds., *Free Movement*, chap. 19. New York: Harvester Wheatsheaf.

31. Ed Diener (1984). "Subjective Well-Being." *Psychological Bulletin* 95: 542–575.

32. Cf. Valerie Møller and Lawrence Schlemmer (1983). "Quality of Life in South Africa." *Social Indicators Research* 12: 225–279.

33. Irving L. Janis (1972). *Victims of Groupthink*, chap. 9. Boston: Houghton Mifflin.

34. Cf. Bruno Latour (1987). *Science and Action*, p. 204. Cambridge, Mass.: Harvard University Press.

35. H. G. Wells (1931). *The Work, Wealth, and Happiness of Mankind*, p. 661. Garden City, N.Y.: Doubleday, Doran.

36. Cf. David Johnson and Roger T. Johnson (1991). *Learning Together and Alone*. Boston: Allyn and Bacon.

37. Yuen Khong Khong (1996). "Confronting Hitler and Its Consequences." In Philip E. Tetlock and Aaron Belkin, eds., *Counterfactual Thought Experiments in World Politics*, chap. 4. Princeton: Princeton University Press.

CHAPTER 10: NEVERTHELESS

1. Cf. Peter M. Haas et al. (1993). *Institutions for the Earth*. Cambridge, Mass.: MIT Press.

2. Eleanor Singer and Phyllis M. Endreny (1993). *Reporting on Risk*, chap. 2, pp. 183–191. New York: Russell Sage Foundation.

3. Cf. Alexander Abdennur (1987). *The Conflict Resolution Syndrome*, chap. 6. Ottawa: University of Ottawa Press.

4. Cf. Richard Seaford (1994). *Reciprocity and Ritual*, chap. 6. Oxford: Clarendon Press.

5. Michael Cole and Sylvia Scribner (1974). *Culture and Thought*, pp. 122, 124. New York: Wiley.

6. Cf. Sylvia Scribner and Michael Cole (1981). *The Psychology of Literacy*, p. 234. Cambridge, Mass.: Harvard University Press.

7. David H. Lumsdaine (1993). *Moral Vision in International Politics*, chaps. 1, 9. Princeton: Princeton University Press.

8. Keith L. Nelson and Spencer C. Olin, Jr. (1979). *Why War?*, chaps. 1, 9. Berkeley: University of California Press.

9. Cf. Robyn M. Dawes (1988). *Rational Choice in an Uncertain World*, pp. 21–31. New York: Harcourt, Brace.

10. Erik H. Erikson (1964). *Insight and Responsibility*, pp. 222, 233, 243. New York: Norton.

11. Cf. Leonard W. Doob (1993). *Intervention*, chap. 6. New Haven: Yale University Press.

12. Cf. C. Fred Alford (1991). *The Self in Social Theory*, p. 121. New Haven: Yale University Press.

Selected Bibliography

Ajzen, Icek, and Martin Fishbein (1980). *Understanding Attitudes and Predicting Social Behavior*. Englewood Cliffs, N.J.: Prentice-Hall.

Allport, Gordon W. (1955). *Becoming*. New Haven: Yale University Press.

Andrews, Frank M., ed. (1986). *Research on the Quality of Life*. Ann Arbor: Institute for Social Research, University of Michigan.

Argyle, Michael (1987). *The Psychology of Happiness*. London: Methuen.

Bauman, Zygmunt (1992). *Mortality, Immortality, and Other Life Strategies*. Stanford, Calif.: Stanford University Press.

Berlin, Isaiah (1996). *The Sense of Reality*. London: Chatto & Windus.

Berry, John W., et al. (1992). *Cross-Cultural Psychology*. Cambridge: Cambridge University Press.

Bettelheim, Bruno (1983). *Freud and Man's Soul*. New York: Knopf.

Bormann, F. Herbert, and Stephen R. Kellert, eds. (1991). *Ecology, Economics, Ethics*. New Haven: Yale University Press.

Chomsky, Noam (1972). *Language and Mind*. New York: Harcourt Brace Jovanovich.

Cole, Michael, and Sylvia Scribner (1974). *Culture and Thought*. New York: Wiley.

Coleman, James S. (1982). *The Asymmetric Society*. Syracuse, N.Y.: Syracuse University Press.

Collins, Harry, and Trevor Pinch (1993). *The Golem*. Cambridge: Cambridge University Press.

Dawes, Robyn M. (1988). *Rational Choice in an Uncertain World*. New York: Harcourt, Brace.

De Jouvenel, Bertrand (1963). *The Pure Theory of Politics*. New Haven: Yale University Press.

Deutsch, Morton (1973). *The Resolution of Conflict.* New Haven: Yale University Press.

Dewey, John (1922). *Human Nature and Conduct.* New York: Henry Holt.

Dollard, John (1937). *Caste and Class in a Southern Town.* New Haven: Yale University Press.

Doob, Leonard W. (1993). *Intervention.* New Haven: Yale University Press.

Edelstein, Alan (1982). *An Unacknowledged Harmony.* Westport, Conn.: Greenwood.

Elias, Norbert (1985). *The Loneliness of Dying.* Oxford: Basil Blackwell.

Erikson, Erik H. (1964). *Insight and Responsibility.* New York: Norton.

Festinger, Leon (1983). *The Human Legacy.* New York: Columbia University Press.

Field, M. J. (1960). *Search for Security.* Evanston, Ill.: Northwestern University Press.

Fromm, Erich (1955). *The Sane Society.* New York: Holt, Rinehart and Winston.

Garcia, Juan R. (1980). *Operation Wetback.* Westport, Conn.: Greenwood.

Garner, Wendell R. (1962). *Uncertainty and Structure as Psychological Concepts.* New York: Wiley.

Glazer, Nathan (1988). *The Limits of Social Policy.* Cambridge, Mass.: Harvard University Press.

Har, Kyung Dark (1930). *Social Laws.* Chapel Hill: University of North Carolina Press.

Heilbroner, Robert L. (1961). *The Future as History.* New York: Grove Press.

James, William (1968). *Pragmatism.* Cleveland: Meridian Books.

Janis, Irving L. (1972). *Victims of Groupthink.* Boston: Houghton Mifflin.

Kagan, Jerome (1989). *Unstable Ideas.* Cambridge, Mass.: Harvard University Press.

Kant, Immanuel (1949). *Fundamental Principles of the Metaphysics of Morals.* Indianapolis: Liberal Arts Press.

Kluckholm, Florence R., and Fred L. Strodtbeck (1961). *Variations in Value Orientations.* Evanston, Ill.: Row, Peterson.

Köhler, Wolfgang (1938). *The Place of Value in a World of Facts.* New York: Liveright.

Kuper, Leo, and M. G. Smith, eds. (1969). *Pluralism in Africa.* Berkeley: University of California Press.

Lewis, Michael, and Carolyn Saarni, eds. (1993). *Lying and Deception in Everyday Life.* New York: Guilford.

Lickona, Thomas (1991). *Educating for Character.* New York: Bantam Books.

Loewenberg, Peter (1985). *Decoding the Past.* Berkeley: University of California Press.

MacKaye, James (1924). *The Logic of Conduct.* New York: Boni & Liveright.

Marshall, James (1968). *Intention in Law and Society.* New York: Funk & Wagnalls.

Marx, Karl, and Frederick Engels (1970). *The German Ideology*. New York: International Publishers.

Meeks, Wayne (1986). *The Moral World of the First Christians*. Philadelphia: Westminster Press.

More, Thomas (1989). *Utopia*. Cambridge: Cambridge University Press.

Niebuhr, Reinhold (1955). *The Self and the Dramas of History*. New York: Scribner's.

Nuland, Sherwin B. (1995). *How We Die*. New York: Vintage Books.

Peplau, Letitia, and Daniel Perlman, eds. (1982). *Loneliness*. New York: Wiley.

Plato (1982). *Republic*. Indianapolis: Hackett Publishing.

Redlich, Frederick, and Daniel X. Freedman (1966). *The Theory and Practice of Psychiatry*. New York: Basic Books.

Rokeach, Milton, ed. (1979). *Understanding Human Values*. New York: Free Press.

Sagan, Carl (1973). *The Cosmic Connection*. Garden City, N.Y.: Anchor.

Schweitzer, Albert (1969). *Reverence for Life*. New York: Harper & Row.

Segall, Marshall H. (1976). *Human Behavior and Public Policy*. New York: Pergamon.

Sharp, Gene (1980). *Social Power and Political Freedom*. Boston: Porter Sargent.

Smith, Adam (1937). *An Inquiry into the Nature and Causes of the Wealth of Nations*. New York: Modern Library.

Smith, John E. (1961). *Reason and God*. New Haven: Yale University Press.

Tauber, Robert T. (1997). *Self-Fulfilling Prophecy*. Westport, Conn.: Praeger.

Tetlock, Philip F., and Aaron Belkin, eds. (1996). *Counterfactual Thought Experiments in World Politics*. Princeton: Princeton University Press.

Veenhoven, Ruut, et al. (1994). *Correlates of Happiness*. Rotterdam: Erasmus University.

Weiner, Bernard (1995). *Judgments of Responsibility*. New York: Guilford Press.

Weischedel, Wilhelm (1976). *Skeptische Ethik*. Frankfurt: Suhrkamp.

Wells, H. G. (1931). *The Work, Wealth, and Happiness of Mankind*. Garden City, N.Y.: Doubleday, Doran.

Wertheimer, Max (1959). *Productive Thinking*. New York: Harper.

Index

The page numbers in **bold face** indicate the text pages in which reference notes are made without mentioning the author's name.

About the Author

LEONARD W. DOOB is Sterling Professor Emeritus of Psychology at Yale University. Throughout his career he has focused his research on interdisciplinary topics and has sought to apply promising scholarly findings to real-life situations, concentrating in particular on psychological warfare and conflicts in Africa and Northern Ireland. He has published numerous articles and books, including *Panorama of Evil* (Greenwood, 1978), *The Pursuit of Peace* (Greenwood, 1981), and *Sustainers and Sustainability* (Praeger, 1995).